Morgenthau, Law and Realism

Although widely regarded as the 'founding father' of realism in International Relations, this book argues that Hans J. Morgenthau's legal background has largely been neglected in discussions of his place in the 'canon' of IR theory. Morgenthau was a legal scholar of German-Jewish origins who arrived in the United States in 1938. He went on to become a distinguished professor of Political Science and a prominent commentator on international affairs. Rather than locate Morgenthau's intellectual heritage in the German tradition of *Realpolitik*, this book demonstrates how many of his central ideas and concepts stem from European and American legal debates of the 1920s and 1930s. This is an ambitious attempt to recast the debate on Morgenthau and will appeal to IR scholars interested in the history of realism as well as international lawyers engaged in debates regarding the relationship between law and politics, and the history of International Law.

OLIVER JÜTERSONKE is Head of Research for the Centre on Conflict, Development and Peacebuilding (CCDP) at the Graduate Institute of International and Development Studies, Geneva, and Research Fellow at the Zurich University Centre for Ethics (ZUCE).

D1730620

Morgenthau, Law and Realism

Oliver Jütersonke

CAMBRIDGE UNIVERSITY PRESS
Cambridge, New York, Melbourne, Madrid, Cape Town,
Singapore, São Paulo, Delhi, Mexico City

Cambridge University Press
The Edinburgh Building, Cambridge CB2 8RU, UK

Published in the United States of America by
Cambridge University Press, New York

www.cambridge.org
Information on this title: www.cambridge.org/9781107407688

First published 2010
First paperback edition 2012

A catalogue record for this publication is available from the British Library

Library of Congress Cataloguing in Publication data
Jütersonke, Oliver.
Morgenthau, law, and realism / Oliver Jütersonke.
    p. cm.
Includes bibliographical references and index.
ISBN 978-0-521-76928-0 (hardback)
1. International relations–Philosophy.   2. Realism.   3. International
law.   4. Morgenthau, Hans J. (Hans Joachim), 1904–1980.   I. Title.
JZ1307.J88 2010
327.101-dc22
2010022110

ISBN 978-0-521-76928-0 Hardback
ISBN 978-1-107-40768-8 Paperback

For my parents,

Elke and Manfred J. Jütersonke

Contents

Preface

Why another monograph on Hans J. Morgenthau? That question, perhaps posed by many picking up this book, is indeed a legitimate one. Ever since his rise to fame in the 1950s with his textbook, *Politics Among Nations: The Struggle for Power and Peace*, plenty has been written on the 'realist theory of international politics' advocated therein. Revolving around the notion of the (national) 'interest defined in terms of power', Morgenthau's work was for decades part of the standard repertoire of practically every introductory course in the field of International Relations, in both the anglophone world and beyond. Moreover, his outspoken views on Vietnam, nuclear deterrence and Middle East peace made Morgenthau a known quantity in foreign policy and media circles. Hans Morgenthau was, in many respects, one of the leading public intellectuals in the United States during the 1960s and 1970s.[1] The multitudinous secondary literature and commentary on the man and his ideas bears testimony to this status.

In short, the present text is a reaction to a recent revival, starting in the late 1990s, of the work of Morgenthau in the academic field of International Relations. With the Cold War over and the global cards reshuffled towards asymmetric warfare and invisible enemies, scholars began looking around for inspiration from the 'classics' to fill the apparent void left by a body of theory that was perceived as being of decreasing utility for the twenty-first century. Hans Morgenthau was one of those rehabilitated. Rereading the texts, his work appeared much more sophisticated than the crude

---

1 He is not to be confused with his namesake Henry Morgenthau Jr (1891–1967), who served in Franklin D. Roosevelt's administration and is best known for his 1944 'Morgenthau Plan' of wanting to deindustrialize and partition post-war Germany into a series of agrarian statelets.

power politics privileged by standard interpretations of his thought, instead offering avenues for addressing issues of morality and ethics in debates on the global war on terrorism, for instance. Such normative considerations, it was argued, tended to be occluded by the more scientific neo-realist approaches that had originally replaced Morgenthau's 'human nature realism'. Yet while this revival of Morgenthau's work is undoubtedly merited and represents, as a whole, an important contribution to the 'disciplinary history' of the relatively new field of International Relations, it continues to mystify why the legal origins of Morgenthau's thought remain unstudied. Before rising to fame at the University of Chicago, Morgenthau was an aspiring legal scholar trying to make a name for himself in Frankfurt, Geneva, Madrid, New York and Kansas City. Bar a number of fragmentary exceptions, the recent literature on Morgenthau has not deemed it worthwhile to formulate – and elaborate upon – the fact that the realist thought of one of its 'founding fathers' was derived from debates that arose in the 1920s and early 1930s as a reaction to the predominant formalist norm-positivism of German and American legal theory. While these intellectual origins have been recognized, and expressed, by a number of scholars in the field of International Law, the consequences of such insights have yet to resonate in International Relations theory.

In a nutshell, Morgenthau's legal formalist heritage incited him to make repeated calls for greater emphasis on the 'reality' of international legal norms, a reality reflected in the restricted scope and weak normativity of the system of sanctions offered by international dispute settlement mechanisms and institutions. His popular American works published in the 1940s and 1950s constitute an attempt to make the convictions he held about the nature of law compatible with his new, non-legal audience. Morgenthau the émigré jurist faced the dual challenge of addressing a readership that was versed in a different literature and used different cultural reference points, and of having to move from the field of Law to Political Science. Works such as *Scientific Man vs. Power Politics* or *In Defense of the National Interest* cannot be understood without taking this institutional and ideational setting into account.

This book does not offer a radically different reading of Morgenthau that necessarily challenges existing, standard renditions of his thought. To be sure, those looking for instances of a rather crude realism that posits international politics as being a pure struggle for power waged by self-interested actors will have no trouble finding such statements in Morgenthau's writings. What I am interested in, however, is fleshing out *why* and *on what basis* Morgenthau came to take on the views that he did. As the following chapters will attempt to show, answering these questions requires a more accurate contextualization of the legal debates Morgenthau was engaged in prior to becoming the advocate of power politics for which he is remembered.

Writing another biography of Morgenthau is not the purpose of this monograph. Although being informed by, and at times drawing on, unpublished material from the Morgenthau archives in Washington, New York, Oxford and Geneva, this book does not attempt to give an exhaustive overview of Morgenthau's thought, his work, or of the man himself. It does not deal critically with the reception of *Politics Among Nations* in subsequent conceptualizations of scientific, structural and neo-realist approaches in International Relations theory. It does not analyse the reception of Morgenthau's realism in US foreign policy circles, and his influence on the likes of George F. Kennan and Henry Kissinger. It does not engage with Morgenthau's strong denunciation of the Vietnam War and the policies of the Johnson administration, and it does not address his at times contradictory views regarding nuclear weapons. What this monograph sets out to do is elaborate on the claim that a revival of Morgenthau's thought is neither particularly interesting nor an added value to the disciplinary history of International Relations if it continues to occlude the law debates within which his ideas were shaped.

The argument of the book can be boiled down to a number of central assertions. First, the Morgenthau remembered in the field of International Relations and in US foreign policy circles is the Morgenthau of the 'six principles of realism'. These were added, upon consultation with his editors, at the beginning of the second edition of *Politics Among Nations* in 1954 to make the book sell better (which it then did). Neither the first edition, nor anything else Morgenthau had written up to that point, contained elements of what was subsequently declared to constitute a 'realist theory of international politics'. Second, what Morgenthau originally meant by 'realism' was the introduction of a dose of 'reality' into the way inter-state disputes were conceptualized. The dominant doctrine of positivist legal formalism detracted from focusing on the underlying distribution of power inherent in any international dispute, and thus also on the empirical enforceability of international legal norms. Third, Morgenthau's use of the term 'legalism' did not imply that international law was irrelevant to the study of international relations, but that it was pernicious to uphold a formalist legal doctrine that was only instrumentalized to suit the requirements of one or more superpowers seeking to depoliticize their underlying claims to ideational supremacy.

Acknowledgements

Writing a monograph is inevitably a somewhat lonely endeavour, perhaps even more so when the subject matter requires digging through archives and hunting down obscure references – rather than, say, engaging in anthropological field work on youth gangs in a Central American suburb. Important are thus those relatively rare moments of 'coming up for air', when certain individuals agree to listen to or read what must have often constituted nonsensical snippets of an argument that was probably as unclear to me as to those on the receiving end of the narrative. My three mentors who regularly put up with this were Keith Krause, Peter Haggenmacher and Martti Koskenniemi, whose words of critique and encouragement, and unbelievable patience, shepherded me over the finishing line. It is to them that I owe the greatest thanks.

Much of the argument of the book revolves around hidden dialogues and implicit influences of one sort or another. The difficulties of pinning down such exchanges are once again apparent when reflecting on the list of scholars I myself was privileged enough to have had conversations with on a variety of aspects related to this monograph. Reconstructing the complete list would be impossible, but I would particularly like to mention and thank George Abi-Saab, Michael N. Barnett, Andrea Bianchi, Thomas J. Biersteker, Curt Gasteyger, Richard Ned Lebow, Joel H. Rosenthal, William E. Scheuerman, David Sylvan, Kenneth W. Thompson, Daniel Warner and Michael C. Williams for their comments, suggestions and encouragement.

My thanks go to John Haslam and Carrie Parkinson at Cambridge University Press, as well as to their design and production teams. Special gratitude also goes to two anonymous reviewers, whose valuable feedback played no insignificant part in shaping the final version of the manuscript. I would moreover like to acknowledge Stephan Kuhr at Axel Springer Publishers in Berlin for assisting in the hunt for the cover image, and also the librarians in the Library of Congress in Washington, DC, the Leo Baeck Institute in New York, the Bodleian Library in Oxford, and the library of the Graduate Institute of International and Development Studies in Geneva, for their tireless efforts in conjuring up the material I was looking for. I also thank Markus Huppenbauer at the Zurich University Centre for Ethics, as well as the Mercator Foundation Switzerland that funded my research over the last three years, for granting me the time to additionally accomplish the publication of this monograph.

Finally, my gratitude goes out to my family, friends and colleagues, who, each in their own way, made the writing of this book possible. It could not have been achieved without you all.

Note on the text

While having also consulted the personal Morgenthau papers in the Leo Baeck Institute in New York, the files of the Academic Assistance Council at the Bodleian Library in Oxford, and various institutional dossiers at the Graduate Institute of International and Development Studies in Geneva, all the unpublished material cited in the following chapters can be found in the Manuscript Division of the Library of Congress, Washington, DC. The collection, entitled *Hans J. Morgenthau Papers*, is divided into numbered containers and will be referenced as 'HJM-Container 110', for instance, in the footnotes.

Unless otherwise stated, all translations from German and French are my own. Where an English translation of the text does exist, yet I felt the need to translate the original text slightly differently, I have added 'my translation, OJ' to the reference. In a few instances, when the original wording is crucial, I have included the German or French text so that the reader may have a direct comparison.

Although significantly rewritten since, a few sections of Chapters 2, 3 and 6 first appeared in Jütersonke, 'Hans J. Morgenthau on the Limits of Justiciability in International Law', *Journal of the History of International Law*, 8:2 (2006), pp. 181–211, and in Jütersonke, 'The Image of Law in *Politics Among Nations*', in M. C. Williams (ed.), *Realism Reconsidered: The Legacy of Hans J. Morgenthau in International Relations* (Oxford University Press, 2007), pp. 93–117. A few lines of two earlier review articles published in the journal *Cooperation and Conflict* – Vol. 40 (2005), pp. 233–41 and Vol. 41 (2006), pp. 463–9 – can also be found in Chapter 1. Thanks go to Brill Publishers, Oxford University Press and SAGE Publications for their permission to draw on this material.

1   Hans J. Morgenthau in International Relations

The benefits to be had from transcending standard renditions of realism as being about crude inter-state power politics have recently been the subject of much debate. After having been proclaimed defunct at the beginning of the 1990s, efforts are now being undertaken to unearth the rich tradition of classical realism that has been lost to the scientific approach of subsequent structuralist, neo-realist approaches and the consequent fragmentation of the tradition.[1] Under the influence of rationalist social science, so the story goes, the European realism taken across the Atlantic by the likes of Hans J. Morgenthau (1904–80) had been transformed into an approach that was no longer based on anthropological foundations revolving around the innate drive for power in human nature, but on rational action expressed in empirical correlations and abstract models. Today, in a time in which a single superpower wages a War on Terror against a largely unidentifiable enemy, the gap between normative (US) foreign policy and International Relations theory is seen by many to be wider than ever before. Robert Kaplan's *Warrior Politics*, Robert Kagan's *Of Paradise and Power*, and Anatol Lieven and John Hulsman's *Ethical Realism* are just three popularistic examples of calls to revert the focus back from scientific theory construction to the 'art' of the realistic statesman, in an effort to link practical politics with ethical principles.[2]

1 S. Guzzini, *Realism in International Relations and International Political Economy: The Continuing Story of a Death Foretold* (London: Routledge, 1998).
2 R. Kaplan, *Warrior Politics: Why Leadership Demands a Pagan Ethos* (New York, NY: Vintage Books, 2002); R. Kagan, *Of Paradise and Power* (London: Atlantic Books, 2003); A. Lieven and J. Hulsman, *Ethical Realism: A Vision for America's Role in the World* (New York, NY: Vintage, 2007).

In the academic field of International Relations, there has been a comparable attempt to reinject the ethics of statecraft into the debate. Echoing earlier work by Greg Russell and Joel H. Rosenthal, Richard Ned Lebow's *The Tragic Vision of Politics* and Michael C. Williams' *The Realist Tradition and the Limits of International Relations* both challenge the adequacy of contemporary International Relations theory and call for a return to some of the fundamental underpinnings of realist thought.[3] Lebow argues that neo-realist theory ignores the importance of justice and the centrality of ethics in foreign policy, thus remaining unaware that it is only through a combination of ethics and interests that order can be obtained. It is not 'hard-nosed egoism' that is most conducive to national security, he claims, but ethical behaviour. A detailed reading of three 'classical' realists – Thucydides, Carl von Clausewitz (1780–1831) and Morgenthau – is used to show to what extent questions of justice played an important role in the formulation of the realist position. Lebow attempts to challenge advocates of *Realpolitik* 'on home turf', by trying 'to persuade readers that ethics are not only instrumentally important, but that it is impossible to formulate interests intelligently outside of some language of justice'.[4]

Michael Williams writes in a similar vein, based on what he calls 'a deep dissatisfaction with the ways in which key figures in the history of political thought have been appropriated in much of International Relations, and the visions of Realism that have been associated with them'.[5] Based on a reading of Morgenthau, Williams was induced to outline a type of realism, which he calls 'wilful' realism, that not only entails a more accurate interpretation of thinkers linked to the tradition, but one that also highlights 'their profound challenge to contemporary understandings of the Realist tradition and its place in International Relations theory today'.[6] Williams identifies three defining features of wilful realism: scepticism, relationality and

---

3 G. Russell, *Hans J. Morgenthau and the Ethics of American Statecraft* (Baton Rouge, LA and London: Louisiana State University Press, 1990); J. H. Rosenthal, *Righteous Realists: Political Realism, Responsible Power, and American Culture in the Nuclear Age* (Baton Rouge, LA: Louisiana State University Press, 1991); R. N. Lebow, *The Tragic Vision of Politics: Ethics, Interests and Orders* (Cambridge University Press, 2003); M. C. Williams, *The Realist Tradition and the Limits of International Relations* (Cambridge University Press, 2005).
4 Lebow, *The Tragic Vision of Power Politics*, p. 16.
5 Williams, *The Realist Tradition*, p. 4.   6 *Ibid.*, p. 5.

power politics. Concerned with the politics of knowledge, wilful realism is sceptical of modern empiricism and rationalism, pointing instead to the limits of reason in the construction of political order. Its emphasis on knowledge also makes wilful realism focus on the constructive relational processes of Self and Other, warning against the dangers of slipping into the dualism of self-identification through antithetical opposition to the Other. Lastly, it argues that the sphere of politics is not only about the destructive potential of the struggle for power, but also about the productive possibilities of self-determination and the establishment of common interests. Williams then uses his vision of wilful realism to examine the link between an ethic of responsibility and the national interest, highlighting how such an understanding relates to recent neo-conservative strands in US foreign policy. Referring to the work of Morgenthau, Williams demonstrates how the national interest functions as a self-reflexive, rhetorical device used as an ethical practice for the construction of a politics of limits.

A number of other recent studies have also been exploring the value added of re-engaging with particular facets of classical realism, and Morgenthau is the common element throughout. Worth mentioning here are monographs by Vibeke Schou Tjalve and Seán Molloy. The first offers a synchronic reading of Morgenthau and the US theologian Reinhold Niebuhr (1882–1971) in order to develop 'an ethical and political language for balancing responsibility and humility' in US foreign policy, one that is akin to the republican sensitivities developed by the founding fathers of the United States.[7] The second uses a reading of E. H. Carr (1892–1982), Morgenthau and Martin Wight (1913–1972) to 'restore humanity' to contemporary conceptualizations of realism by focusing on the inherited language, philosophies and meta-narratives that have 'contained and constrained' realism in International Relations theory.[8] A further interesting monograph recently came from the pen of Robbie Shilliam, who explored the thought of Immanuel Kant (1724–1804), Georg Wilhelm Friedrich Hegel (1770–1831), Max Weber (1864–1920) and Morgenthau with the aim of illuminating the way these German thinkers tried to

7 V. S. Tjalve, *Realist Strategies of Republican Peace: Niebuhr, Morgenthau, and the Politics of Patriotic Dissent* (New York, NY and Basingstoke: Palgrave Macmillan, 2008).

8 S. Molloy, *The Hidden History of Realism: A Genealogy of Power Politics* (New York, NY and Basingstoke: Palgrave Macmillan, 2006).

reconcile the liberal project with realist thought within an historical context delineated by the problem of 'alterity', or 'the interaction between differentially developed societies'.[9] Morgenthau also plays a prominent role in Duncan Bell's recent edited volume exploring 'realist orientations' in contemporary (international) political theory.[10]

Rediscovering the virtues of classical realist thought, then, has been a popular activity of late, both within narrower theoretical debates in International Relations, as well as in more general narratives about the requirements and prerequisites of sound foreign policy decision-making. Yet because of the inward-oriented means by which the field of International Relations tends to write its own 'disciplinary' history, the fact that 'classical' authors were writing in different socio-historical and disciplinary mindsets is often occluded. As this book seeks to demonstrate, the German and US legal theoretical debates out of which emerged the 'realist theory of international politics', based on 'interest defined in terms of power', are the missing context in the case of Morgenthau. Arguably, ignoring or downplaying the legal background on which Morgenthau's ideas are founded is to the detriment of the stated purpose of rehabilitating the thought of such scholars precisely because of their intellectual richness and analytical depth.

Career prospects for German-Jewish jurists in US law schools were exceedingly limited in the 1930s and 1940s. The result was that many lawyers were forced to switch discipline and take up posts in Political Science, or in the newly created field of International Relations, which at the time spanned courses in international law, international organization, diplomatic history and international politics. Morgenthau was no exception to this trend, eventually becoming the Albert A. Michelson Distinguished Service Professor of Political Science and Modern History at the University of Chicago. This book sets out to show that what Morgenthau and a host of other émigré jurists brought across the Atlantic was not simply Bismarckian *Realpolitik* based on anthropological foundations revolving around the innate drive for power in human nature, but

---

9   R. Shilliam, *German Thought and International Relations: The Rise and Fall of a Liberal Project* (Basingstoke: Palgrave Macmillan, 2009).
10 D. S. Bell, *Political Thought and International Relations: Variations on a Realist Theme* (Oxford University Press, 2009).

a sophisticated understanding of the relationship between law and politics derived from the type of theoretical-historical analysis practiced by German *Staatsrechtslehre*. It is simply misleading to declare that Morgenthau, together with the likes of Hannah Arendt (1906–1975), Leo Strauss (1899–1973) and Herbert Marcuse (1898–1979), was one of the most influential refugee 'political theorists and philosophers'.[11] Versed as he may have been in the literature, Morgenthau was not a political theorist, nor a philosopher. The unfortunate result of such generalizations is that potentially very useful appropriations of 'classical' thinkers for contemporary purposes are stunted by a lack of engagement with reference points and contexts that lie outside of, in this case, the International Relations sphere. Analysing Morgenthau's work using the conceptual toolkit of International Relations theory alone, while at the same time calling for a greater emphasis on context, intellectual origins, and a more profound understanding of his thought, does not make for a particular effective – or useful – exercise.

Realism

In general terms, realism implies having a certain, sober outlook on a particular set of circumstances, without being influenced by interests or preferences, or misled by ephemera of one sort or another.[12] Although varyingly employed, realism is a position that can be found in the visual arts, in literature and in various strands of philosophical thought. In political theory, realism is generally identified with an approach focusing on the sources, modalities and effects of power. In International Relations theory, realism posits that international politics involves self-interested actors operating in a self-help system with no overarching authority.

Realism is a relational concept, in that a claim to being 'realist' defines itself and is evaluated with regard to an opposing conception

---

11 As does P. G. Kielmansegg, 'Introduction', in P. G. Kielmansegg, H. Mewes and E. Glaser-Schmidt (eds.), *Hannah Arendt and Leo Strauss: German Emigrés and American Political Thought after World War II* (Washington, DC: The German Historical Institute and Cambridge University Press, 1995), pp. 1–8, at 1.

12 See Duncan Bell's useful discussion of realism in his 'Introduction: Under an Empty Sky – Realism and Political Theory', in Bell (ed.), *Political Thought and International Relations*, pp. 1 25, at 1.

that is less realistic, i.e. idealistic or utopian.[13] This is also reflected in the status of realism in International Relations. In his import-ant book, *The Power of Power Politics*, John A. Vasquez demonstrates empirically that the realist paradigm has indeed dominated the field since the early 1950s, showing how it has guided theory construc-tion, data-making and research.[14] And even if many contempor-ary theoretical approaches advocated or applied in journal articles or monographs differ sharply from realist assumptions, that fact is made clear precisely in explicit contradistinction to realism. As Jeffrey W. Legro and Andrew Moravcsik write, realism remains 'the primary or alternative theory in virtually every major textbook and article addressing general theories of world politics, particularly in security affairs'.[15]

Of course, realism in International Relations is far from anything resembling a coherent and unified theoretical framework: not only is there a temporal split between classical realism (Morgenthau), neo-realism (Waltz)[16] and even postclassical realism,[17] but the lit-erature also distinguishes between the offensive realism of John J. Mearsheimer and Robert Gilpin and the defensive realism of Kenneth N. Waltz, Robert Jervis and others.[18] Yet the overall sali-ence of realist theories has meant that the position and function of realism in International Relations has been the subject of continued discussion, and is part of a discourse on what Steve Smith calls the

13 On this point, see B. S. Chimni, *International Law and World Order: A Critique of Contemporary Approaches* (New Delhi: SAGE Publications, 1993), p. 30.
14 J. H. Vasquez, *The Power of Power Politics: From Classical Realism to Neotraditionalism* (Cambridge University Press, 1998).
15 J. W. Legro and A. Moravcsik, 'Is Anybody Still a Realist?', *International Security*, 24 (1995), pp. 5–55, at 5.
16 The neo-realism of Waltz is often equated with structural realism, although some leading members of the English School have tried to draw a distinction; see B. Buzan, C. Jones and R. Little, *The Logic of Anarchy: Neorealism to Structural Realism* (New York, NY: Columbia University Press, 1993).
17 See S. G. Brooks, 'Dueling Realisms', *International Organization*, 51 (1997), pp. 445–77.
18 J. H. Mearsheimer, 'Back to the Future: Instability in Europe after the Cold War', *International Security*, 15 (1991), pp. 5–57; J. H. Mearsheimer, *The Tragedy of Great Power Politics* (New York, NY: W.W. Norton, 2001); R. Gilpin, *War and Change in World Politics* (Cambridge University Press, 1981); K. N. Waltz, *Theory of International Politics* (Reading, MA: Addison-Wesley, 1979); R. Jervis, 'Cooperation under the Security Dilemma', *World Politics*, 30 (1978), pp. 167–214. For an overview of some of the literature on these, and other strands of realism, see G. H. Snyder, 'Mearsheimer's World – Offensive Realism and the Struggle for Security. A Review Essay', *International Security*, 27 (2002), pp. 149–73, at 149–50.

'self-images' of International Relations theory.[19] A widely accepted characterization of the field of International Relations involves the chronological division of its history into dominant theoretical positions, with the periods of transition marking 'great debates'. Thus one supposedly witnessed the first great debate between idealism and realism in the 1930s and 1940s, and the second between realism/traditionalism and behaviouralism in the 1950s and 1960s. Recently, there has been talk of a third debate between positivism and post-positivism, or what are effectively post-modernist approaches.

The accuracy of such depictions has increasingly been called into question. As Duncan Bell points out, '[e]ven a minimally contextualist reading of the respective periods demonstrates that the "debates" are illusory anachronisms, based on an inaccurate interpretation of the scope, coherence and interests of the field'.[20] Indeed, as Peter Wilson has shown, the first great debate between idealism and realism did not actually take place,[21] and discussion between traditionalists and behaviouralists was confined to a brief exchange of views between Hedley Bull and Morton A. Kaplan in the journal *World Politics* in 1966.[22] In short, one can only agree with Ole Wæver that 'the way the discipline [of International Relations] usually reflects its own development falls embarrassingly behind standards developed in sociology of science and historiography'.[23]

None of this should really surprise us, however. In its efforts to attain the status of an academic discipline, the field of International Relations has, right from the start, attempted to define its existence through a stringent categorization of its supposed content: no pigeon-holes, no discipline. Debates between seemingly opposing theoretical views are a way of constituting disciplinary knowledge through

19 S. Smith, 'The Self-Images of a Discipline: A Genealogy of International Relations Theory', in K. Booth and S. Smith (eds.), *International Relations Theory Today* (Cambridge: Polity Press, 1995), pp. 1–37.

20 D. S. Bell, 'Political Theory and the Functions of Intellectual History: A Response to Emmanuel Navon', *Review of International Studies*, 29 (2003), pp. 151–60, at 154.

21 P. Wilson, 'The Myth of the "First Great Debate"', *Review of International Studies*, 24 (1998), pp. 1–15.

22 H. Bull, 'International Theory: The Case for a Classical Approach', *World Politics*, 18 (1966), pp. 361–77; M. A. Kaplan, 'The New Great Debate: Traditionalism vs. Science in International Relations', *World Politics*, 19 (1966), pp. 1–20.

23 O. Wæver, 'The Sociology of a Not So International Discipline: American and European Developments in International Relations', *International Organization*, 52 (1998), pp. 687–727, at 689.

processes of 'field construction' and 'boundary work'.[24] This work is necessarily exclusionist, as it 'entails the development of both arguments to justify particular divisions of knowledge and the strategies to use in constructing and maintaining them'.[25] The result of this is twofold. On the one hand, the field is depicted as made up of a number of schools of thought, characterized by means of overly simplistic conceptualizations of opposing positions (realism–idealism, for instance). As Richard K. Ashley writes, '[e]very great scholarly movement has its own lore, its own collectively recalled creation myths, its ritualized understandings of the titanic struggles fought and challenges still to be overcome in establishing and maintaining its paramountcy'.[26] On the other hand, these schools of thought stake out their terrain by establishing themselves as 'traditions', through recourse to 'classical' authors deemed to have already analysed the relations between political entities in a way compatible with that particular theory of international politics. Whether this was really the case – one need only think of realism's appropriation of Thomas Hobbes (1588–1679) – is not the issue. Morgenthau is thus also taken to be part of a realist canon stretching all the way back to Thucydides, with certain transcending themes they supposedly shared forming the basis for realist theorizing.

Part of the current rehabilitation of classical realism, undertaken in good interpretivist fashion, is therefore also the initiation of new debates on how the likes of Thucydides, Thomas Hobbes, Jean-Jacques Rousseau (1712–1778) and Morgenthau ought to be appropriated for the benefit of the 'canon', and whether we are doing justice to their work by doing so. There is a growing unease with the way classical authors continue to be claimed by proponents of a particular tradition, with little appreciation for the gaping chasm between standard renditions and a more nuanced, contextualized reading of works considered part of that canon. The following chapters share this unease, not only with standard renditions, but with the apparent unwillingness of many of these 'new', 'contextualized'

---

24 E. Messer-Davidow, D. R. Shumway and D. J. Sylvan, 'Introduction: Disciplinary Ways of Knowing' in Messer-Davidow, Shumway and Sylvan (eds.), *Knowledges: Historical and Critical Studies in Disciplinarity* (Charlottesville, VA and London: University Press of Virginia, 1993), pp. 1–21.

25 *Ibid.*, p. 9.

26 R. K. Ashley, 'The Poverty of Neorealism', *International Organization*, 38 (1984), pp. 225–86, at 230.

readings – indeed, almost all of the new readings of Morgenthau – to move beyond the Political Science-oriented field of International Relations. Rehabilitating Morgenthau requires us to engage with the discourses he was part of, even if this means delving into German and US public law debates.

An example may illustrate this deficiency further. The most notable attempt to date to construct a critical disciplinary history of the field of International Relations is Brian C. Schmidt's *The Political Discourse of Anarchy*.[27] The rationale of Schmidt's approach, which he calls 'critical internal discursive history', is that the field itself, and not the general political universe, is the most appropriate context for reconstructing the 'actual conversation among political scientists and other professional scholars who institutionally thought of themselves as participating in a formalized academic setting devoted to the study of international politics'.[28] While this may indeed serve his purpose well, what it also does, however, is occlude the intellectual baggage that many of these conversing scholars brought along before entering the field and engaging in its discourse. This is particularly so in the case of the German-Jewish émigrés who were to populate US International Relations departments in the 1940s. Schmidt only takes a scholar into account once he has entered the discourse, without considering that person's intellectual development. While Schmidt does seem to be aware of this dilemma, he arguably fails to problematize it sufficiently in his analysis.

Hans J. Morgenthau

John Vasquez's empirical analysis of classical realism also highlighted the centrality of Morgenthau's textbook, *Politics Among Nations*, in the development of the realist position in International Relations, asserting that, '[w]ith the advantage of hindsight, there can be no doubt that Morgenthau's work was the single most important vehicle for establishing the dominance of the realist paradigm within the field'.[29] Yet in a sense, the Morgenthau reception seems to follow an intellectual version of Gresham's law: Morgenthau continues to

27 B. C. Schmidt, *The Political Discourse of Anarchy: A Disciplinary History of International Relations* (Albany, NY: State University of New York Press, 1998).
28 *Ibid.*, p. 1.
29 Vasquez, *The Power of Power Politics*, p. 36.

be cited as a part of a realist canon, but not necessarily for reasons with a higher intrinsic value. As Michael C. Williams writes, 'it is difficult to escape the impression that for several decades Morgenthau was more often cited than read, and that in the process he has been reduced by both his supporters and his critics primarily to an implacable opponent of liberalism and an advocate of power politics'.[30] Even more recent efforts to rehabilitate the 'real' thought of those belonging to the tradition continue to block out, misunderstand or simply overlook crucial elements of the intellectual environments of those they are studying. Yes, Morgenthau is indeed worth rereading, but not necessarily for the reasons usually stated.

Morgenthau is above all remembered as the author of one of the most successful textbooks in International Relations, *Politics Among Nations: The Struggle for Power and Peace*.[31] First published in 1948, *Politics Among Nations* was explicitly designed to be an undergraduate text – its closest competitor, which *Politics Among Nations* indeed came to replace, as Morgenthau never tired of pointing out, was Frederick L. Schuman's *International Politics*.[32] An almost immediate success, *Politics Among Nations* went through a variety of reprints and editions – a process that, since Morgenthau's death, has been judiciously upheld by his student, assistant and then colleague and friend, Kenneth W. Thompson.[33]

By February 1962, *Politics Among Nations* had sold 75,100 copies[34] and made its author famous for the 'Realist Theory of

---

30 Williams, *The Realist Tradition*, p. 82.
31 H. J. Morgenthau, *Politics Among Nations: The Struggle for Power and Peace* (New York, NY: Alfred A. Knopf, 1948).
32 F. L. Schuman, *International Politics: An Introduction to the Western State System* (New York, NY: McGraw-Hill, 1933). See, for instance, the letter from Morgenthau to John T. Hawes of Alfred A. Knopf, dated 15 October 1953, HJM-Container 126. Indeed, Morgenthau originally wanted his book to be called 'International Politics' as well, but this met with 'strong objections' from Schuman, who was also publishing all his books with Alfred A. Knopf. See the letter from Roger W. Shugg, Editor at Alfred A. Knopf, to Morgenthau, dated 19 June 1946, HJM-Container 121.
33 See O. Jütersonke, 'Book Review Essay: Morgenthau and the Return to Ethics in a Realist Theory of Power Politics', *Cooperation and Conflict*, 41 (2006), pp. 463–9. *Politics Among Nations* was first published by Alfred A. Knopf in 1948, and reprinted eight times before a second, revised and enlarged edition came out in 1954 (reprinted six times), a third in 1960 (reprinted eight times), a fourth in 1967 (reprinted three times) and a fifth in 1973 (all published with Alfred A. Knopf). Kenneth W. Thompson then posthumously published a sixth edition in 1985, a brief edition in 1992, and, with W. David Clinton, a seventh edition in 2006 (with McGraw-Hill, Boston, MA).
34 Cited in a letter from Joseph G. Sutton of Alfred A. Knopf to Hans Morgenthau, dated 12 April 1962, HJM-Container 121.

International Politics' it proposed, based on the 'Six Principles of Political Realism' Morgenthau had added, upon consultations with the editors, in the second edition. These claim that politics is governed by objective laws having their roots in human nature (1st principle). Realism's key concept is that of interest defined in terms of power (2nd), which is considered an objective category of universal validity (3rd); realism is aware of the moral significance of political action (4th), but 'refuses to identify the moral aspirations of a particular nation with the moral laws that govern the universe' (5th) – in short, it represents 'a distinctive intellectual and moral attitude to matters political' (6th).[35] These principles continue to be mentioned in many, if not most, introductory courses to International Relations theory, where Morgenthau is taken to represent 'classical', 'traditional', 'human nature' realism, in distinction to later versions of 'scientific', 'structural' or 'neo-' realism that, so the story goes, were to take its place.

Those claiming to know Morgenthau and his work beyond the scope of the undergraduate lecture on classical realism will probably begin by pointing out that Morgenthau also played his part in popularizing the notion of the 'national interest', that he was a staunch critic of the Vietnam War,[36] and that, actually, his most interesting book was the often overlooked (and at the time of publication heavily criticized) *Scientific Man vs. Power Politics*.[37] Those growing up in the United States and old enough to remember might also mention Morgenthau's televised confrontation with Special Presidential Assistant McGeorge Bundy (1919–1996) in a debate hosted at Georgetown University in June 1965. And the real connoisseurs may also whisper something about his affection for a certain Hannah Arendt.

35 H. J. Morgenthau, *Politics Among Nations: The Struggle for Power and Peace*. Third edition (New York, NY: Alfred A. Knopf, 1960), pp. 4–11. The book went through plenty of changes during its lifetime. For present purposes, and unless otherwise stated, use will be made primarily of the first edition of 1948 and the third edition of 1960. These represent the two most important versions of the text.

36 On Morgenthau and the Vietnam War see in particular J. W. See, 'A Prophet Without Honor: Hans Morgenthau and the War in Vietnam, 1955–1965', *Pacific Historical Review*, 70 (2001), pp. 419–47; E. G. Rafshoon, 'A Realist's Moral Opposition to War: Hans J. Morgenthau and Vietnam', *Peace and Change*, 26 (2001), pp. 55–77; and W. E. Scheuerman's perceptive chapter, contra Rafshoon, in his *Hans Morgenthau: Realism and Beyond* (Cambridge: Polity Press, 2009), pp. 165–95.

37 H. J. Morgenthau, *Scientific Man vs. Power Politics* (Chicago, IL: University of Chicago Press, 1946).

Biographical curiosities aside, however, Morgenthau generally had for a long time the status of a tedious anachronism, representing long-refuted views expressed in arguments that did not meet the methodological requirements of Political Science. Until recently, the secondary literature on Morgenthau, usually taking the form of articles in periodicals or thematic chapters in books on International Relations theory or the history of the 'discipline', isolated and evaluated certain key concepts – 'interest defined in terms of power', the 'balance of power', the 'national interest', and so on. Little attempt was made to delineate the evolution of these concepts, or to connect the central claims of *Politics Among Nations* with the rest of Morgenthau's work, in particular with what came before it.

A number of lengthier studies that have been appearing recently do try to pay greater attention to Morgenthau's intellectual development and heritage. I have already mentioned some of the most important ones above – others include an edited volume by Michael Williams[38] and a recently published book by William Scheuerman.[39] Yet when it comes to Morgenthau's European background, even these more 'refined', 'detailed' and 'contextualized' readings of Morgenthau still tend to rely on the existing anglophone secondary literature and on Morgenthau's own account of his life in the 'Fragment of an Intellectual Biography' and his interview with Bernhard Johnson, both produced towards the end of Morgenthau's life and published by Kenneth W. Thompson and Robert J. Myers.[40] Thus we have tended to accept Morgenthau's assertion that his doctoral dissertation was a reaction to Carl Schmitt (1888–1985), that everyone was conspiring against him in Geneva, and that his anti-scientific stance in *Scientific Man vs. Power Politics* and *Politics Among Nations* stems from a long-held scepticism about the merits of empiricist research. I will attempt to tackle each of these issues in Chapters 2, 3 and 4.

What will emerge from our efforts is a picture of Morgenthau that, rather than scolding him for argumentative inconsistency and

38 M. C. Williams (ed.), *Realism Reconsidered: The Legacy of Hans J. Morgenthau in International Relations* (Oxford University Press, 2007).

39 Scheuerman, *Hans Morgenthau*.

40 H. J. Morgenthau, 'Fragment of an Intellectual Autobiography: 1904–1932' and 'Interview with Bernhard Johnson', in K. W. Thompson and R. J. Meyers (eds.), *Truth and Tragedy: A Tribute to Hans J. Morgenthau*. Second edition with new Postscript (New Brunswick, NJ: Transaction Books), pp. 1–17 and 333–86.

blatant contradictions in his 'oeuvre', actually brings out the ad hoc nature and heterogeneity of his thinking as positive (and in no way unnatural) elements in the path of the intellectual. Colin Loader has made a similar argument in his impressive study of the sociologist Karl Mannheim (1893–1947), pointing to

> the tendency to overlook Mannheim's experimental attitude and to take the heterogeneity of his work simply as a weakness. Even those who recognize Mannheim's experimental approach still generally view him as a confused thinker who has exhausted the patience of many commentators. Those who have tried to defend Mannheim without really taking this heterogeneity into account have actually done him more harm than good.[41]

The same can be said of Morgenthau. Contextualization does not simply entail inserting Morgenthau's work into its social environment of production, but also includes identifying supposed as well as real interlocutors and debates and, in the special case of the intellectual émigré, also the tensions and competing mindsets Morgenthau was confronted with.

Classics and redescriptions

Morgenthau, then, is commonly taken as representative of classical, 'human nature' realism in International Relations, and his textbook *Politics Among Nations* is deemed a central pillar of the International Relations canon. As Niklas Luhmann (1927–1998) has repeatedly pointed out, however, there are still no thorough investigations of the functions of classics in academic, literary and artistic practice, although they are generally deemed to be central to the identity of disciplines.[42] Indeed, the role of classic texts goes beyond the common 'justification-surrogating footnote reference to an unread citation fossil',[43] and is, as Luhmann writes, a 'multifunctional invention': classics facilitate teaching, they offer a way of ordering redundant material by tying it to a particular 'exemplary' name

---

41 C. Loader, *The Intellectual Development of Karl Mannheim: Culture, Politics, Planning* (Cambridge University Press, 1985), p. 3; notes omitted.
42 See J. C. Alexander, 'The Centrality of the Classics', in A. Giddens and J. H. Turner (eds.), *Social Theory Today* (Cambridge: Polity Press, 1987), pp. 11–57.
43 As Jens Kersten, *Georg Jellinek und die klassische Staatslehre* (Tübingen: Mohr Siebeck, 2000), p. 3, so brilliantly puts it in German: 'begründungs-surrogierendes Fussnotenzitat auf ein ungelesenes Zitierfossil'.

and, perhaps most significantly, they are a way of turning substantive problems into textual ones, thereby avoiding answers to potentially difficult contemporary questions through recourse to what has already been said regarding a certain 'transcending' issue.[44]

These functions are all present in the case of *Politics Among Nations*. The book continues to be the standard example of classical realism in most undergraduate courses on International Relations theory. Morgenthau is also commonly cited when scholars and students feel the need to engage in name-dropping when referring to the balance of power, power politics or the national interest. And, indeed, calls for a 'return to the roots' are prominent in recent attempts to rehabilitate classical realism in favour of more contemporary frameworks that are deemed inadequate in one way or another. 'What would Hans Morgenthau say?' becomes a useful starting point for a variety of reflections on both current international affairs and the state of the 'discipline' of International Relations.[45]

Moreover, the functions of classics are quite particular in International Relations. In contrast to the more established, 'canonized' social science disciplines, the relatively recent creation that is the field of International Relations is still struggling to attain a comparable status – and some (including Morgenthau) might even argue that given the heterogeneous nature of the subject matter dealt with and the methods applied, any such attempt would be futile, or at least misplaced.[46] Indeed, it seems appropriate to speak of the scientific study of international politics or of social scientists studying international relations, as does Richard Ashley, for instance.[47] Yet in the absence of its own proper canon, International Relations scholars inevitably engage in a 'disciplining' process involving the

---

44 N. Luhmann, *Die Wissenschaft der Gesellschaft* (Frankfurt a.M.: Suhrkamp, 1992), p. 452.

45 See M. C. Williams, 'Introduction', in Williams (ed.), *Realism Reconsidered*, pp. 1–17, at 1.

46 As Morgenthau would go on to write: 'To establish an academic discipline with the adjective "international" as its focus is obviously no more possible than to centre one on the adjective "national". Such attempts, on the national or international level, will either lead to the restoration, by dint of their own logic, of the traditional academic disciplines and consequently to the frustration of interdisciplinary integration, or else to the drowning of all discipline in a chaotic mass of unrelated data which will at best receive from the ever-changing whims of public opinion a semblance of order and direction'; H. J. Morgenthau, 'Area Studies and the Study of International Relations', *Social Science Research Bulletin*, 4 (1952), pp. 647–55, at 653.

47 Ashley, 'The Poverty of Neorealism', p. 285.

frantic search and hopeful appropriation of classical texts from history, theology, political theory, sociology, psychology, and so on. Hence Thucydides, Kautilya, Hobbes, Niccolò Machiavelli (1469–1527), Clausewitz and Vladimir Ilyich Lenin (1870–1924) all became classics of the realist paradigm. Now, a few decades later, a more genuine list of so-called classics is emerging, including the likes of E. H. Carr, John H. Herz (1908–2005), Hans Morgenthau, Kenneth N. Waltz and Arnold Wolfers (1892–1968), to name but a few. How these texts became standard works – indeed, it may be argued that Waltz's *Theory of International Politics* only became representative of the label 'neo-realism' because of Richard Ashley's poignant critique (and inevitable pigeonholing) of it – is no longer the central issue.[48]

A few examples may help illustrate this trend. Both John Vasquez, in his *Classics of International Relations*, as well as Chris Brown, Terry Nardin and Nicolas Rengger, in their *International Relations in Political Thought*, assemble excerpts ranging from antiquity to the present for their stated purpose of providing an overview of thought on International Relations. Vasquez writes:

I have tried to select those works that are regarded as classics in Western civilization and essential to a liberal education. In selecting more recent works, I have tried to select classics of the discipline – representatives of the most influential work published on international relations in each of the last four decades.[49]

Chris Brown and his colleagues begin with the following:

In recent years there has been a revival of interest in the classical theory of international relations, or, as we will call it here, 'international political theory.' We define international political theory as that aspect of the discourse of International Relations which addresses explicitly issues concerning norms, interpretation, and the ontological foundations of the discipline.[50]

The jury is still out as to whether Marcus Aurelius or Dante Alighieri were really discussing the ontological foundations of International

---

48 K. N. Waltz, *Theory of International Politics* (Reading, MA: Addison-Wesley, 1979); Ashley, 'The Poverty of Neorealism'.
49 J. A. Vasquez, *Classics of International Relations*. Second edition (Englewood Cliffs, NJ: Prentice Hall, 1990), p. xv.
50 C. Brown, T. Nardin and N. Rengger, *International Relations in Political Thought. Texts from Ancient Greeks to the First World War* (Cambridge University Press, 2002), p. 1.

Relations, but, be that as it may, the presumption seems to be that through recourse to the great names of 'Western civilization' (whatever happened to the likes of Kautilya and Lao Tzu?), we are able to get to the bottom of this mysterious creature called 'International Relations' with which many of us strive to earn a living.

This is not to say, of course, that the field of International Relations should work any differently than any other academic field, and that it should not engage in the construction of traditions and theoretical positions that build on foundational texts. Indeed, Kenneth W. Thompson offers a useful introduction to the field in his *Masters of International Thought*.[51] For a start, there are no 'classical' authors – everyone included is from the period after the field was institutionally established in the early decades of the twentieth century. Nonetheless, it is telling that even Thompson, one of Morgenthau's closest collaborators, starts the latter's bibliography with *Scientific Man vs. Power Politics*, as if none of what Morgenthau wrote before – and as this book attempts to demonstrate, there was plenty of it – mattered for our understanding of the scholar and his work.

Recently, there have been a number of quite sophisticated attempts at rewriting the history of realist thought. The outstanding instance here is Jonathan Haslam's book, *No Virtue Like Necessity*.[52] Haslam convincingly shows that realist notions can indeed be found in the expressions of numerous scholars and diplomats from the sixteenth century to the present, writing from a variety of philosophical perspectives, and in ever-changing contexts. The book's important message is that elements of the realist position are not only contained in the writings of usual suspects such as Machiavelli and Otto von Bismarck (1815–1898), but also in the work of Rousseau and Kant, or even Giovanni Botero (c.1544–1617) and Samuel von Pufendorf (1632–1694), for example, scholars who are usually not immediately associated with realism in International Relations theory. Haslam thus points to the inadequacy of pigeonholing so-called canonical texts and their authors into mutually exclusive traditions, or schools of thought, a procedure that may be conducive to social-scientific

51 K. W. Thompson, *Masters of International Thought: Major Twentieth-Century Theorists and the World Crisis* (Baton Rouge, LA and London: Louisiana State University Press, 1980).
52 J. Haslam, *No Virtue Like Necessity: Realist Thought in International Relations since Machiavelli* (New Haven, CT and London: Yale University Press, 2002).

theorizing, but that nonetheless leads to significant exclusion, occlusion and inevitable misinterpretation. Yet for all his efforts, Haslam is never far from engaging in precisely what he is criticizing – not least through the choice of historical figures he decides to address. And by reading realist notions into the texts, Haslam is always on the brink of falling into the same trap of 'abstract and dogmatic generalization' himself, by over-emphasizing the apparent continuity in realist thought. Whereas he very rightly warns against referring to something called realist 'theory', as 'this imposes upon a loose and fragmented assemblage of thought a degree of coherence which is arguably unjustified and unnecessary', one page later he claims that Robert Tucker's 'main alignment reaches back to Machiavelli and the Reasons of State tradition', and that Kenneth Waltz 'stands furthest along a continuum dating from Botero'.[53] It is precisely these kinds of assertions that must be avoided, for they strengthen the hand of those who are looking for an intellectual justification for their own theories by grazing through the 'classics' in the hunt for glimmers of some enduring (though artificially constructed) question or dilemma.

However to the point Luhmann's critique may be, the recourse to the classics need not only be deconstructed as a negative practice. Morgenthau has been receiving renewed attention that stems from a substantive dissatisfaction with the way mainstream schools of thought in International Relations fail to pay enough attention to the production of foreign policy, from the sense that rational choice approaches are unable to adequately explain cooperation, and from an overall feeling that in the face of a single superpower waging a War on Terror, International Relations theory requires a return to ethics and insights from the humanities.

In the conclusion to Michael Williams' recently published edited volume on Morgenthau, Richard Ned Lebow outlines four rather more positive reasons why scholars continue to be drawn to older texts.[54] The first is 'justification': being able to show how one's own work fits into a discourse associated with famous authors can go beyond the practice of name-dropping, and can indeed be a source

---

53 *Ibid.*, pp. 249–50.
54 R. N. Lebow, 'Texts, Paradigms, and Political Change', in Williams (ed.), *Realism Reconsidered*, pp. 241–68, at 246–50.

of legitimacy and respect in the eyes of the potential reader. The second reason is 'delegitimization': here, the idea is that one refers back to the famous authors of a discourse that one profoundly disagrees with, in order to show that these household names have actually been misinterpreted, and do not really stand for what they have been (often over centuries) taken to argue. 'Reclaiming texts', Lebow's third reason, is then a combination of the first two: it is legitimate to continue focusing on a particular author, but the reasons for doing so are not the crucial ones. As Lebow points out, this is indeed what I am doing in my own work here.[55] As I have argued before[56] and continue to argue in this book, Morgenthau is indeed still worth reading, but not in order to cite his six principles of realism or make him part of a hidden discourse with a Carl Schmitt or Max Weber, but rather to use him as a vehicle to flesh out a number of important issues on the relationship between (international) law, ethics and politics. Morgenthau's academic career saw him continuously grappling with the tensions pertaining to the threshold between law and politics, and uncovering the details of these tensions will not only further our understanding of Morgenthau (a valid justification in its own right), but will moreover (re)open avenues for making sense of the discursive incommensurability between the fields of International Law and International Relations.

The fourth and final reason Lebow outlines is that of 'texts as inspirations'. This is when thorough, hermeneutical readings of older texts are forgone for looser interpretations serving the purpose of inspiring the author into originality by using the classic as a platform or springboard from which to leap into creative thought. Hegel's reading of *Antigone* and Sigmund Freud's (1856–1939) use of *Oedipus Tyrannus* are obvious examples.[57]

Inspiration aside, perhaps aiming for hermeneutically precise interpretation of the classics is not the way forward anyway. In his address commemorating sixty years since Edmund Husserl's (1859–1938) famous Viennese Lectures, Niklas Luhmann argued

55 *Ibid.*, p. 248.
56 O. Jütersonke, 'Book Review Essay: Morgenthau and the Return to Ethics'; Jütersonke, 'Hans J. Morgenthau on the Limits of Justiciability in International Law', *Journal of the History of International Law*, 8 (2006), pp. 181–211; Jütersonke, 'The Image of Law in *Politics Among Nations*', in Williams (ed.), *Realism Reconsidered*, pp. 93–117.
57 See also D. J. Schmidt, *On Germans and Other Greeks: Tragedy and Ethical Life* (Bloomington, IN: University of Indiana Press, 2001).

that, from a sociological point of view, the time distance was too great to engage fruitfully in a textual exegesis along hermeneutical directives.[58] Instead, Luhmann proposed to situate Husserl's text back into the communicative situation of its time, in order for it to be possible to determine towards what, without it necessarily being specified in the text itself, the text was aimed. In other words, Luhmann proposed to read Husserl's text as communicative actions, formulated in a particular period, that reacted with its descriptions to the society of that period. This procedure, borrowing a term from Mary Hesse's work on the function of metaphoric language in scientific explanations,[59] Luhmann called 'redescription':

> The theoretical redescription of redescriptions of descriptions is an autological concept, one that is applicable to itself. It does not claim to give a justification – and even less a better justification. The concept therefore does not leave itself open to infinite redress. It does what it does, and constitutes itself that way. It operates, itself, autopoietically, without aiming for a calm-instilling, conclusive formula.[60]

Redescriptions of descriptions do not aim for progress, for an amelioration or increase of knowledge, for a hermeneutical exegesis of the actual meaning, nor for critique. Rather, what happens in this way is a continuous transformation of necessity into contingency (in the sociological sense of the term): what was accepted as obvious and *lebensweltlich* is now conceived as a particularity of a certain approach or way of observation.

To illustrate: the renewed focus on Morgenthau can arguably be linked to growing interest in the anglophone social sciences and law, over the past decade or so, in the exceptionally rich – both culturally and intellectually – period of the Weimar Republic. This may have something to do with the fact that the period produced very stimulating debates on the virtues (or otherwise) of liberalism. In a world in which the ideological battle of the Cold War is over, and with liberalism supposedly enjoying unchallenged supremacy, a coherent and substantial critique of liberalism has been received with open arms. Hence a sudden resurgence of Carl Schmitt, as

---

58 N. Luhmann, *Die neuzeitlichen Wissenschaften und die Phänomenologie* (Vienna: Picus, 1996).
59 M. B. Hesse, *Models and Analogies in Science* (Notre Dame, IN: University of Indiana Press, 1966).
60 Luhmann, *Die neuzeitlichen Wissenschaften*, p. 58.

well as Hans Kelsen (1881–1973), Walter Benjamin (1892–1940), Franz L. Neumann (1900–1954), Hermann Heller (1891–1933) – the list is remarkably long. As Michael Stolleis rightly points out, however, when engaging in such exercises, it is important not to forget that those who were part of these rich discussions in Weimar did not think in the same mindset as later generations of scholars who, with hindsight, have generally been guided by the question 'how could it have come to that?'.[61] Post-1945 scholarship on the Weimar Republic was predominantly interested in the origins of National Socialism, and many details were unearthed that may otherwise not have surfaced. Yet it also shifted our mode of thought on the subject 'Weimar' as a whole. The 'open horizon' (a term Stolleis borrows from Husserl) of the Weimar intellectuals is precisely what this book is trying to redescribe.

In this vein, the proposed redescription of Morgenthau in the following chapters will not hunt after the 'real' or 'right' meaning of his writings, nor will it engage in the quest for continuity in his thought – and thus develop a critical stance on rupture and contradiction. Just as Richard Ashley redescribed Morgenthau's classical realism from the position of the structuralist response – Louis Althusser (1918–1990), Pierre Bourdieu (1930–2002) – in the 1970s,[62] my aim will likewise be to offer a redescription in a time of communicative reason (Jürgen Habermas) and autopoietic social systems (Niklas Luhmann).

Such a relativist approach means that earlier redescriptions of Morgenthau cannot simply be labelled as wrong or false. Yet they can be characterized as inadequate or incomplete *with respect to my own redescription of Morgenthau*. Existing work was obviously written with a particular aim in mind, and may indeed have served its purpose well. Factual mistakes and contradictions in the argument can, of course, be flagged and corrected. Yet the demands of and standards set by this monograph cannot be used to claim that the reading herein proposed is the right one, with all existing interpretations of Morgenthau thereby being disqualified. The present work may go into Morgenthau's juridical works in greater detail than

---

61 M. Stolleis, *Geschichte des öffentlichen Rechts in Deutschland: Weimarer Republik und Nationalsozialismus* (Munich: C. H. Beck, 2002), p. 153.
62 Ashley, 'The Poverty of Neorealism'.

anything that has been written before and, from the perspective of International Relations, it may venture further into legal debates than has been the case previously. But this in no way rules out other redescriptions of Morgenthau's thought, written in another time for a different purpose. Producing 'the last words' on Morgenthau is not the aim here. Much remains to be addressed, in particular regarding the under-studied impact of German-Jewish émigré scholars on US academia in general.

Biography

Given Morgenthau's centrality in the understanding and perception of realism in International Relations, it is all the more interesting to observe that his intellectual origins have only recently moved into the spotlight – and a rather dim bulb it is at best. Morgenthau, it must be said, did not help our cause, downplaying his past and deliberately trying to break with his earlier European career, either by not talking about it at all, or by leaving out decisive references. As Richard Ned Lebow writes, Morgenthau 'was protective of his personal life, and questions about his German past were taboo'.[63]

So who was this Hans Joachim Morgenthau? Hans was born in Coburg, a small town that was at the time the capital of the Duchy of Saxony-Coburg and Gotha (Bavaria), on 17 February 1904. An only son of Ludwig Morgenthau, a medical doctor with his own practice in Coburg, and Frieda Bachmann, an apparently caring mother who continuously had to save him from his 'rather neurotic and oppressive father',[64] Hans seemed to have led a somewhat lonely childhood, experiencing the all-too-common incidents associated with his Jewish background. Indeed, Coburg became a hotbed for radicalism following the end of the First World War, and was even the first German town to bestow honorary citizenship on Adolf Hitler in 1933. For Morgenthau, all this seemingly led to him becoming the introvert outsider who, although excelling in school, had trouble interacting positively with his social environment.

After a stint of one semester in the philosophy faculty of the University of Frankfurt, Morgenthau eventually opted for law in

---

63 Lebow, *The Tragic Vision of Politics*, p. 219.
64 Morgenthau, 'Interview with Bernhard Johnson', p. 337.

Munich, as his father thought literature, Morgenthau's subject of choice, to be an unprofitable occupation. He passed his first law exam on 12 February 1927, and decided to go for the three-year 'dunce's tour' of the conventional training as legal assessor, to the great pleasure of his father.[65] On Christmas Day 1927, Morgenthau came down with tuberculosis and needed to have one of his lungs removed. Already physically weak to begin with, this episode led him to become even more fragile, a trait that would characterize him until the end of his life.

In May 1928 Morgenthau transferred to Frankfurt am Main, where he would work for three years with the prominent Hugo Sinzheimer (1875–1945), the 'father of German labour law'[66] and undoubtedly one of Morgenthau's most significant mentors.[67] During this period, he also completed his doctorate under the supervision of Karl Strupp (1886–1940), a reputed international lawyer at the University of Frankfurt.[68] Although his dissertation, which will be dealt with in Chapter 2, met with all-round praise (including from such lofty heights as the pen of Hersch Lauterpacht (1897–1960) and Carl Schmitt), Morgenthau failed to do well in his oral exams, thus earning him only a *magna cum laude*, and not the *summa cum laude* he had expected.[69]

Whereas the story of most German-Jewish émigrés contains the crucial bit when the National-Socialist regime dismisses them from their positions or puts them into early retirement, Morgenthau's biography followed a somewhat different trajectory. In October 1931, Morgenthau himself requested to be released from his work

65 C. Frei, *Hans J. Morgenthau: An Intellectual Biography* (Baton Rouge, LA: Louisiana State University Press, 2001), p. 34.

66 K. Kubo, *Hugo Sinzheimer – Vater des deutschen Arbeitsrechts: eine Biographie* (Cologne: Bund-Verlag, 1995).

67 In a letter Morgenthau wrote to Sinzheimer from Geneva on 27 Janaury 1943, he speaks of the 'inner relations that bind me to you and always will bind me ... after all, I was not only your employee, but I breathed the intellectual and moral air that you exhaled', HJM-Container 197. The influence of Sinzheimer on Morgenthau has been nicely analysed by William Scheuerman in his 'Realism and the Left: The Case of Hans J. Morgenthau', *Review of International Studies*, 34 (2008), pp. 29–51; see also Scheuerman, *Hans Morgenthau*, pp. 11–39. Other notable German-Jewish jurists who worked under Sinzheimer at the time included Otto Kahn-Freund (1900–79) and Franz L. Neumann.

68 Strupp lost his position in 1933 and fled first to Istanbul and then to France, where he committed suicide upon the arrival of invading German troops.

69 See Frei, *Hans J. Morgenthau*, p. 40.

in the service of the Prussian judicial system in order to 'prepare for a university career'.[70] Yet at the time there was a severe over-supply of law graduates looking for positions in academia. Arthur Baumgarten (1884–1966), professor of legal philosophy at the University of Frankfurt with whom Morgenthau had begun think-ing about his habilitation, thus helped Morgenthau obtain a vacant teaching position at the University of Geneva, where Baumgarten himself had taught earlier in his career. On his twenty-eighth birth-day, on 17 February 1932, Morgenthau had left of his own accord for Switzerland.

This move did not have the immediate positive effect Morgenthau had anticipated. Not only did he fare miserably at the University in Geneva with his habilitation (a story, starring Hans Kelsen and Paul Guggenheim (1899–1977), that will be outlined in Chapter 3), but the fact that he had left Germany in 1932 also meant that he was no longer classified as an academic refugee: his application in late 1933 was turned down by the Rockefeller and Carnegie Foundations in New York, by the Academic Assistance Council in London, and the International Jewish Committee in Amsterdam.[71] By a stroke of good fortune, the Emergency Committee for German Scholars Abroad inquired in early 1935 whether Morgenthau would be interested in a position at the *Instituto de Estudios Internacionales y Económicos* in Madrid, which Leo Gross (1903–1990), a student of Kelsen in Vienna, had turned down.[72] Morgenthau gladly accepted the offer.

The joy was short-lived, however. While on holiday in Italy with his wife Irma Thormann in July 1936, civil war broke out in Spain, and the Morgenthaus were unable to return to Madrid. All books,

---

70 *Ibid.*, p. 42.
71 For the sake of accuracy, it ought to be mentioned that Morgenthau remained a mem-ber of the labour court in Frankfurt until the end of 1933, when he was indeed 'retired' from his position as a consequence of the infamous Law for the Reconstitution of the Professional Civil Service of 7 April 1933. Morgenthau would later use this fact to demand financial reparation, which he received in the form of retroactive pension payments for a district court magistrate until 1951. Frei, *Hans J. Morgenthau*, pp. 49–50.
72 Leo Gross would also emigrate to the United States, becoming Professor of International Law and Organization at the Fletcher School of Law and Diplomacy, Tufts University. Unsurprisingly, he is one of the few that did situate the intellectual origins of Morgenthau in the German law debates of the 1920s; L. Gross, 'On the Justiciability of International Disputes', in Thompson and Meyers, *Truth and Tragedy*, pp. 203–19.

manuscripts and research materials were out of reach, and, as part of the Popular Front's measures taken against German citizens, their safe at the Viscaya Bank was confiscated – lost was all their money, the family jewellery, Hans' golden watch: 'In an ironic twist of fate', Frei writes, 'Morgenthau, who had already become an unwelcome citizen in Germany, now lost everything in Republican Spain because of his German citizenship'.[73]

This time, the only offer of the Emergency Committee for German Scholars Abroad entailed becoming the manager of a new settlement in Venezuela. Morgenthau declined. The United States now seemed the only option, even though the prospects were bleak, with Karl Löwenstein (1891–1973) pointing out that New York City was teeming with young German jurists already.[74] Helped in Geneva by the affidavit of his wife's rich cousin Samuel Rothschild, the Morgenthaus eventually managed to obtain immigration visas. They boarded the *SS Königstein* in Antwerp on 17 July 1937, bound for New York.

After five months of fruitless job-hunting, Morgenthau was finally offered a position as instructor at Brooklyn College. There, for $3.50 an hour, he would work for an entire year before being offered a job at the University of Kansas City in January 1939. Again, Morgenthau spent a miserable time in Kansas, with a huge teaching load of eighteen hours per week and a tiny office that had previously been used

---

73 Frei, *Hans J. Morgenthau*, p. 57. When the remnants of his belongings were finally shipped to him in the United States, the *Kansas City Times* published a short article about the issue on 20 January 1941. Showing a picture of Morgenthau unpacking the boxes that were sent to him and entitled 'Seven Vests From General Franco', the article reads: 'Strung on the arms of Dr. Hans Morgenthau of the University of Kansas City law school are all he will ever see of the seven suits he was forced to abandon in his Madrid apartment when the Franco rebellion broke out in July, 1936. The vests and a few other things arrived last week at the Morgenthau apartment, 303 Brush Creek boulevard, after four years of trying to persuade the Spanish government to release the family's property and household furnishings. The boxes at Dr. Morgenthau's feet hold such valuable things as a pair of broken scales and half a tube of toothpaste.'

74 Letter from Karl Löwenstein to Morgenthau, dated 28 March 1935, HJM-Container 37. Also cited in Frei, *Hans J. Morgenthau*, p. 59. Löwenstein, thirteen years older than Morgenthau and already a reputed, 'habilitated' jurist at the time of the Nazi crackdown, was offered a professorship in the Department of Government at Yale in December 1933, with half of his salary coming from the funds of the Emergency Committee in Aid of Displaced Foreign Scholars; see E. C. Stiefel and F. Mecklenburg, *Deutsche Juristen im amerikanischen Exil (1933–1950)* (Tübingen: Mohr, 1991), pp. 101–4.

for a quite different purpose.[75] As Morgenthau complained to the university president Clarence Decker (1904–1969), the office was

during the heating period filled with hot steam which settles down on wall, floor and all objects in form of water. The smell, a composite of toilet and laundry, leads not infrequently to situations embarrassing for myself when visitors demonstrate their displeasure. There is sitting space for only one person; when more than one person wants to see me, we have either all to stand up or two persons have to use one chair.[76]

Instead of improving his plight, however, his confrontation with Decker eventually got him fired. Although he would go on to win the subsequent appeal he presented to the American Association of University Professors and the Association of American Law Schools, what really saved him were two simultaneous offers in August 1943, the same year he passed the Missouri bar exam and became a naturalized US citizen. The first was a temporary research position with Frederick S. Dunn (1893–1962) at Yale's Institute of International Studies; the second was the offer to replace Quincy Wright (1890–1970) for six months at the University of Chicago. Morgenthau opted for the latter, and when Wright's absence went from six to eighteen months, Morgenthau was able to establish himself firmly enough for Chicago to offer him a teaching position upon Wright's return.

The rest is known, and well summarized by Christoph Frei.[77] Between 1946 and 1951 alone, Morgenthau published six books and thirty-four articles, including his most famous monographs *Scientific Man vs. Power Politics*, *Politics Among Nations* and *In Defense of the National Interest*.[78] He became a full professor in Chicago in 1949, and founded the Center for the Study of American Foreign and Military Policy there in 1950. When forced to retire in 1971, he moved to New York, where he would continue teaching at the City University and the New School for Social Research. Between 1949 and 1977, Morgenthau also held twenty guest professorships at ten

---

75 These early years in the United States are also crucial for our understanding of Morgenthau's intellectual development – see Chapter 4.
76 Letter from Morgenthau to Clarence Decker, dated 19 September 1941, HJM-Container 88; also cited in Frei, *Hans J. Morgenthau*, p. 66.
77 *Ibid.*, pp. 74–80.
78 H. J. Morgenthau, *In Defense of the National Interest: A Critical Examination of American Foreign Policy* (New York, NY: Alfred A. Knopf, 1951).

US universities, including Harvard, Yale, Columbia and Princeton. Moreover, he was guest professor in Salzburg, Madrid, Geneva, New Delhi and Haifa. In addition, his biographer Frei counted more than 1,300 formal guest lectures between 1950 and 1980. Walter Scheel, President of the Federal Republic of Germany, awarded him the High Order of Merit (*das Große Bundesverdienstkreuz*) in 1975. Hans Morgenthau died, at the age of seventy-six, on 19 July 1980.

Delving into Morgenthau's past

That there was a story about Morgenthau worth telling was first recognized by Niels Amstrup, who published an article on the 'early Morgenthau' in the journal *Cooperation and Conflict* in 1978. 'It seems to have been forgotten', he wrote, 'that before his departure to the United States in 1937 he [Morgenthau] had written several books and articles on international law and on the relations between law and politics'.[79] Amstrup's short analysis correctly concluded that the origins of realism were not to be found in US debates between utopians (or idealists) and realists, but rather in debates of continental European *Staatslehre*.

Nothing more would come of it, however. Amstrup was unable to interview the elderly Morgenthau because of the latter's ill health (Morgenthau would die a year later), and failed to excavate any new material in response to a series of written enquiries. It would need another decade before Christoph Frei started out on his endeavour of writing an intellectual biography of Morgenthau, a useful book that I already cited in the previous section.[80] Frei collaborated with Morgenthau's children, Matthew and Susanna, interviewed a whole host of relatives, friends and colleagues of Morgenthau, and was the first to delve into the wealth of archival material that can today be found in the Library of Congress in Washington, DC, and in the Leo Baeck Institute in New York. And Frei's book (first published in German in 1993, later translated into English in 2001), does not do a bad job of elaborating on the steps in Morgenthau's life. We also have Frei to thank for pointing out not only the link between

---

79 N. Amstrup, 'The "Early" Morgenthau: A Comment on the Intellectual Origins of Realism', *Cooperation and Conflict*, 13 (1978), pp. 163–75, at 163.
80 Frei, *Hans J. Morgenthau*.

Morgenthau and Max Weber, but also the influence of the work of Friedrich Nietzsche (1844–1900) on Morgenthau's thought. Yet the main shortcoming of Frei's monograph is that it is too general to be able to draw any clear conclusions from the research: though an historical account, it does not adequately situate Morgenthau in the academic controversies and debates of the time, neither in Law nor in the fledgling field of International Relations. Frei analyses Morgenthau's early legal works, for instance, but does not capture the overarching themes prevalent in the 1920s. The same goes for Morgenthau's emigration to the United States, where neither the institutional constraints nor the intellectual circumstances Morgenthau was confronted with are clearly recognized.

In the field of International Law, our insights on Morgenthau were given a boost through the publication of Martti Koskenniemi's *Gentle Civilizer of Nations: The Rise and Fall of International Law 1870–1960*.[81] Indeed, it would be no exaggeration to declare that Koskenniemi's book is the only one until now to have been able to effectively situate Morgenthau in the history of both International Law and International Relations. Koskenniemi had already used Morgenthau as exemplary of the rule-scepticist position in his conceptualization of the structure of international legal argument in his opus *From Apology to Utopia*.[82] Then, in the year 2000, Koskenniemi returned to Morgenthau in an essay entitled 'Carl Schmitt, Hans Morgenthau, and the Image of Law in International Relations',[83] a precursor to the argument he would go on to elaborate in the *Gentle Civilizer*. Although Koskenniemi may be over-emphasizing the link with Carl Schmitt somewhat, his work is alone to date in convincingly demonstrating the intricate links between legal debates in the Weimar Republic and Morgenthau's political realism. The present

---

81 M. Koskenniemi, *The Gentle Civilizer of Nations: The Rise and Fall of International Law 1870–1960* (Cambridge University Press, 2002). Other, shorter works on Morgenthau from an international law perspective include Chimni, *International Law and World Order*, pp. 22–72; and A. Carty, 'The Continuing Influence of Kelsen on the General Perception of the Discipline of International Law', *European Journal of International Law*, 9 (1998), pp. 344–54.

82 M. Koskenniemi, *From Apology to Utopia: The Structure of International Legal Argument* [1989]. Reissue with a new Epilogue (Cambridge University Press, 2005).

83 M. Koskenniemi, 'Carl Schmitt, Hans Morgenthau, and the Image of Law in International Relations', in M. Byers (ed.), *The Role of Law in International Politics: Essays in International Relations and International Law* (Oxford University Press, 2000), pp. 17–34.

book can be seen as an elaboration of some of Koskenniemi's core insights, but from the perspective of International Relations.

Another set of relevant pieces on Morgenthau's move from law to politics comes from the pen of Alfons Söllner, a specialist in intellectual migration.[84] Söllner shows that if one takes into account those émigré academics who were still able to complete their studies (usually a doctorate) at German-speaking universities, and who attained a teaching position (usually a professorship) in Political Science (including International Relations) in their host country, one reaches a number of at least sixty-four. Over half of them had studied law, the rest came mostly from philosophy faculties or the *Staatswissenschaften*. Ninety per cent ended up in the United States, and more than half in International Relations.[85] Söllner focuses on Hans Kelsen, Morgenthau, John H. Herz and Karl W. Deutsch (1912–1992). As will be spelt out in more detail in Chapter 4, however, it is worth differentiating what this move to Political Science actually entailed. Indeed, Deutsch is one of the few who was able to immerse himself in the behaviouralist social sciences successfully. Morgenthau campaigned against them aggressively, Herz was somewhat of a bystander in this respect during his time at the Office of Strategic Studies, and the elderly Kelsen, though endowed with a chair in Political Science at the University of California (Berkeley), came nowhere near to changing his perspective.

Worth mentioning are also articles by Jan Willem Honig, Hans-Karl Pichler, Ulrik Enemark Petersen and Robert Schuett.[86] Honig argues that the realism Morgenthau would develop from *Scientific Man vs. Power Politics* onwards entailed a rejection of the 'optimism

---

84 A Söllner, 'From Public Law to Political Science? The Emigration of German Scholars after 1933 and their Influence on the Transformation of a Discipline', in M. G. Ash and A. Söllner, *Forced Migration and Scientific Change: Émigré German-Speaking Scientists and Scholars After 1933* (Cambridge University Press, 1996), pp. 246–72; Söllner, 'German Conservatism in America: Morgenthau's Political Realism', *Telos*, 72 (1987), pp. 161–72; Söllner, 'Vom Völkerrecht zum *science of international relations*. Vier typische Vertreter der politikwissenschaftlichen Emigration', in I. Srubar (ed.), *Exil, Wissenschaft, Identität: Die Emigration deutscher Sozialwissenschaftler 1933–1945* (Frankfurt a.M.: Suhrkamp, 1988), pp. 164–80.

85 *Ibid.*, pp. 164–5.

86 J. W. Honig, 'Totalitarianism and Realism: Hans Morgenthau's German Years', *Security Studies*, 5 (1995/6), pp. 283–313; H.-K. Pichler, 'The Godfathers of "Truth": Max Weber and Carl Schmitt in Morgenthau's Theory of Power Politics', *Review of International Studies*, 24 (1998), pp. 185–200; U. E. Petersen, 'Breathing Nietzsche's Air: New Reflections on Morgenthau's Concepts of Power and Human Nature', *Alternatives*, 24 (1999), pp. 83–119; R. Schuett, 'Freudian Roots of Political

and idealism' of his earlier writings on international law, in favour of insights drawn from the nineteenth-century German tradition of *Realpolitik*, coupled with lessons learned from 'paleorealist' conceptions of international politics advocated by the far-right in Weimar and the National-Socialist regime. Pichler attempts to show how Morgenthau uses the thought of Max Weber and Carl Schmitt to overcome the value determinacy of social science in order to analyse international politics 'objectively' as the ultimate pursuit and preservation of the national interest, but unfortunately does not go into the legal debates that Schmitt and Morgenthau were part of. Petersen does a good job of fleshing out the Nietzschean elements in Morgenthau's conception of power and human nature and, in the process, manages to debunk the view (expounded by Pichler and others), that Morgenthau's thought is simply a rephrasing of the ideas of Max Weber. Schuett, finally, tries to show Morgenthau's intellectual indebtedness to Sigmund Freud, who did indeed influence the way those engaged in German *Staatslehre* – including Hans Kelsen – thought about law and politics in the 1920s.

This discussion would be incomplete without devoting a paragraph to William E. Scheuerman, whose work on Morgenthau I already mentioned above. It would be no exaggeration to claim that we have Scheuerman to thank for kick-starting the revival of Morgenthau's ideas to which this book is a critical reaction. In the mid-1990s, anglophone Political Science (and subsequently also International Relations) discovered the 'forbidden' German jurist Carl Schmitt, the 'crown jurist' of the Third Reich. Schmitt's writings appeared to offer a critique of liberalism that suited the purposes – of interestingly both the right and the left – of generating a theoretical counter-argument to the end-of-history assertion proclaimed at the end of the Cold War.[87] Scheuerman contributed to this literature with his insightful book *Carl Schmitt: The End of Law*.[88] The book ends with a discussion of a supposed 'hidden dialogue' between Schmitt and a certain Hans J. Morgenthau, who had asserted on a number of occasions that Schmitt had 'stolen' his

Realism: The Importance of Sigmund Freud to Hans J. Morgenthau's Theory of International Power Politics', *History of the Human Sciences*, 20 (2007), pp. 53–78.

87 See in particular F. Fukuyama, *The End of History and the Last Man* (London: Penguin Books, 1992).

88 W. E. Scheuerman, *Carl Schmitt: The End of Law* (Lanham, MD: Rowman & Littlefield, 1999).

concept of intensity from his doctoral thesis. I will focus on Schmitt and critically assess Morgenthau's claim in the next chapter. The point here is that Scheuerman's portrayal of a 'hidden dialogue' contributed to the interest in Schmitt in the field of International Relations,[89] while also paving the way for more serious reflections on how that field writes its own history.[90] The debate about Schmitt and Morgenthau did much to raise the issue of whether standard renditions of canonical thinkers such as Morgenthau do not actually under-utilize their ideas by occluding their intellectual origins.

Two remarks are worth making at this stage. The first is that the above review of the literature does not in any way cover the qualitative and quantitative scope of writings dealing with Morgenthau's brand of realism, or the way standard readings of his work portray him in the canon of International Relations theory. Such readings generally focus on the six principles of realism from the second edition of *Politics Among Nations*, coupled with concepts from *In Defense of the National Interest* and an array of journal articles and commentaries. But tackling this literature that 'applies' Morgenthau is not the issue here, as my focus is on complementing, rather than negating, the standard renditions of his thought. What I am interested in is not to argue that the realist label is misplaced, but rather offer a redescription of how he came to take on the views that he did. The works mentioned here are thus simply those that substantively engage, in one way or another, with the legal theoretical aspects of Morgenthau's past. Painting a more comprehensive picture of that heritage is the aim of this book.

Second, it seems worth pointing out again that what follows is not intended to be a comprehensive intellectual biography of Morgenthau. Of course, Morgenthau's *Werdegang* is central to the analysis of particular concepts for the establishment of which he is representative. Yet Morgenthau the man is in a sense secondary to the social and intellectual environment he lived through, was influenced

---

89 For a recent discussion of this trend, see D. Chandler, 'The Revival of Carl Schmitt in International Relations: The Last Refuge of Critical Theorists?', *Millennium – Journal of International Studies*, 37 (2008), pp. 27–48.

90 Indeed, as Scheuerman himself writes: 'There is now a significant cottage industry on Morgenthau's relationship to Schmitt.' To his credit, Scheuerman has come to acknowledge that it is easy to over-state this relationship and thereby occlude other interlocutors of Morgenthau – notably Hersch Lauterpacht and Hans Kelsen. See Scheuerman, *Hans Morgenthau*, pp. 205–6.

by, and helped shape in turn. Hence the approach taken relates to contemporary theory of biography, which no longer maintains the myths of a coherent, closed historical personality, but is rather based on a sociological concept of personality in which the collective is reflected in the individual by means of the production of a 'narrative of transindividual occasions'.[91] One might be reminded of Hannah Arendt's early book on Rahel Varnhagen,[92] which, though focusing on one characteristic personage, was intended to be an historical-sociological study of the motives and origins of first-generation Jewish assimilation in Germany. This book, however, has no such aspirations, even though aspects of a theory of biography seem fairly compatible with Luhmann's notion of redescriptions and the overall aims followed here.

Thought style and thought collective

My central claim, then, is that the Morgenthau reception in International Relations continues to ignore, or at least underestimate, the significance of the fact that Morgenthau was originally a legal scholar. Either his origins as a jurist are simply occluded and his German origins interpreted as meaning that he is another proponent of Prussian-style *Realpolitik*,[93] or his legal heritage is recognized, but then shrugged off with the assertion that there was an inherent 'break' in the work of the émigré: first a European Morgenthau engaged with international legal theory, and then an American Morgenthau disillusioned with liberal internationalism and preaching the virtues of power politics. In both cases, Morgenthau's early writings are ignored.[94] This book is an attempt to highlight the ways in which such inaccurate portrayals limit the usefulness and scope of

---

91 J. Clifford, '"Hanging up Looking Glasses at Odd Corners": Ethnobiographical Prospects', in D. Aaron (ed.), *Studies in Biography* (Cambridge, MA: Harvard University Press, 1978), pp. 41–56; cited in H. E. Bödeker, 'Biographie: Annäherungen an den gegenwärtigen Forschungs- und Diskussionsstand', in Bödeker (ed.), *Biographie schreiben* (Göttingen: Wallstein, 2003), pp. 9–63, at 26.

92 H. Arendt, *Rahel Varnhagen: Lebensgeschichte einer deutschen Jüdin aus der Romantik. Mit einer Auswahl von Rahel-Briefen* (Munich: R. Piper, 1962).

93 This is the case for both Russell, *Hans. J. Morgenthau*, and M. J. Smith, *Realist Thought from Weber to Kissinger* (Baton Rouge, LA: Louisiana State University Press, 1986).

94 An instance of this is the otherwise very fascinating study on Morgenthau's 'Jewish experience' by B. M. Mollov, *Power and Transcendence: Hans J. Morgenthau and the Jewish Experience* (Lanham, MD: Lexington Books, 2002).

potentially fruitful engagement with Morgenthau, skew our understanding of the origins and development of the field of International Relations, and ultimately undermine any attempts at understanding the 'image of law' held by the mainstream discourse in that field.

In order to be armed with an appropriate conceptual toolkit for the reading of Morgenthau proposed in the following chapters, it is useful to return to the first pages of Karl Mannheim's *Ideology and Utopia* on the sociological notion of thought. There, Mannheim begins by elaborating on the historical-social situation out of which individually differentiated thought emerges:

> it is not men in general who think, or even isolated individuals who do the thinking, but men in certain groups who have developed a particular style of thought [*Denkstil*] in an endless series of responses to certain typical situations characterizing their common position.
>
> Strictly speaking it is incorrect to say that the single individual thinks. Rather it is more correct to insist that he participates in thinking further what other men have thought before him. He finds himself in an inherited situation with patterns of thought which are appropriate to this situation and attempts to elaborate further the inherited modes of response or to substitute others for them in order to deal more adequately with the new challenges which have arisen out of the shifts and changes in his situation.[95]

Mannheim's assertion, then, is that there are modes of thought that cannot be captured or understood without reference to their social context. The individual, speaking the language of a particular group, inevitably thinks and expresses herself in the manner of the group, in the words and meaning accessible and thus comprehensible to it.

This basic sociological conception of human thought was also employed by Ludwik Fleck (1896–1961) in his fascinating study, first published in 1935, entitled *Genesis and Development of a Scientific Fact*.[96] The book, which is at once a theoretical contribution to scientific change and a detailed historical analysis of syphilis and the discovery of the Wassermann reaction, was also the inspiration for Thomas S. Kuhn's (1922–1996) *The Structure of Scientific Revolutions*,

---

95 K. Mannheim, *Ideology and Utopia: An Introduction to the Sociology of Knowledge* [1936] (London: Routledge & Kegan Paul, 1968), p. 3.

96 L. Fleck, *Genesis and Development of a Scientific Fact* (Chicago, IL and London: University of Chicago Press, 1979). Originally published as *Entstehung und Entwicklung einer wissenschaftlichen Tatsache: Einführung in die Lehre vom Denkstil und Denkkollektiv* (Basel: Benno Schwabe & Co, 1935).

as Kuhn himself acknowledged.[97] Armed with the epistemological insight that knowledge is never possible in and of itself, but always only under the condition of content-specific presuppositions about the object, Fleck introduced the conceptual pairing of 'thought collective' (*Denkkollektiv*) and 'thought style' (*Denkstil*): the first denotes the social unity of the scientific community of a particular field of study, the latter the thought-related assumptions on which the collective bases its structured reflections. In other words, the thought style sociologically conditions cognition within the thought collective.[98]

For present purposes, Fleck's discussion of the intercollective communication of thought is most relevant. Just as Fleck traces the passage of the syphilis concept from the mystical, via the empirical and the pathogenetical, to the etiological, this book looks at what happens when Morgenthau's theorizing about the limits of justiciability in international dispute settlement confronts the thought collective of empiricist, pragmatist Political Science in the United States. Such communication, Fleck writes, 'never occurs without a transformation, and indeed always involves a stylized remodelling, which intracollectively achieves corroboration and which intercollectively yields fundamental alteration'.[99]

The argument can now be expressed more concretely: Morgenthau, coming from the thought collective of German *Staatsrechtslehre*, transposes his thought style onto the thought collective of US social science. Finding his thought style to be fundamentally at odds with the behaviouralist currents gaining momentum at the time, moreover being confronted with an increasing aversion to German 'goose-step' theorizing, Morgenthau reacts by transforming substantive elements of his juristic thought style into a critique, expressed in *Scientific Man vs. Power Politics* and in a range of other publications and lectures, of rationalist, positivist Political Science and the image of international law it entails. I shall demonstrate that the underlying assumptions, arguments and structure of *Politics Among*

---

97 T. S. Kuhn, *The Structure of Scientific Revolutions* (University of Chicago Press, 1962), pp. viii–ix; see also Kuhn, 'Foreword', in Fleck, *Genesis and Development of a Scientific Fact*, pp. vii–xi.

98 See T. J. Trenn, 'Preface', in Fleck, *Genesis and Development of a Scientific Fact*, pp. xiii–xix, at xiii.

99 Fleck, *Genesis and Development of a Scientific Fact*, p. 111.

Nations show an undeniable link with Morgenthau's earlier work in international law on the peaceful settlement of disputes and the validity and reality of international legal norms. For those not familiar with these debates, however, Morgenthau's transformation reads exactly like what it has generally been perceived as being: an ode to the centrality of power politics in the name of the national interest.

But what exactly is Morgenthau's juristic thought style? Here, Martti Koskenniemi's important work on the structure of international legal argument, elaborated in his book *From Apology to Utopia*,[100] provides a useful conceptualization that can be employed throughout the following chapters. In their constant concern to demonstrate that their subject matter is distinct from politics, Koskenniemi argues, international lawyers attempt to show that international law is both concrete and normative. The concreteness of international law refers to its responsiveness to changes in the behaviour, will and interests of states, while normativity refers to international law's degree of autonomy from state behaviour. Without concrete processes, international law would face the charge of being utopian, as it would mean assuming the existence of a natural morality independent of the behaviour, will and interests of states. Without normative rules, however, international law would be unable to demonstrate its independence from state policy, hence opening up to the charge of being apologist. This gives rise to a matrix of exhaustive and logically exclusive positions, outlined in Figure 1.1.

From the perspective of the lawyer who attempts to make his or her work appear coherent, 'modern discourse will appear as the constant production of strategies whereby threats to the argument's inner coherence or to its controlling assumptions are removed, or hidden from sight, in order to maintain the system's overall credibility'.[101] The international lawyer may prefer concreteness or normativity, reject both, or claim them to be compatible. Whatever the position taken, it will fit somewhere along the two axes of binding force and material scope, whose range, it must be emphasized, is continuous. The four positions in Figure 1.1 are thus relational, and represent typical characterizations of possible standpoints. The identification

---

100 Koskenniemi, *From Apology to Utopia*.   101 *Ibid.*, p. 158.

binding force

		strong	weak
material scope	wide	Idealism (Alvarez)	Policy approach (McDougal)
	restricted	Rule approach (Schwarzenberger)	Scepticism (Morgenthau)

Figure 1.1 The structure of international legal argument

of each position with a particular international lawyer, moreover, 'is not intended to be fixed, permanent classification but only to demonstrate typical ways of trying to construct better doctrines by lawyers who have been relatively "theoretical" and consistent'.[102]

The modern rule approach, exemplified by Georg Schwarzenberger (1908–1991), another émigré jurist who ended up at the London School of Economics and Political Science (LSE), established itself out of a series of critiques of the apologist nature of pre-First World War international doctrine. As I will outline in Chapter 2, Georg Jellinek's (1851–1911) doctrine of auto-limitation (*Selbstverpflichtungslehre*) and the consequent distinction between legal and political disputes led Hersch Lauterpacht, Hans Kelsen and others to advocate a position that instead prioritized the normativity of the law, and the autonomy of international legal rules from state policy. Yet this position, which logically culminates in a holistic conception of international law as a complete system of independent rules, remains open to the charge of being utopian. The resulting policy approach – an issue taken up in Chapter 4, which touches upon the work of Myers S. McDougal (1906–1998) and Harold D. Lasswell (1902–1978) – was first advocated by the likes of Georges Scelle (1878–1961) in Europe and Roscoe Pound (1870–1964) in the United States, who called for a social conception of law that focuses on the effectiveness, rather than the validity, of legal norms. This distinction will be elaborated upon in Chapter 3. The remaining two positions are either

102 *Ibid.*, p. 189.

sceptical of both the normativity and applicability of international law – Morgenthau – or 'have continued writing as if both the law's binding force as well as its correspondence with developments in international practice were a matter of course'.[103] This idealist position is exemplified by the work of Alejandro Alvarez (1869–1960), which focuses on global interdependence and the functions of supranational organizations such as the United Nations.

'The descriptive project *of From Apology to Utopia*', Koskenniemi writes in a new epilogue, 'was to reconstruct the argumentative architecture of international law in its many variations so as to produce an account of it as a language and a professional competence'.[104] Rather than constituting an account of how legal decisions are actually made, Koskenniemi's conceptualization looks at how these decisions are justified – expressed differently, Koskenniemi examines the conditions of possibility in the language of international law. This will also be the central concern throughout my usage of Koskenniemi's framework in the following chapters. The additional, normative part of his project, of providing 'resources for the use of international law's professional vocabulary for critical or emancipatory causes',[105] need not concern us for the present purpose.

---

103 M. Koskenniemi, 'The Politics of International Law', *European Journal of International Law*, 1 (1990), pp. 4–32, at 11.
104 Koskenniemi, *From Apology to Utopia*, p. 589.
105 *Ibid.*

2   The justiciability of disputes

This and the following chapter will begin to sketch out the academic debates that Morgenthau's early European publications and
manuscripts were feeding into. While these works were in the field of
international law, our reading will require a number of short detours
into the history of German public law. Late nineteenth-century and
early twentieth-century public law debates, usually running under
the labels of *allgemeine Staatslehre* (general theory of the state) and
Staatsrechtslehre (legal theory of the state), were steeped in historical-
philosophical analysis that did not yet make the clear distinction
between domestic/constitutional and international law that is made
today. Instead, the prevalent distinction was one between private/civil
law and public law. Moreover, the nature of the academic training
of the legal scholars involved in these fields meant that the resulting
debates had a deep, philosophical spin to them that their French and
Anglo-Saxon counterparts did not.[1] As Martti Koskenniemi writes,
the history of international law in Germany during the period since
1871 'is a narrative about philosophy as the founding discipline for
reflecting about statehood and what lies beyond. In this narrative
"concrete reality" sometimes appears as State power, sometimes as
the power of a cosmopolitan history – and "social ideals" sometimes intensively romantic-national, sometimes liberal-individu-
alist. This debate came to an end by the Second World War'.[2] Of

---

1 Indeed, Anglo-Saxon legal and political theory – by the likes of John W. Burgess (1844–
   1931), William James (1841–1910) and John Dewey (1859–1952) – was frowned
   upon and generally not studied at all. See F. L. Neumann, 'Intellektuelle Emigration
   und Sozialwissenschaft (1952)', in Neumann, *Wirtschaft, Staat, Demokratie: Aufsätze
   1930–1954*. Edited by Alfons Söllner (Frankfurt a.M.: Suhrkamp, 1978), pp. 402–23,
   at 416.
2 M. Koskenniemi, *The Gentle Civilizer of Nations: The Rise and Fall of International Law
   1870–1960* (Cambridge University Press, 2002), p. 182.

course, no claim will be made to provide a comprehensive outline of these discourses. Every stage in this historical process, and many actors in it, have been the subject of an immense body of literature – mostly, inevitably, in German. The task of contextualizing the likes of Morgenthau as a disciplinary outsider, so to speak, is thus indeed a daunting one, and perhaps the main reason why those concerned with rehabilitating Morgenthau in International Relations have generally thought it wiser not to engage too rigorously with these aspects of his intellectual development.

Those versed in German legal debates may judge the following exposition to be incomplete, though hopefully not misleading. The aim here is to situate Morgenthau for the benefit of those not familiar with legal theory, and thus less in order to rewrite a chapter in the history of International Law. Readers from International Relations might find themselves on unexplored terrain, whereas the jurist might find herself confronted with an at times incomplete map of the ground being ventured into. Hopefully, the footnotes will contain sufficient references to point the interested reader in the direction of more detailed literature.

This chapter sets out to do two things. First, it will seek to contextualize Morgenthau's doctoral dissertation on the justiciability of international disputes by briefly exploring legal debates in the late-Wilhelmine and Weimar periods. It will show how his engagement with the issue of justiciability led to the differentiation between 'disputes' and 'tensions', a theme that will continue to resonate in his US publications, notably *Politics Among Nations*. The analysis will also show how his subsequent resort to psychological reflections on the will to power, another Morgenthau trademark, was the result of criticism he had received for his dissertation, in particular from Hersch Lauterpacht.

The second, subsidiary but arguably very important task of this chapter is to address Scheuerman's supposed 'hidden dialogue' between Morgenthau and Carl Schmitt – an issue already touched upon in the previous chapter. I will attempt to situate Schmitt's work within the legal debates that are relevant to the argument, and portray the link between some of Schmitt's ideas and Morgenthau's early writings. Ultimately, Morgenthau's allegation that Schmitt had stolen his notion of intensity from his doctoral dissertation is not as obvious as Morgenthau, and those who are now taking this assertion

at face value, would like it to be. More to the point, I will argue that
the emphasis on Schmitt should not detract from other sources of
influence, especially Lauterpacht, that may be even more significant
for contextualizing Morgenthau's early works than his direct and/or
hidden dialogue with Schmitt.

The rise and fall of legal positivism

Already before the so-called German Revolution that began in
March 1848, the academic treatment of public law was a highly
politicized affair – not least because the majority of legal scholars
at the time were also engaged in practical politics.[3] After the events
of 1848, however, any remaining Hegelian idealism was irrevocably
shattered, instead giving way to the sobering realization that political influence required economic and military power.[4] For decades
to come, this *Realpolitik* would continue to underlie all efforts in the
field of German public law.[5] One of the main features of post-1848
legal theory was the attempt to consolidate its position by ridding its
subject matter from all non-legal (i.e. political and social) elements.
In parallel to developments in civil law, *Staatsrechtslehre* thus also
took a drastic positivist turn – Carl Friedrich von Gerber (1823–
1891) is perhaps the most important scholar linked with this development. Similar to the time of the pandectics a generation or two
earlier in the field of civil law – notably Friedrich Carl von Savigny
(1779–1861) – when legal theory was based on interpretations of
Roman law, *Staatsrechtslehre* now became the study of existing legal
norms, with the aim of bringing these norms into a coherent logical
system.[6] Hans Kelsen's subsequent 'pure theory of law' would
represent the culmination of this methodological approach.

---

3 M. Stolleis, *Geschichte des öffentlichen Rechts in Deutschland 2: Staatsrechtslehre und
  Verwaltungswissenschaft 1800–1914* (Munich: C. H. Beck, 1992), p. 119.
4 *Ibid.*, p. 275.
5 Indeed, this would be the entry point for an argument that tries to make the link between
  someone like Morgenthau and Bismarckian *Realpolitik*: not Machiavellian notions but
  the switch from 'might is right' to 'right is might' is central to this backdrop. As I mentioned in Chapter 1, J. W. Honig, 'Totalitarianism and Realism: Hans Morgenthau's
  German Years', *Security Studies*, 5 (1995/6), pp. 283–313, comes closest to making this
  argument, but arguably misses out the crucial stages of such a redescription.
6 See E.-W. Böckenförde, *Gesetz und gesetzgebende Gewalt: Von den Anfängen der deutschen Staatsrechtslehre bis zur Höhe des staatsrechtlichen Positivismus* (Berlin: Duncker &
  Humblot, 1958), p. 212.

Yet the move to formalist positivism did not imply that German public law became any less politicized. Exemplary here is the work of Paul Laband (1838–1918), which came to dominate the field throughout the later decades of the nineteenth century. Like von Gerber, Laband posited the methodological irrelevance of non-legal reflections (theory of the state, philosophy, history, sociology) for the *Staatsrechtswissenschaft*. More importantly, he also empha-sized the centrality of the will of the state as the actual object of this academic field. Laband conceived there to be two independent 'will spheres': that of the monarchic-bureaucratic state, and that of bourgeois society. This strategy allowed Laband to focus exclusively on the monarchic executive when he reflected on the will of the state: because the state precedes the legal order, and the law postu-lated by it delimits the will sphere of the bureaucratic administration from the private will sphere of its subjects, Laband introduced a highly context-specific, apologist legal doctrine that played the role of justifying and consolidating Wilhelmine constitutional monarchy.[7] As Morgenthau's mentor, Hugo Sinzheimer wrote, '[t]he basis for Labandian positivism is the affirmation of Bismarckian politics. Just as for Hegel the *Weltgeist* took on its ultimate and highest form in the Prussian state, so too did Laband and the positivists of that era consider the political spirit to find its highest form in Bismarck and his *Reich*'.[8] In the realm of international law, the question was how to relate such an understanding of the state with a normative order that lies beyond it, but that nonetheless entails a notion of obli-gation. The particular problem faced by any conceptualization of international law was how to overcome the fact that in the absence of a central authority establishing and enforcing norms, the creators and subjects of international law were identical. Late nineteenth-century debates in German-speaking academic circles thus oscil-lated between the 'objective principle' of Karl Baron Kaltenborn von Stachau (1817–1866), according to which the community of states represented a supranational legal community in which states

7 See C. Schönberger, 'Ein Liberaler zwischen Staatswille und Volkswille: Georg Jellinek und die Krise des staatsrechtlichen Positivismus um die Jahrhundertwende', in S. L. Paulson and M. Schulte (eds.), *Georg Jellinek: Beiträge zu Leben und Werk* (Tübingen: Mohr Siebeck, 2002), pp. 3–32, at 6.
8 H. Sinzheimer, *Jüdische Klassiker der deutschen Rechtswissenschaft* (Amsterdam: Menno Hertzberger, 1938), pp. 197–8.

functioned as organs of this legal order, and the Hegelian 'subjective principle' that considered international law to be based on a voluntarism derived from the will of sovereign states.[9]

This was the situation when Georg Jellinek, perhaps the most significant German public lawyer of his time, began making his mark on the scene with the publication of his early work, *Die rechtliche Natur der Staatenverträge*.[10] In this and subsequent publications, notably his *System der subjektiven öffentlichen Rechte*[11] and his *Allgemeine Staatslehre*,[12] Jellinek began thinking critically about the foundations and methods of public and international law. One of his aims was to give the private sphere, so effectively excluded in Laband's framework, a more positive spin. According to his theory of autolimitation (*Selbstverpflichtungslehre*), which parallels state action with the submission of the Kantian subject to moral law (*Sittengesetz*), the state makes itself a subject of the law it creates – expressed differently, the state only realizes itself completely by means of the legal bindingness of the laws it imposes on itself.[13]

Jellinek also advocated a pluralistic conception of the state.[14] Of course, as a jurist, Jellinek was very conscious of the need to adhere to the legal approach to the state, but he nonetheless wanted to place the state on social-scientific foundations. To achieve this, he introduced a two-sided conception of statehood (*Zwei-Seiten-Lehre*), according to which the state exists both in empirical reality (*Sein*) and, through the will of the *Volk*, in the normative 'ought' (*Sollen*).

---

9 See J. von Bernstorff, *Der Glaube an das universale Recht: Zur Völkerrechtstheorie Hans Kelsens und seiner Schüler* (Baden-Baden: Nomos, 2001), pp. 13–37; also J. von Bernstorff, 'Georg Jellinek – Völkerrecht als modernes öffentliches Recht im *fin de siècle?*', in Paulson and Schulte, *Georg Jellinek: Beiträge zu Leben und Werk*, pp. 183–206, at 185–6.

10 G. Jellinek, *Die rechtliche Natur der Staatenverträge: Ein Beitrag zur juristischen Konstruktion des Völkerrechts* (Vienna: Alfred Hödler, 1880).

11 G. Jellinek, *System der subjektiven öffentlichen Rechte* (Freiburg i.B.: Mohr (Siebeck), 1892).

12 G. Jellinek, *Allgemeine Staatslehre* [1900] (Berlin: Julius Springer, 1921). The edition of 1921, edited by his son Walter Jellinek, will be cited hereon.

13 *Ibid.*, p. 480; C. Schönberger, 'Ein Liberaler zwischen Staatswille und Volkswille', pp. 20–1. This reflexivity of the will that Jellinek introduces in the *Allgemeine Staatslehre* contrasts with his earlier approach employed in his *System der subjektiven öffentlichen Rechte*, although an elaboration of such nuances goes far beyond present purposes; but see J. Kersten, *Georg Jellinek und die klassische Staatslehre* (Tübingen: Mohr Siebeck, 2000), pp. 439–40.

14 Jellinek, *Allgemeine Staatslehre*, pp. 174–83.

Underlying this conceptualization is the neo-Kantian maxim that the choice of method determines cognition of the object.

Coupled with the theory of auto-limitation, Jellinek's *Zwei-Seiten-Lehre* enabled him to conceive of domestic and international law as two separate normative systems that are in a relation of coordination, not subordination, to one another. In other words, he was able to characterize inter-state relations as being both a struggle for power and the administration of a legal system.[15] Through what he called the 'normative power of the factual' (*die normative Kraft des Faktischen*), Jellinek argued that every legal order was based on the practical validity (*praktische Geltung*) of legal norms that received their binding force through the psychologically conceived will of the legal subject.[16] As I will show in Chapter 3, this practical validity, or 'effectiveness' of norms would be the topic of Morgenthau's book *La réalité des normes*.[17]

Standard renditions of the history of German public law generally portray the late-Wilhelmine era as culminating in the work of Jellinek, which was then subject to sustained attack during the Weimar period by, on the one hand, more radical normativists focusing almost exclusively on the 'ought' (Hans Kelsen and the Vienna School), and, on the other, by a variety of anti-normativists who focused more on decisions, interests and the sociology of law (Carl Schmitt, Rudolf Smend (1882–1975), Hermann Heller, etc.). While sufficient for most purposes, this chapter requires a somewhat more nuanced description. First, as Massimo La Torre points out, the 'crisis' of legal positivism and legal formalism was already declared by Jellinek himself, even though he would later often be the target of anti-positivist polemics.[18] Second, while the advent of the First World War is generally taken to be the crucial watershed, the real crisis of German *Staatsrechtslehre* had already occurred a decade earlier. Indeed, rapid social and political change made the apologist justification of the monarchical state increasingly less tenable. In

15 Koskenniemi, *The Gentle Civilizer of Nations*, p. 200.
16 Jellinek, *Allgemeine Staatslehre*, pp. 337–41.
17 H. Morgenthau, *La réalité des normes, en particulier des normes du droit international: Fondements d'une théorie des normes* (Paris: Félix Alcan, 1934).
18 M. La Torre, 'Der Kampf des "neuen" Rechts gegen das "alte" – Georg Jellinek als Denker der Modernität', in Paulson and Schulte, *Georg Jellinek: Beiträge zu Leben und Werk*, pp. 33–52, at 49.

their early works, Hans Kelsen,[19] Carl Schmitt,[20] as well as others such as Erich Kaufmann (1880–1972) and Rudolf Smend, were all already chipping away at the crumbling foundations of the system long before the advent of the Weimar Republic and a democratic constitution brought about de facto change to the system.[21] Third, it is also worth pointing to the fact that, as Michael Stolleis demonstrates, the group of legal scholars termed 'anti-normativist' were actually far too heterogeneous to categorize[22] – indeed, the most difficult to place was, and continues to be, a certain Carl Schmitt.

Jellinek's doctrine of self-limitation was one of the main targets of this new generation of legal scholars. For why should the state adhere to its own legal bindingness? And was it useful to suppose (both historically and conceptually) the existence of a 'pre-legal' holder of power, embodied in the state?[23] Such contestations were then brought to a head with the very specific constellation created by the Weimar Constitution, and in particular the infamous Article 48, which allowed the President to rule by emergency decree (*Notverordnung*) without consent of the *Reichstag* if 'public security and order' were under threat. The main forum for these debates was the *Vereinigung der deutschen Staatsrechtslehrer*, whose sessions have been well documented and published, and represent an invaluable source for the historian.[24] All the household names of German public law were regularly present at these conventions, including Hans Kelsen, Carl Schmitt, Rudolf Smend, Hermann Heller, Heinrich Triepel (1868–1946), Richard Thoma (1874–1957) and Gerhard Anschütz (1867–1948), to name but a few of the most prominent.

Interpretations of Article 48 inevitably took up much of the debate. Indeed, Paragraph 5 of the article stipulated that particulars would be specified by forthcoming legislation, legislation that failed

19 H. Kelsen, *Hauptprobleme der Staatsrechtslehre, entwickelt aus der Lehre vom Rechtssatze* [1911]. Second edition (Tübingen: Mohr, 1923).
20 C. Schmitt, *Gesetz und Urteil. Eine Untersuchung zum Problem der Rechtspraxis* (Berlin: Liebmann, 1912).
21 See S. Korioth, 'Erschütterungen des staatsrechtlichen Positivismus im ausgehenden Kaiserreich: Anmerkungen zu früheren Arbeiten von Carl Schmitt, Rudolf Smend und Erich Kaufmann', *Archiv des öffentlichen Rechts*, 117 (1992), pp. 212–38.
22 Stolleis, *Geschichte des öffentlichen Rechts in Deutschland 2*, p. 158.
23 For a useful discussion of these points see C. Möllers, 'Skizzen zur Aktualität Georg Jellineks: Vier theoretische Probleme aus Jellineks Staatslehre in Verfassungsrecht und Staatstheorie der Gegenwart', in Paulson and Schulte, *Georg Jellinek: Beiträge zu Leben und Werk*, pp. 155–71, at 163–4.
24 See Stolleis, *Geschichte des öffentlichen Rechts in Deutschland 2*, pp. 186–202.

to materialize. The debate over the status of the *Reichspräsident* thus continued – though with a number of shifts in focus[25] – right up to the moment when Adolf Hitler used the article for his all too famous purposes in 1933. I will not go into these debates in any detail here. Suffice it to say that the fragile set-up of the Weimar Constitution led to increasing calls for a move away from the 'neutralized' legal positivism of the Wilhelmine period, and towards an acknowledgement of the link between norms of constitutional law and political powers and interests.[26] It was one thing to 'depoliticize' public law to further the status quo when that status quo was deemed worth consolidating. Yet the Constitution of the Weimar Republic was an altogether different affair, and the need for legal scholars to incorporate the realities and dynamics of the ever-changing political situation became increasingly and threateningly apparent.

A landmark in this debate was Heinrich Triepel's lecture 'Staatsrecht und Politik', held when he became Rector of the Friedrich Wilhelm University (Berlin) in October 1926.[27] Called by Richard Thoma a '*Programmschrift für die deutsche Staatsrechtswissenschaft*',[28] Triepel's lecture is a true call to arms for a public law that incorporated 'the political' into its field of study:

> It is impossible to arrive at an understanding of legal rules without grasping the purposive relations (*Zweckbeziehungen*) that construe the 'legal', the interests, whose acceptance, reprobation and balancing represent the first aim or, if you will, the prerequisite of a legal order. If we now call 'political' ... everything that relates to the purposes of the state (*Staatszwecke*) or to their delimitation with regard to individual purposes, it is clear that a comprehensive ascertainment of the norms of public law is not even possible without incorporation of the political.[29]

Unsurprisingly, Carl Schmitt makes reference to Triepel's lecture at the outset of his 'Begriff des Politischen', a first version of which

25 *Ibid.*, pp. 114–15.
26 See U. Scheuner, '50 Jahre deutsche Staatsrechtswissenschaft im Spiegel der Verhandlungen der Vereinigung der Deutschen Staatsrechtslehrer', *Archiv des öffentlichen Rechts*, 97 (1972), pp. 349–74, at 359–60.
27 W. Triepel, *Staatsrecht und Politik. Rede beim Antritte des Rektorats der Friedrich Wilhelms-Universität zu Berlin am 15. Oktober 1926* (Berlin and Leipzig: Walter de Gruyter & Co., 1927).
28 R. Thoma, 'Gegenstand – Methode – Literatur', in G. Anschütz and R. Thoma (eds.), *Handbuch des Deutschen Staatsrechts, Vol. 1* (Tübingen: Mohr (Siebeck), 1930), pp. 1–13, at 5.
29 Triepel, *Staatsrecht und Politik*, p. 20.

appeared not long after.[30] Schmitt was, above all, concerned with the way Triepel and others equated the political with the state, a strategy that had allowed the likes of von Gerber, Laband and, later, Kelsen to 'depoliticize' and 'purify' public law. 'The concept of the political has already been thought [sic] in the concept of the state', Jellinek had written in his *Allgemeine Staatslehre*.[31] In his famous first sentence of 'The Concept of the Political', Schmitt now turns this around: 'The concept of the state presupposes the concept of the political'.[32]

That the concept of the political was high on people's agenda at the time also had something to do with the fact that, as Triepel rightly pointed out, the distinction between legal and political disputes was dominating debates over justiciability in international law.[33] The Treaty of Arbitration and Conciliation between Germany and Switzerland of 3 December 1921, for example, foresaw decision by a court of justice for disputes deemed justiciable according to Article 36 of the Statute of the Permanent Court of International Justice (adopted in Article 14 of the Covenant of the League of Nations), and by a permanent conciliation board for matters considered 'political' by one or more of the disputing parties because they involved the vital interests or integrity of the state in question.[34]

Indeed, the entire debate was steeped at the time in what came to be called the doctrine of non-justiciable disputes.[35] This doctrine

30 C. Schmitt, 'Der Begriff des Politischen', *Archiv für Sozialwissenschaft und Sozialpolitik*, 58 (1927), pp. 1–33.
31 [*Im Begriff des Politischen hat man bereits den des Staates gedacht*]. Jellinek, *Allgemeine Staatslehre*, p. 180.
32 [*Der Begriff des Staates setzt den Begriff des Politischen voraus.*] Schmitt, 'Der Begriff des Politischen', p. 1. See also E. Vollrath, 'Wie ist Carl Schmitt an seinen Begriff des Politischen gekommen?', *Zeitschrift für Politik*, 36 (1989), pp. 151–68.
33 W. Triepel, 'Streitigkeiten zwischen Reich und Ländern. Beiträge zur Auslegung des Artikels 19 der Weimarer Reichsverfassung', in *Festgabe der Berliner Juristischen Fakultät für Wilhelm Kahl zum Doktorjubiläum am 19. April 1923* (Tübingen: Mohr (Siebeck), 1923), pp. 15–17.
34 See H.-J. Schlochauer, 'Die Entwicklung der internationalen Schiedsgerichtsbarkeit', *Archiv des Völkerrechts*, 10 (1962/3), pp. 1–41, at 23–4; also C. B. Gosnell, 'The Compulsory Jurisdiction of the World Court', *Virginia Law Review*, 14 (1928), pp. 618–43.
35 The literature on this issue is unsurprisingly vast, and no attempt will be made here to give a representative overview. Instead, focus will be primarily on the works of Hersch Lauterpacht, who wrote extensively on the subject in a series of publications starting with the article 'The Doctrine of Non-Justiciable Disputes in International Law', *Economica*, 24 (1928), pp. 277–317, and culminating in his opus *The Function of Law in the International Community* (Oxford: Clarendon Press, 1933). This choice

of the inherent limitations of the international judicial process, Lauterpacht writes, is 'the work of international lawyers anxious to give legal expression to the state's claim to be independent of law'.[36] It is thus the logical consequence of the concept of state sovereignty, which found expression in positivist international law through the right of a state to determine which rules it accepts as binding and, by implication, which inter-state disputes it is willing to submit to international arbitration. Based on 'the alleged fundamental difference' between two categories of disputes, varyingly termed 'legal and non-legal, legal and political, justiciable and non-justiciable, disputes as to rights and disputes arising out of conflicts of interests', the doctrine connotes that there are certain disputes that, owing to the nature of the international system, are outside of the field of judicial settlement.[37] As Hans Kelsen would go on to write, '[t]he distinction between legal and political conflicts plays a role analogous to that of the notorious *clausula rebus sic stantibus* [changed conditions may warrant revision]. Just as the latter invalidates the rule *pacta sunt servanda* [treaties must be respected] so the former abolishes the duty of obligatory jurisdiction'.[38]

The origins of the modern doctrine of the non-justiciability of disputes, Lauterpacht informs his readers, can be traced back to the proceedings surrounding three decisive events for international arbitration: the Alabama arbitration of 1872, the foundation of the Institut de droit international in 1873, and the Hague Peace Conferences of 1899 and 1907. Already in 1865, Thomas Balch, in a letter addressed to the *New York Tribune*, articulated what would become 'the seed from which sprang subsequent writings on the distinction between legal and political questions'.[39] Balch argued that the reciprocal claims of those involved in the Alabama case were claims pertaining to individuals, thereby implicitly stating that they did not include the vital interests of Great Britain and the

    can be justified on the basis of Lauterpacht's status as one of the influential names in
    the debate of the time, and also makes practical sense in the context of the argument
    made in this chapter, as will become clear in the following pages.
36 Lauterpacht, *The Function of Law*, p. 6.
37 *Ibid.*, pp. 3–4; also Lauterpacht, 'The Doctrine of Non-Justiciable Disputes', p. 277.
38 H. Kelsen, 'Compulsory Adjudication of International Disputes', *American Journal of International Law*, 37 (1943), pp. 397–406, at 404.
39 T. W. Balch, 'Différends juridiques et politiques dans les rapports des nations', *Revue générale de droit international publique*, 21 (1914), pp. 137–82, at 144.

United States. When James Goldschmidt was then called upon by the *Institut de droit international* to prepare the Draft Regulations for International Arbitration in 1873, he asserted that because arbitral decisions were essentially judicial decisions, they generally only pertain to those conflicts 'which, through ensured restriction to a point of dispute decidable by legal principles, are suitable for judicial settlement'.[40] By the time of the first Hague Conference, finally, it was clear from the refusal to embody the principle of obligatory arbitration in a rule of positive law that the distinction between legal and political disputes had become part and parcel of mainstream international law discourse.[41]

Of course, the debate has meanwhile moved on, and already Lauterpacht's famous work, *The Function of Law in the International Community*, was an attempt to transcend the dichotomy between legal and political disputes. Indeed, the distinction is essentially an apologist doctrine, for it allows the state to decide, by reference to its 'vital' interests, whether a dispute is justiciable or not. Yet an objective rule to decide the matter would require the presence of a constraining hierarchy of interests that overrides the subjective interests of any particular state. This would assume the existence of some sort of natural morality, leaving it open to the charge of being utopian.[42] While the distinction has thus today largely been abandoned – H. L. A. Hart's (1907–1992) notion of relative indeterminacy may provide one way of overcoming the dilemma[43] – it was still part and parcel of international law debates in the late 1920s when Morgenthau was writing his doctoral dissertation.

40 J. Goldschmidt, 'Ein Reglement für internationale Schiedsgerichte', *Zeitschrift für das Privat- und Öffentliche Recht der Gegenwart*, 2 (1875), pp. 714–49, at 718.

41 Lauterpacht, *The Function of Law*, p. 10. That the question of justiciability continues to be an issue is demonstrated by, for instance, the 1986 Nicaragua case, in which the International Court of Justice rejected the claim that the dispute should be declared non-justiciable because it did not fall into the category of 'legal disputes' within the meaning of Article 36, Paragraph 2, of the Statute of the Court. See 'Military and Paramilitary Activities in and against Nicaragua' (*Nicaragua v. United States of America*), Merits, Judgment, I.C.J. Reports 1986, pp. 26–7; also E. McWhinney, *Judicial Settlements of International Disputes: Jurisdiction, Justiciability and Judicial Law-Making on the Contemporary International Court* (Dordrecht: Martinus Nijhoff, 1991), pp. 37–46.

42 See M. Koskenniemi, *From Apology to Utopia: The Structure of International Legal Argument*. Reissue with a new Epilogue (Cambridge University Press, 2005), pp. 28–9.

43 H. L. A. Hart, *The Concept of Law* [1961]. Second edition with a new Postscript (Oxford University Press, 1994), Koskenniemi, *From Apology to Utopia*, pp. 36–41.

Carl Schmitt

Before turning to the dissertation, however, a few words on Carl Schmitt may now be appropriate. The author of forty books and over 200 essays and articles,[44] Schmitt is undoubtedly one of the heavyweights of twentieth-century German legal theory. Rhetorically outstanding, both orally and in writing, the young Schmitt would soon enjoy considerable prominence in the law circles of the Weimar Republic. His popularity, however, would also be his downfall, as an attempt to collaborate with Hitler's regime – exemplified by his article 'Der Führer schützt das Recht' ['The Führer Upholds the Law'],[45] and his closing speech of a conference he organized on the subject of removing the Jewish influence from German jurisprudence[46] – led first to internment by the United States and then banishment from German public life until his death in 1985.[47] Nonetheless, his thought remained influential, with his critique of the Constitution of the Weimar Republic playing a not insignificant role in the drafting of the *Grundgesetz* (the Basic Law of the Federal Republic of Germany), in particular as to the constructive no-confidence vote and the protection of core elements of the constitution. Articles 67 and 79 of the *Grundgesetz* were specifically designed as a reaction to Articles 54 and 76, respectively, of the Weimar Constitution, the weaknesses and possible interpretations of which had perceptively been analysed by Schmitt.[48]

44 For a complete bibliography see A. Koenen, *Der Fall Carl Schmitt: Sein Aufstieg zum "Kronjuristen des Dritten Reiches"* (Darmstadt: Wissenschaftliche Buchgesellschaft, 1995), pp. 850–61.

45 C. Schmitt, 'Der Führer schützt das Recht', *Deutsche Juristen-Zeitung*, 39 (1 August 1934), cols. 945–50; reprinted in Schmitt, *Positionen und Begriffe im Kampf mit Weimar – Genf – Versailles 1923–1939* [1940] (Berlin: Duncker & Humblot, 1994), pp. 227–32.

46 'Die deutsche Rechtswissenschaft im Kampf gegen den jüdischen Geist. Schlußwort auf der Tagung der Reichsgruppe Hochschullehrer des NSRB vom 3. und 4. Oktober 1936', *Deutsche Juristen-Zeitung*, 41 (1936), cols. 1193–9.

47 For an English biography of Schmitt, see G. Balakrishnan, *The Enemy: An Intellectual Portrait of Carl Schmitt* (London: Verso, 2000). Schmitt spent the remaining forty years of his life living in the small German town of Plettenberg, in Westphalia.

48 See D. van Laak, *Gespräche in der Sicherheit des Schweigens. Carl Schmitt in der politischen Geistesgeschichte der frühen Bundesrepublik* (Berlin: Akademie Verlag, 2002), pp. 157–64; also R. Mußgenug, 'Carl Schmitts verfassungsrechtliches Werk und sein Fortwirken im Staatsrecht der Bundesrepublik Deutschland', in H. Quaritsch (ed.), *Complexio Oppositorum – Über Carl Schmitt. Vorträge und Diskussionsbeiträge des 28. Sonderseminars 1986 der Hochschule für Verwaltungswissenschaften Speyer* (Berlin: Duncker & Humblot, 1988), pp. 517–28.

Outside of the realm of legal scholarship, Schmitt is best known for his essay 'Der Begriff des Politischen', which I already touched upon in the previous section. First published as a journal article in 1927, it was expanded into a book in 1932, again modified to suit the new regime in Berlin in 1933, and finally republished, in its 1932 version, in 1963.[49] *Der Begriff des Politischen* was a continuation of an issue Schmitt had already taken up in his 1921 book on dictatorship,[50] which entails an intellectual history on the legitimacy of emergency powers from early modern Europe to the nineteenth century, or from Jean Bodin (1529–1596) to Vladimir Lenin. There, Schmitt had traced out the way in which the state lost its 'monopoly over the political' as other political entities, especially a new revolutionary class – the '*Industrie-Proletariat*' – challenged this monopoly and thus became new and effective subjects of the political.[51] It is this crucial change in the relation between the concepts of state and politics that induced Schmitt to write *Der Begriff des Politischen*, as he explained in the introduction to the Italian edition in 1971.[52] In this introduction, Schmitt argues that within the space of fifty years Europe had lost its place as the centre of world politics, a process that brought with it the unsettling of specific juridical concepts such as 'state' and 'sovereignty', 'constitution' and 'law', 'legality' and 'legitimacy'. These concepts, according to Schmitt, are the product of a long symbiosis of theological, philosophical and juridical thought, forming an important part of occidental rationalism culminating in the *Jus Publicum Europaeum*. With the writings of Machiavelli, Bodin and Hobbes, the classical European state had attained a decisive monopoly by becoming the only subject of politics. Once the state

---

49 C. Schmitt, 'Der Begriff des Politischen', *Archiv für Sozialwissenschaft und Sozialpolitik*, 58 (1927), pp. 1–33; Schmitt, *Der Begriff des Politischen* (Munich and Leipzig: Duncker & Humblot, 1932); Schmitt, *Der Begriff des Politischen* (Hamburg: Hanseatische Verlagsanstalt, 1933); Schmitt, *Der Begriff des Politischen. Text von 1932 mit einem Vorwort und drei Corollarien* (Berlin: Duncker & Humblot, 1963); in English: Schmitt, *The Concept of the Political*. Translation, introduction, and notes by George Schwab, foreword by Tracy B. Strong (Chicago, IL and London: The University of Chicago Press, 1996).

50 C. Schmitt, *Die Diktatur, von den Anfängen des modernen Souveränitäts-Gedankens bis zum proletarischen Klassenkampf* [1921] (Leipzig: Duncker & Humblot, 2006).

51 See Schmitt's own summary of *Die Diktatur* in Schmitt, *Politische Theologie II: Die Legende von der Erledigung jeder Politischen Theologie* (Berlin: Duncker & Humblot, 1970), p. 21.

52 C. Schmitt, 'Introduction to the Italian edition of *Der Begriff des Politischen* (1971)', in Quaritsch, *Complexio Oppositorum*, pp. 269–73.

began to lose this monopoly over decision-making, however, politics came to be distinguished from the political. Specifying the new subject of the political consequently became the central issue, as Heinrich Triepel had already recognized in his 1926 lecture.

Schmitt argued that a conceptualization of the political could only be obtained through the detection and establishment of the specifically political categories.[53] The political had to be regarded as an independent sphere (*Gebiet*) distinct from other spheres of human thought and action, such as the moral, the aesthetic and the economic. Just as the moral rested on the distinction between good and evil, the aesthetic on that between beautiful and ugly, and the economic on that between beneficial and harmful, or profitable and unprofitable, the 'specific political distinction to which political actions and motives can be reduced is that between *friend* and *foe*'.[54] What is more, this distinction could hold, both in theory and in practice, without it being necessary to draw upon any moral, aesthetic, economic or other distinction: the political foe need not be morally evil, aesthetically ugly, or take the form of an economic competitor: 'He is simply the Other, the stranger, and it is sufficient for his nature that he is, in a specially intense way, existentially something different and alien, so that in a case of conflict he represents the negation of one's own form of existence, and therefore will be repulsed or fought to retain one's proper, ontological form of life.'[55]

A discussion of all the changes Schmitt made to the text from one version to another need not distract us here; suffice it to say that whereas in the 1927 version the political had been an independent sphere of human thought and action, alongside other spheres such as the moral, the aesthetic and the economic, in the 1932 edition the political was now defined according to its own set of criteria that express themselves in a characteristic way: 'The political must therefore rest on its own ultimate distinctions, to which all action with a specifically political meaning can be traced.'[56] The political is no longer unrelated to other spheres of cultural life, but can rather emerge in every sphere of human existence: 'The distinction of friend and enemy denotes the utmost degree of intensity of a union

---

53 Schmitt, 'Der Begriff des Politischen', p. 3.
54 *Ibid.*, 4; emphasis in the original.   55 *Ibid.*
56 C. Schmitt, *The Concept of the Political* (1996), p. 26.

or separation, of an association or dissociation.'[57] By thus highlighting the notion of the intensity of a dispute, Schmitt was able to
incorporate domestic conflicts into his model, and take into consideration civil war as well as revolution.[58] Alongside the Platonic
distinction between πολέμιος ('public' foe) and ἐχϕρός ('private'
enemy) one now also finds the antithesis of πολέμος (war) and
στάσις (civil war, or insurrection).[59] Any antagonism, if intense and
extreme enough, the reader was now told, can become political,
and 'every concrete antagonism becomes more political the closer
it gets to the most extreme point, namely that of the friend–foe
grouping'.[60]

Morgenthau would later claim that it was precisely this novel
emphasis that Schmitt had taken from his doctoral dissertation without giving him credit for it; an assertion that Scheuerman picked up
on and that continues to excite the Schmitt–Morgenthau 'cottage
industry'. But before discussing this matter any further, let us now
look more closely at Morgenthau's doctoral thesis, and on the elements that were to have a lasting place in his subsequent work.

Disputes and tensions

Entitled *Die internationale Rechtspflege, das Wesen ihrer Organe und die
Grenzen ihrer Anwendung; insbesondere der Begriff des Politischen im
Völkerrecht*,[61] Morgenthau's doctoral dissertation dealt with the topic
I discussed above, namely the extent to which states felt obliged to
submit their disputes to international settlement. True to his liking for political philosophy and social scientific thought in general,
Morgenthau chose the topic, he would later claim, because 'while
legal in nature, it lent itself to philosophical and political considerations', the latter being far more interesting than 'run-of-the-mill legal

---

57 *Ibid.*
58 See H. Meier, *Carl Schmitt, Leo Strauss und "Der Begriff des Politischen": Zu einem
Dialog unter Abwesenden* (Stuttgart and Weimar: Metzler, 1998).
59 Schmitt, *Der Begriff des Politischen* (1963), p. 29. In an added footnote, Schmitt now
mentions that real war for Plato is a war between those who are 'by nature enemies'
(i.e. Hellenes and Barbarians) while conflicts among Hellenes are only considered as
discords (στάσεις).
60 *Ibid.*, p. 30.
61 [The judicial function in the international realm, the nature of its organs and the limits of its application; in particular, the concept of the political in international law.]

problems'.[62] In his late autobiographical sketch Morgenthau would also assert that his doctoral dissertation was a reply to Schmitt's 'Concept of the Political', even though 'the final title did not show it'.[63] This is somewhat of a puzzling assertion, for Schmitt's 1927 article on the concept of the political is not cited at all – indeed, the only work by Schmitt that does appear in the references is *Die Kernfrage des Völkerbundes*.[64] In any event, the dissertation was published in March 1929 in the academic series *Frankfurter Abhandlungen zum Kriegsverhütungsrecht* under the abbreviated title *Die internationale Rechtspflege, ihr Wesen und ihre Grenzen*.[65] Amongst the book's reviewers were Paul Guggenheim, Hersch Lauterpacht, Otfried Nippold (1864–1938) and Hans Wehberg (1885–1962) – all household names in the international law debates of the 1920s and 1930s.

The starting point for Morgenthau's dissertation was the clause relating to matters of honour and (national) interest (*die sogenannte Ehren- und Interessenklausel*), which represented the classical expression of the attempt by states to give their international obligations a form that allowed them 'to avoid unforeseen, unwanted consequences of the obligation without breaking the law, by means of a contractual disregard of the agreement':[66] if a state could not ignore its obligations under international law, then it had to be made sure that issues of 'vital' interest were formally acknowledged to lie outside of the law's scope. The content of this clause, and the theoretical framework of the concept of the political which it is based upon in order to delineate the area of non-justiciable disputes, were to be the subject matter of the work.

---

62 H. J. Morgenthau, 'Fragment of an Intellectual Autobiography: 1904–1932', in K. W. Thompson and R. J. Meyers (eds.), *Truth and Tragedy. A Tribute to Hans J. Morgenthau*. Second edition with new Postscript (New Brunswick, NJ: Transaction Books, 1984), pp. 1–17, at 9.

63 *Ibid.*, p. 15.

64 C. Schmitt, *Die Kernfrage des Völkerbundes* (Berlin: Dümmler, 1926). Paradoxically, when Morgenthau finally broke the prolonged silence concerning his relation to Carl Schmitt, he talks of Schmitt's 'Concept of Politics', a complete mistranslation of the German '*Begriff des Politischen*'. The elderly Morgenthau also falsely remembered Schmitt to have published the 'book' in 1921 (it came out in 1932).

65 [The Judicial Function in the International Realm, its Nature and its Limits.] H. J. Morgenthau, *Die internationale Rechtspflege, ihr Wesen und ihre Grenzen* (Leipzig: Noske, 1929).

66 *Ibid.*, p. 4.

Morgenthau began his analysis by 'proving', as he called it, that the area of competence of international dispute-settlement bodies – with the criterion of justiciability based objectively on the ability of judges to settle a dispute through a decision in a material sense – had indeed no limitations.[67] For his reviewers, this formalistic reasoning was uncontroversial, and 'in conformity with the view now gaining general acceptance'.[68] Wehberg, however, pointed out that there was no need to first prove this at all, and that the fact that Morgenthau nonetheless did so set him off in the wrong direction. For instead of distinguishing between cases that can be decided by means of existing legal norms, and those for which such norms must still be created or for which the judge only has the option of deciding on the grounds of equity (*nach Billigkeit*), Morgenthau, in what Wehberg called '(potentially lethal) intellectual acrobatics' (*einen geistigen Saltomortale*), based his analysis on the far more general issue of whether a dispute can be solved using generally applicable norms, i.e. with the decision being based either on strict law or on equity.[69] Similarly, Lauterpacht claimed that Morgenthau's book 'suffers from an obviously imperfect first-hand knowledge of international arbitration', and that this was 'perhaps the reason why the author does not seem to be aware of the possibilities of the judicial function as an agency in developing the law and in adapting it to new conditions'.[70]

Of far greater importance, however, is the second part of Morgenthau's thesis, the main claim of which, as Martti Koskenniemi points out, 'deviated from (and was in part directed against) the type of legal formalism represented by the works of his supervisor [Karl] Strupp'.[71] Morgenthau began by stating the obvious: although in theory all international disputes could be solved by resort to international judicial settlement bodies, it was by no means the case in practice that all inter-state disputes were submitted to international arbitration. Following the thought of another well-known jurist of the time, the Swiss internationalist Otfried Nippold, he asserted

---

67 *Ibid.*, p. 42.
68 H. Lauterpacht, 'Review of Morgenthau, *Die internationale Rechtspflege*', *British Year Book of International Law*, 12 (1931), pp. 229–30, at 229.
69 H. Wehberg, 'Review of Morgenthau, *Die internationale Rechtspflege*', *Die Friedens-Warte*, 30 (1930), pp. 30–1.
70 Lauterpacht, 'Review of Morgenthau, *Die internationale Rechtspflege*', p. 229.
71 Koskenniemi, *The Gentle Civilizer of Nations*, p. 445.

that while the common 'vertical' distinction between legal disputes and disputes over conflicts of interests might hold in theory, it was of no value for a practice-oriented analysis.[72] Instead, he advocated a 'horizontal' distinction that singled out certain disputes from the set of legal disputes and disputes over conflicts of interests, namely 'political' disputes, defined as those related to the honour and vital interests of the disputing parties. All disputes are obviously related to the interests of the parties involved; of importance is whether the interests are such that international judicial settlement is deemed too risky. The concepts of the legal and the political should not be understood as opposing terms, Morgenthau claimed, and the antithesis of political questions is non-political questions, and not legal questions, which themselves could be of a political or non-political nature.[73]

In principle and by definition, Morgenthau continued, there was no issue of state action to which the word 'political' could not be applied. Only through an empirical analysis was it possible to assert that in a particular situation, a given issue attained a political character; in a different context, the same issue might not be political in nature. This was because the concept of the political has no substance of its own, but is rather a quality that can adhere to all substances – in other words, the field of political disputes cannot be determined through its subject matter: any dispute can, under certain circumstances, be or become a political one. In order to identify this quality, what is thus required is a more precise conceptualization of the political, reaching beyond the more general concept relating 'political' to the purpose of state action (*Staatszweck*). The essential characteristic of this more nuanced concept of the political is, according to Morgenthau, the degree of intensity with which an object of state action is related to the substantiality, or individuality, of the state itself.[74]

---

72 O. Nippold, *Die Fortbildung des Verfahrens in völkerrechtlichen Streitigkeiten* (Leipzig: Duncker & Humblot, 1907), pp. 181 and 186. Nippold argued that talk of the legal limits to judicial settlement is worthless, as they are not related to the nature of the process of arbitration itself, nor to the nature of modern state disputes: if there are limits to justiciability, these would be found in the realm of practical politics (*im praktisch-politischen Gebiet*), and are hence outside of the scope of international law altogether.

73 Morgenthau, *Die internationale Rechtspflege*, pp. 58 and 62.

74 *Ibid.*, pp. 65–9. At this point, p. 67, Morgenthau again quotes Nippold's *Die Fortbildung des Verfahrens in völkerrechtlichen Streitigkeiten*, p. 143, who writes: 'A legal dispute can

Central to the argument is thus Morgenthau's claim that the concept of the political, as it had hitherto been formulated, was inadequate in its function of objectively categorizing a particular type of juridical question within a given legal system. This was because 'its content, which cannot be completely resolved in a conceptual formulation, goes against the nature of the contractual obligation that fulfils its function of securing legal harmony precisely from the possibility of specifying its content on the basis of generally applicable principles'.[75] Consequently, Morgenthau argued that it was necessary to distinguish between 'objective' and 'subjective' limits to judicial settlement, a distinction that, he proposed, could be captured by the concept of 'tensions' (*Spannungen*): a disagreement between states would be called a 'dispute' if it can be expressed in legal terms, whereas the word 'tension' refers to a situation 'involving a discrepancy, asserted by one state against another, between the legal situation on the one hand and the actual power relation on the other'.[76] Due to the static nature of the international legal order, formal dispute settlement bodies could not adequately deal with such tensions, and thus, as Martti Koskenniemi succinctly sums up Morgenthau's argument, the law needed to be changed from a static to a dynamic order by equipping it 'with a (legislative) mechanism that would reflect the underlying political transformations and integrative new values and power relations into itself while at the same time limiting States' unilateral right to resort to war'.[77]

This distinction between objective and subjective limits of judicial settlement did not sit well with Morgenthau's reviewers, generally because to them it did not do justice to recent developments in regard to what Guggenheim called 'an ever denser network of

---

turn into a political, and a political dispute into a legal one.' Nippold then proceeds to cite Goldschmidt, 'Ein Reglement für internationale Schiedsgerichte', who urges that one must not forget 'that the major international conflicts seldom exist in their full intensity from the outset, that originally meagre sprouts can grow into serious threats to the peace' [*daß die großen Völkerkonflikte selten von vornherein in voller Intensität bestehen, daß ursprünglich dürftige Keime allmählich zu schweren Friedensbedrohungen heranwachsen*].

75 Morgenthau, *Die internationale Rechtspflege*, p. 71.
76 *Ibid.*, p. 78.
77 M. Koskenniemi, 'Carl Schmitt, Hans Morgenthau, and the Image of Law in International Relations', in M. Byers (ed.), *The Role of Law in International Politics: Essays in International Relations and International Law* (Oxford University Press, 2000), pp. 17–34, at 20.

international legal treaties'[78] – hence the criticism that Morgenthau either had an inadequate knowledge of, or at least did not pay enough attention to, actual practice.[79] While Lauterpacht was the most conciliatory, merely hinting that he deemed Morgenthau's treatment of the subjective side of the justiciability of disputes to be 'less satisfactory', Guggenheim rather more bluntly asserted that at this point 'the author's analysis starts to become particularly original, but also particularly problematic': Morgenthau's argument that in disputes of a political nature an international settlement body would either unconsciously choose the decision that would restore the balance of power, or, in recognition of its responsibility, would make the tension itself a constituent of the decision, was, according to Guggenheim, 'exaggerated and not completely thought through'.[80] Lauterpacht agreed: 'A close acquaintance with the history of international arbitration', he wrote, 'would also have saved him from attaching, as he does, decisive importance to the argument as to the impossibility of securing impartial international judges in matters of high political importance'.[81]

78 Guggenheim, 'Review of Morgenthau, *Die internationale Rechtspflege*', *Juristische Wochenschrift*, 58 (1929), pp. 3469–70, at 3470.

79 Interestingly, Wehberg nonetheless used the same terminology of 'objective' and 'subjective' limits a few years earlier, in his reply to the report by Marshall-Brown and Politis regarding 'La classification des conflits comportant un reglement judicaire'. After also referring to Nippold's *Die Fortbildung des Verfahrens in völkerrechtlichen Streitigkeiten*, he goes on to write: 'The reasons for which certain disputes, emerging in the life of states, are not submitted to a tribunal of arbitration are based only on their political nature, and the existence of their political nature is solely determined by the subjective appreciation of the state. There is no touchstone, no basis for objective appreciation which determines when a dispute is not susceptible to a judicial solution', H. Wehberg, 'Reply to Marshall-Brown and Politis, "La classification des conflits comportant un reglement judicaire"', *Annuaire de l'Institut de droit international*, 29 (1922), pp. 57–8, at 57.

80 Guggenheim, 'Review of Morgenthau, *Die internationale Rechtspflege*', pp. 3469–70.

81 Lauterpacht, 'Review of Morgenthau, *Die internationale Rechtspflege*', p. 230. Ironically, at just this time (1931) the Permanent Court of International Justice was asked to give an Advisory Opinion on the Austro-German Customs Union controversy – it was decided by eight voices against seven! Undoubtedly aware of the tension between his own 'idealistic' theoretical view and reality, Lauterpacht argued, in a lengthy footnote in *The Function of Law*, pp. 156–8, that much of the criticism voiced against the Court for having ruled on a matter that was 'highly political' was misguided, because given 'the indefiniteness of the term "political"', every judgment or advisory opinion of the Court was political to a certain degree. What was more important, Lauterpacht argued, was that the Court 'was called upon to exercise a typically judicial function consisting in the interpretation of a contractual obligation'. He thus concluded: 'The fact that the Opinion was given by a majority of six against a minority of five [Lauterpacht seems to have erred on the numbers], gave rise to some exaggerated criticism.'

In sum, the reviewers – with the exception of Nippold[82] – were sceptical about the way Morgenthau sought to grapple with the observation that while all disputes could theoretically be dealt with through international arbitration, reality told a rather different story. The idea that there were certain political tensions which overruled, or preceded, international law's claim of relevance in addressing inter-state disputes was not what those insisting on the binding force and material scope of the law in the international realm wanted to hear. As Wehberg wrote, 'It is unclear how one would want to promote the authority of international law by advocating that tensions among states be taken even more into consideration than has already been the case in practice. Here, the author shows himself as a politician of power, rather than one of law'.[83] True to their discipline of International Law, the likes of Lauterpacht tried to undermine the realism of the view that there were practical limits to justiciability by arguing that 'it is the refusal of the state to submit the dispute to judicial settlement, and not the intrinsic nature of the controversy, which makes it political'.[84] Morgenthau, most certainly less attached to the well-being of his chosen trade of International Law than Lauterpacht, had far less inhibition to take the analysis to intellectual plains that were beyond the realm of international legal scholarship altogether. Evidently, the rule-scepticism that, according to Martti Koskenniemi's framework outlined in the preceding chapter, will come to represent Morgenthau's position later on is already at work here. Wehberg's statement about the author's predisposition as an advocate of the centrality of power turned out to be a most perceptive one indeed.

The will to power

When Morgenthau moved to Geneva in February 1932, and had finally managed to overcome the troublesome hurdle of passing his inaugural lecture,[85] he reacted to the reviews he had received for his

---

82 Nippold's review of sixteen lines takes the form of a complete endorsement of Morgenthau's dissertation, and offers no critical commentary whatsoever. One might wonder whether the fact that Morgenthau cited him seventy times had any bearing on this; in any event, Nippold's influence on Morgenthau's thought is fairly clear.
83 Wehberg, 'Review of Morgenthau, *Die internationale Rechtspflege*', p. 31.
84 Lauterpacht, *The Function of Law*, p. 164.
85 See Chapter 3.

dissertation with a small volume in French, *La notion du 'politique' et la théorie des différends internationaux.*[86] A large part of the text is basically a translation of sections of his dissertation, but without the impressive list of footnotes which, it is clear from the reviews, made the reception of *Die internationale Rechtspflege* more favourable.[87] Yet whereas the aim of the dissertation had been to associate the work with the ongoing debate over international judicial settlement, Morgenthau was now out to distance himself from it, asserting that his reflections were of a purely theoretical nature, focused solely on the sociological structure on which international disputes were founded, but drew no consequences for practice with respect to the issue of justiciability:

> We believe it necessary to insist on this last point, given that the dominant doctrine has the habit of confusing the empirical and normative points of view, identifying legal disputes with justiciable disputes and political disputes with non-justiciable disputes, and that it is thus tempted to draw, by way of classification only, certain immediate practical consequences.[88]

Obviously Morgenthau believed attack to be the best means of defence: positive international law did not have the necessary tools to fully grasp the concept of the political, he charged. All attempts to do so, including those of Lauterpacht, consequently had to resort to defining the concept of the political in opposition to the notion of legal questions or questions susceptible to a juridical solution[89]– and this, Morgenthau would continue to argue throughout his career, was precisely the problem of the 'internationalism' that had corrupted inter-war thought on international relations. As he would later write in *Scientific Man vs. Power Politics*, 'liberal foreign policy' had, wrongly in his view, 'developed two distinct methods of dealing with the two types of international disputes: compromise for the

---

86 H. J. Morgenthau, *La notion du 'politique' et la théorie des différends internationaux* (Paris: Sirey, 1933).

87 Guggenheim, 'Review of Morgenthau, *Die internationale Rechtspflege*', acknowledged that Morgenthau's work was, for a first publication, characterized by an astonishing familiarity with the literature. Similarly, Lauterpacht, 'Review of Morgenthau, *Die internationale Rechtspflege*', wrote that the book 'shows an extensive knowledge of the literature on the subject'.

88 Morgenthau, *La notion du "politique"*, p. 5.

89 *Ibid.*, p. 38.

so-called "political" disputes or conflicts of interests and the rule of international law for the so-called "legal" disputes'.[90]

Morgenthau's initial stab at Lauterpacht, however, was rather misguided. Having read and reviewed Morgenthau's dissertation, Lauterpacht cited the work on numerous occasions between 1930 and 1933.[91] Morgenthau was aware of this, and in *La notion du 'politique'* remarked in the conclusion that Lauterpacht was undoubtedly the one who had devoted the most attention to his theory.[92] Yet what Morgenthau failed to appreciate sufficiently, it seems, was that Lauterpacht was just as opposed to the distinction between legal and political, justiciable and non-justiciable, as he was himself. The difference, rather, lay in the consequences each drew from the recognition of this inadequacy: whereas Lauterpacht concluded that 'all international disputes are, irrespective of their gravity, disputes of a legal character in the sense that, so long as the rule of law is recognized, they are capable of an answer by the application of legal rules',[93] Morgenthau chose to take the apologist route of arguing that the substance of the 'political' falls into the domain of social reality.[94]

The word 'apologist', of course, refers us back to Koskenniemi's structure of international legal argument outlined in Chapter 1. Both Lauterpacht and Morgenthau were opposed to the distinction between legal and political disputes. Lauterpacht still tried to reconcile the demands of normativity and concreteness by positing a wide material scope of the law, thereby downplaying the role that political considerations had on the actual workings of the international legal system. Morgenthau, by contrast, decided to prioritize the analysis of this social reality of the political, and in *La notion du 'politique'* proposed to unravel what he called the concept's philosophical and

90 H. J. Morgenthau, *Scientific Man vs. Power Politics* (University of Chicago Press, 1946), p. 94.
91 See, in particular, Lauterpacht, 'The Absence of an International Legislature and the Compulsory Jurisdiction of International Tribunals', *British Year Book of International Law*, 11 (1930), 134–57; Lauterpacht, 'La théorie des différends non justiciable en droit international', *Recueil des cours de l'Académie de droit international* (RCADI), 34 (1930-IV), pp. 493–654; and Lauterpacht, *The Function of Law*.
92 Morgenthau, *La notion du "politique"*, p. 89.
93 Lauterpacht, *The Function of Law*, p. 158.
94 For a short comparison of Lauterpacht and Morgenthau on this issue, see M. Koskenniemi, 'Hersch Lauterpacht (1897–1960)', in J. Beatson and R. Zimmermann (eds.), *Jurists Uprooted: German-Speaking Emigré Lawyers in Twentieth-century Britain* (Oxford University Press, 2004), pp. 601–61, at 620–1.

sociological foundations.[95] Morgenthau was no longer trying to produce a strategy that would uphold a sense of internal coherence and order that is vital for international legal practice. By doing so, he slid into the disciplinary chasm between legal and political theory, into a grey zone in which, though embedding his argument into the legal language of international dispute settlement, he was no longer addressing his supposed target audience of international lawyers. Although responding to Lauterpacht, Morgenthau had made himself the external critic.

In 1930, Morgenthau produced a manuscript that attempted to relate the notion of intensity, with which he had defined the concept of the political, with the primordial lust for power in the human psyche.[96] The paper itself is somewhat of a disaster, as Morgenthau himself would later acknowledge. In his autobiographical fragment, he writes: 'The result was a manuscript that I did not even try to publish, either then or later, so certain have I been of the failure of this undertaking.'[97] Nevertheless, in *La notion du 'politique'* his psychological reflections would become the starting point for the refinement of the concept of the political, analysed on the level of the individual. All political action, he asserted, is based on the psychological factor of the will to power (*la volonté de puissance*). This will to power can take on three forms: it can aim at maintaining the acquired power, increasing it, or demonstrating it.[98] As Frei rightly notes,[99] and Morgenthau would later admit,[100] one finds much the same in Max Weber's 1919 lecture 'Politik als Beruf' ['Politics as Vocation']:

When we say that a question is 'political', that a minister or official is 'political,' or that a decision has been made on 'political' grounds, we always mean the same thing. This is that the interests involved in the distribution or preservation of power, or a shift in power, play a decisive role in resolving that question, or in influencing that decision or defining the sphere of

---

95 Morgenthau, *La notion du "politique"*, p. 42.
96 Morgenthau, 'Über die Herkunft des Politischen aus dem Wesen des Menschen' [On the Derivation of the Political from Human Nature], 1930, HJM-Container 151.
97 Morgenthau, 'Fragment of an Intellectual Autobiography', p. 14.
98 Morgenthau, *La notion du 'politique'*, p. 43.
99 C. Frei, *Hans J. Morgenthau: An Intellectual Biography* (Baton Rouge, LA: Louisiana State University Press, 2001), p. 130.
100 In a letter to Max Bodilson, 3 May 1976, HJM-Container 6.

activity of the official concerned. Whoever is active in politics strives for power, either power as a means in the service of other goals, whether idealistic or selfish, or power 'for its own sake,' in other words, so as to enjoy the feeling of prestige that it confers.[101]

While the first two forms of the will to power are related to objects which themselves, independent of the will in question, have an objective value, the will to demonstrate one's power entails an often 'grotesque' disproportion between its objective value and the intensity of the will to affirm it, Morgenthau continued. In the words of Hamlet: 'Rightly to be great / Is not to stir without great argument, / But greatly to find quarrel in a straw / When honour's at the stake'.[102]

Contrary to this view, Morgenthau wrote, is the theory expounded by Carl Schmitt, to whose concept of the political he now turned for a discussion, somewhat irrelevant to his argument, that spans eighteen pages.[103] It is the only time in his career that Morgenthau engages substantively with the writings of Schmitt and, alas, it seems to be in line with Aurel Kolnai's assertion that 'in view of the immense effect, which this exceedingly profound and energetic text by *Carl Schmitt* [*Der Begriff des Politischen*] has exercised ... the exponent of a diverging position must deal with the aforementioned work in particular detail'.[104] Morgenthau seemed to have been very aware of the necessity of engaging with Schmitt's conceptualization of the political in order for his work to be deemed academically sound, although this in itself, he also knew, was not reason enough for devoting space to him. The result is a rather rambling (and

101 M. Weber, 'Politics as a Vocation', in Weber, *The Vocation Lectures*. Edited and with an Introduction by D. Owen and T. B. Strong (Indianapolis, IN: Hackett, 2004), pp. 32–94, at 33–4. Frei, *Hans J. Morgenthau*, p. 130, goes further, arguing that almost identical formulations can be found in the works of Friedrich Nietzsche, with the work of whom Morgenthau was familiar.

102 Morgenthau, *La notion du 'politique'*, pp. 43–4. Shakespeare's quote is from *Hamlet*, Act 4, Scene 4, of the Second Quarto manuscript of 1604–5. It is a rather unfamiliar passage, as it is not included in the First Folio manuscript of 1623, which has been taken as the control text in recent editions of the play. On this point see G. R. Hibbard, 'Textual Introduction', in William Shakespeare, *Hamlet* (Oxford University Press, 1987), pp. 67–130.

103 Morgenthau, *La notion du 'politique'*, pp. 44–61. The section closely follows a German manuscript from the year 1932, entitled 'Einige logische Bemerkungen zu Carl Schmitt's Begriff des Politischen' [A Few Logical Remarks on Carl Schmitt's Concept of the Political], HJM-Container 110.

104 A. Kolnai, 'Der Inhalt der Politik', *Zeitschrift für die gesammte Staatswissenschaft*, 94 (1933), pp. 1–38, at 2; emphasis in the original.

perhaps ultimately unsuccessful) qualification in which Morgenthau argued that not only was Schmitt's theory worth discussing because it exerted considerable influence on public opinion,

but also because it served as a basis for a metaphysics of the role of elementary forces in international relations, a metaphysics which, according to Schmitt, would follow with inescapable necessity from his concept of the political pushed to its logical extremes. It is clear that such a conception of the political, if it were founded, would exercise the greatest influence on the theory of international disputes.[105]

The soundness of the reasoning aside, the above at least reveals the core of Morgenthau's critique, namely that Schmitt's 'doctrine', as he called it, is a metaphysical one, and is very far from historical and psychological reality.

Morgenthau's analysis of Schmitt's concept of the political is not very profound, unlike for example the reflections by Leo Strauss,[106] known to Morgenthau and explicitly praised in a footnote.[107] Much less ambitious, Morgenthau seemed content to focus on questioning the validity of the friend–foe distinction, which, as I outlined earlier, Schmitt had established as the fundamental dichotomy in the realm of the political. Schmitt's distinction between friend and foe, Morgenthau asserted, was of little scientific value for a derivation of a definition of the substance of the political. The opposing pairs of good and evil, beautiful and ugly, represent tautological relations derived from the quality of the respective value spheres of the moral and the aesthetic, and are of no use to an analysis attempting to delineate one sphere from another.[108] Such an analysis would have as its substance the relations moral–non-moral (= the aesthetic, the political, the economic), aesthetic–non-aesthetic (= the moral, the political, the economic), and so on. The problem with Schmitt was that he confounded the two levels of analysis: he declared the

105 Morgenthau, *La notion du 'politique'*, pp. 45–6.
106 L. Strauss, 'Anmerkungen zu Carl Schmitt, Der Begriff des Politischen', *Archiv für Sozialwissenschaft und Sozialpolitik*, 67 (1932), pp. 732–49.
107 Morgenthau, *La notion du 'politique'*, p. 46. Indeed, Morgenthau continued to recommend Strauss' article to his students at the University of Chicago; see also Frei, *Hans J. Morgenthau*, p. 174.
108 Exactly the same critique, it must be pointed out, was already made by another important figure of the constitutional debates in the Weimar Republic, Hermann Heller, in 1928. H. Heller, 'Politische Demokratie und soziale Homogenität', in Heller, *Gesammelte Schriften. 2. Band: Recht, Staat, Macht* (Leiden: A. W. Sijthoff, 1971), pp. 421–33.

distinction between friend and foe to be the essential quality of the political sphere, but then used it to distinguish between what is political and what is not. Moreover, the level-of-analysis problem aside, Morgenthau argued that the distinction between friend and foe was based on a completely different conceptual logic than the pairing good–evil, or beautiful–ugly. For the latter were founded on a value judgment of what is morally or aesthetically valuable (good, beautiful) as opposed to the absence of such worth (evil, ugly). Yet it was by no means the case that the friend is necessarily politically valuable, while the foe is not. Rather, the political friend is an actor who promotes (latently or explicitly) one's political aims, whereas a foe is someone who works against them. Although not in the least irrelevant to an elaboration of the content of the political sphere, Morgenthau concluded, Schmitt's distinction between friend and foe was not particularly helpful for the stated goal of distinguishing the political from other spheres of human action.

Having thus dismissed Schmitt's conceptualization, Morgenthau proceeded to go back to his own argument, and his typology based on the will to power. Now, he claimed that the insights that were made in the domain of human life could 'find their verification' in the external relations of states:

All foreign policy is nothing but the will to maintain, increase or demonstrate its power, and these three manifestations of political will denote the fundamental empirical forms of the policy of the status quo, the policy of imperialism, and the policy of prestige.[109]

If Morgenthau ever made what Wehberg called a '*geistigen Salto-mortale*', this was it. Throughout his doctoral dissertation, Morgenthau had circumscribed a concept of the political that was compatible with the doctrine of the non-justiciability of disputes in international law, i.e. one formulated for the actions of sovereign states. He then completely left the field of International Law to indulge in psychological reflections on the nature of human desire, only to then transpose his insights back onto the field of international dispute settlement. Now armed with the 'will to power' of states, and the triad of maintaining, increasing or demonstrating that power, Morgenthau heavy-handedly closed the door on any hope of reconciling his views with

109 Morgenthau, *La notion du 'politique'*, p. 61.

those in the legal profession. For the static and dynamic elements in international law were now aligned with the goal of maintaining and increasing one's power respectively. Given the complete lack of any enforcement mechanisms, international law, he charged, was bound by the willingness of states, and this willingness was only present when the distribution of power was such that maintaining one's share was the policy to follow. The moment this 'balance of power' was in jeopardy, international law lacked the necessary rules of peaceful change – hence Morgenthau's distinction between 'disputes' and 'tensions'. According to this logic, there are two levels of conflict, the first covered by mechanisms of international law, and correspondingly termed 'disputes', the second being out of the grasp of 'rational regulation', a lower level of generally latent conflict which only manifests itself indirectly – save for the occasional 'violent explosion'.[110]

Schmitt's concept of the political

So where does this leave us on the issue of the 'hidden dialogue' between Morgenthau and Schmitt? One thing is certain: it would have been almost unthinkable for any young scholar studying *Staatsrechtslehre* in the 1920s not to have come into contact with the writings of Carl Schmitt, and it thus does not come as a surprise that Morgenthau was no exception. From his publications and correspondence it is clear that as much as Morgenthau came to despise Schmitt for the way the prominent scholar treated the young enthusiast during their only meeting – 'When I walked down the stairs from Schmitt's apartment, I stopped on the landing between his and the next floor and said to myself: "Now I have met the most evil man alive"'[111] – he continued reading him well after emigrating to the United States, though practically never citing what he read.[112]

110 *Ibid.*, p. 78.
111 Morgenthau, 'Fragment of an Intellectual Autobiography: 1904–1932', p. 16.
112 Leo Strauss, for instance, gave Morgenthau Schmitt's *Theorie des Partisanen: Zwischenbemerkung zum Begriff des Politischen* (Berlin: Duncker & Humblot, 1963) to read not long after it was published. Morgenthau replied in a thank-you note to Strauss that he deemed the book to be 'one of the shoddiest pieces of thinking and writing I have ever seen'; letter from Morgenthau to Leo Strauss, 14 January 1965, HJM-Container 52. Morgenthau repeated his remarks in a letter to Hannah Arendt (also dated 14 January 1965), in which he writes that Schmitt's

But given Schmitt's reputation as 'crown jurist' of the Third Reich and Morgenthau's subsequent status as Jewish émigré, this lack of explicit reference should hardly come as a surprise.

As I tried to illustrate earlier in this chapter, Schmitt's short text on the concept of the political was responding to no insignificant degree to Heinrich Triepel, and to the demands of the very specific circumstances created by the constitutional settings of the Weimar Republic. The anglophone appropriation of Schmitt 'the political theorist' or 'political philosopher' seems to want to avoid all such allusions to obscure German law debates, however, and instead tends to treat Schmitt's text and the friend/foe distinction as a stand-alone, 'existential' theory of politics.

It is important to point out again that contrary to widespread opinion, especially in Political Science and the field of International Relations, the 'concept of the political' was not invented by Carl Schmitt, whose text is but one of a series of conceptualizations – other notable attempts came from Rudolf Smend[113] and Gerhard Leibholz (1901–82)[114] – to grapple with the way political considerations were re-injected into the dominant, formalistic legal positivism in a time of constitutional turmoil in the Weimar Republic and the very specific German debate in international law created by the Versailles Treaty. Once again, however, Schmitt's conceptualization had the right mixture of intellectual sharpness and layman's comprehensibility to steal the show, to the point where it became impossible to discuss the concept of the political without referring to Schmitt.

What seems to fascinate people is Morgenthau's claim that Schmitt appropriated his notion of intensity and worked it into the 1932 edition of the *Begriff des Politischen*, a charge that continues to be taken at face value in the current literature. Indeed, Morgenthau made this claim repeatedly, in the first version of his inaugural lecture in Geneva, in *La notion du 'politique'*, and again in his autobiographical

---

text 'is interesting but unbelievably shoddy, both in thought and exposition'; HJM-Container 5.

113 R. Smend, *Die politische Gewalt im Verfassungsstaat und das Problem der Staatsform* (Tübingen: Mohr, 1923).

114 G. Leibholz, 'Zur Begriffsbildung im öffentlichen Recht', *Blätter für Deutsche Philosophie*, 5 (1931), pp. 175 89.

fragment.[115] Yet as I tried to demonstrate in this chapter, the notion of intensity, the way Morgenthau used it in his dissertation in the context of the justiciability of disputes, was not terribly original, and can already be found in the work of James Goldschmidt in 1875. Moreover, present at Morgenthau's only meeting with Schmitt in 1930 was a certain Carl Bilfinger (1879–1958), Professor of Law at the University of Halle, who also used the notion of intensity in his own work.[116] And let us not forget the ever-present Georg Jellinek and his opus *Allgemeine Staatslehre*, a book these people all knew off by heart. What do we find there? Nothing less than the assertion that 'the intensity of an association varies according to the strength and significance of the purposes that constitute this association ... it attains its highest degree in the state'.[117]

We will probably never know for sure whether Schmitt became hooked on the notion of intensity from the discussion he had with Morgenthau – and indeed, it is perhaps not all that important, at least not for those of us interested in Morgenthau. Still, the Morgenthau–Schmitt 'cottage industry' enjoys using this story as a springboard for launching into a discussion of how Morgenthau was influenced by the work of Schmitt,[118] even though Morgenthau's assertion does not actually serve as a basis for such a claim, but for the opposite: how Schmitt was influenced by Morgenthau.

What is perhaps of greater interest, however, is to reflect upon the way the literature on Morgenthau and Schmitt has tended to occlude other scholars Morgenthau conversed with, and to again call for a more nuanced picture of who or what may have had a bearing on the young Morgenthau's thought. Chris Brown, Martti Koskenniemi,

115 Morgenthau, 'Der Kampf der deutschen Staatslehre um die Wirklichkeit des Staates' ['The Struggle of German Theory of the State over the Reality of the State'], Geneva, 1932, in HJM-Container 110; Morgenthau, *La notion du 'politique'*, p. 35; Morgenthau, 'Fragment of an Intellectual Autobiography: 1904–1932', p. 16.
116 K. Bilfinger, 'Betrachtungen über politisches Recht', *Zeitschrift für ausländisches öffentliches Recht und Völkerrecht*, 1 (1929), pp. 57–76.
117 *(Die Intensität des Verbandes ist eine verschiedene nach Stärke und Bedeutung der den Verband konstituierenden Zwecke ... sie erreicht ihren höchsten Grad im Staat.)* Jellinek, *Allgemeine Staatslehre*, p. 179; see also Vollrath, 'Wie ist Carl Schmitt an seinen Begriff des Politischen gekommen?', p. 153.
118 Recent examples of this are C. Brown, '"The Twilight of International Morality"? Hans J. Morgenthau and Carl Schmitt on the End of the *Jus Publicum Europaeum*', and W. E. Scheuerman, 'Carl Schmitt and Hans Morgenthau: Realism and Beyond?', both in M. C. Williams (ed.), *Realism Reconsidered: The Legacy of Hans J. Morgenthau in International Relations* (Oxford University Press, 2007), pp. 42–92.

William Scheuerman, Michael Williams and others are certainly correct in pointing to the obvious parallels between the writings of Schmitt and Morgenthau,[119] and these certainly merit further investigation. But Schmitt was by no means the only one of Morgenthau's interlocutors – be it in a 'hidden dialogue' or not – visibly shaping his thought. In this chapter I have tried to show that Hersch Lauterpacht played a crucial role for the young Morgenthau, and Chapter 3 will try a similar exercise with Hans Kelsen. Moreover, these influences need not, by any means, be internally consistent: already the briefest of introspective reflection on one's own development will undoubtedly show the haphazard and unsystematic way ideas and arguments make their way into one's thought process, only to be digested and reproduced in some form or other in subsequent work. So why should Morgenthau's thoughts have been any more coherent?

Of course, those who have been in direct personal contact with Carl Schmitt report of the fascination evoked by the man and his ideas.[120] But one of the central talents of Schmitt was precisely his ability to boil down complex arguments and debates to seemingly comprehensible and thus attractive expressions and phrases: the concept of the political formulated as the distinction between friend and foe; sovereignty as based on deciding over the state of exception;[121] the crisis of parliamentary democracy in Weimar diagnosed by means of the distinction between legality and legitimacy;[122] or the story of the origins of law, told in his *Nomos der Erde*,[123] as resting on the act of land appropriation, or *Landnahme*. While this goes some way to explaining his rise to fame (or infamy), it is only part of the story. For Schmitt's tactic of breaking everything down to the smallest common denominator also means that the end result

---

119 John P. McCormick, in his book *Carl Schmitt's Critique of Liberalism: Against Politics as Technology* (Cambridge University Press, 1997), p. 304, even goes to the extreme of declaring Morgenthau to be a 'Schmitt student'.

120 Most astonishing is still the story of Alexandre Kojève (1902–68), perhaps the most important Hegelian philosopher of his generation. According to Jacob Taubes, *Ad Carl Schmitt: Gegenstrebige Fügung* (Berlin: Merve, 1987), p. 69, Kojève, on a visit to Berlin in 1967, when asked what else he would do during his stay, replied that he would go to Plettenberg – 'with whom else is it worth talking to in Germany?'

121 C. Schmitt, *Politische Theologie: Vier Kapitel zur Lehre von der Souveränität* [1922] (Munich: Duncker & Humblot, 2009).

122 C. Schmitt, *Legalität und Legitimität* [1932] (Berlin: Duncker & Humblot, 1998).

123 C. Schmitt, *Der Nomos der Erde im Völkerrecht des Jus Publicum Europaeum* [1950] (Berlin: Duncker & Humblot, 1997).

is open to particularly broad interpretation. This is why many still find him so useful for contemporary debates. But this is also why it is easy to try to read Schmittian elements into the work of someone like Morgenthau.

Oppenheim's balance of power

Before proceeding with Morgenthau's turn to Hans Kelsen's theory of norms, it is insightful to have a look at Morgenthau's US textbook, *Politics Among Nations*.[124] Not only will we find a repeat of many of the major themes of his doctoral dissertation and *La notion du 'politique'*, but also a further episode of his engagement with Lauterpacht, in what constitutes a fascinating, and very telling, anecdote.

The purpose of *Politics Among Nations*, Morgenthau wrote in the first edition, was 'to detect and understand the forces which determine political relations among nations, and to comprehend the ways in which those forces act upon each other and upon international political relations and institutions'.[125] Written with a continuous eye on US foreign policy in 'an age of two worlds and of total war', the book, his readers were told, revolved around the two concepts of power and peace. In light of the power aspirations of sovereign states, Morgenthau sought to discuss the value of the two devices through which peace could be maintained, one being 'the self-regulatory mechanism of the social forces which manifests itself in the struggle for power on the international scene, that is the balance of power', the other consisting of 'normative limitations upon that struggle in the form of international law, international morality, and world public opinion'.[126]

In exactly the same terms as in 1933, Morgenthau then asserted that this struggle for power, the manifestation of all politics, could be reduced to three 'basic types': 'A political policy seeks either to keep power, to increase power, or to demonstrate power.' Moreover, to these three patterns of politics correspond three foreign policies: the policy of the status quo, the policy of imperialism, and the policy of

---

124 H. J. Morgenthau, *Politics Among Nations: The Struggle for Power and Peace*. First edition (New York, NY: Alfred A. Knopf, 1948).
125 *Ibid.*, p. 3.   126 *Ibid.*, pp. 8–9.

prestige, respectively.[127] Again, just as in 1933, Morgenthau highlights the ad hoc nature of this typology, warning that '[i]t should
be noted that these formulations are of a provisional nature and are
subject to further refinement'.[128] Refine them, however, he never
did – even though the conceptual triad of maintaining, increasing
and demonstrating power was a formula Morgenthau would reiter-
ate until the end of his career.[129]

Moving on, the last part of *Politics Among Nations* discussed the
issue of attaining international peace. The usual way of solving the
problem, Morgenthau argued, had been by trying to limit the power
aspirations of states. The possible remedies outlined are disarma-
ment, collective security and the establishment of an international
police force; judicial settlement and peaceful change; and finally
international government through the creation of the Holy Alliance,
the League of Nations, and then the United Nations – all of which
had little hope of success given the 'conditions of the modern state
system'.[130] The chapter on judicial settlement is taken straight from
his doctorate: an analysis of international conflict needed to distinguish between disputes (i.e. legally formulated conflicts) and
tensions (or 'unformulated conflicts of power').[131] Shakespeare's
Hamlet is again cited, and it is concluded that 'political disputes –
disputes which stand in relation to a tension and in which, therefore,
the over-all distribution of power between two nations is at stake –
cannot be settled by judicial means'.[132]

It is all too evident that Morgenthau's debate with Hersch
Lauterpacht continued to have a bearing on what he considered

---

127 *Ibid.*, pp. 21–2.
128 *Ibid.*, p. 22; see also Frei, *Hans J. Morgenthau*, pp. 131–2.
129 It can be found, for instance, in *Scientific Man vs. Power Politics*, pp. 167–8, as well
   as in H. J. Morgenthau, *Science: Servant or Master?* (New York, NY: New American
   Library, 1972), pp. 14 and 32. Interestingly, the first chapter of the latter book is
   based on a German manuscript entitled 'Über den Sinn der Wissenschaft in dieser
   Zeit und über die Bestimmung des Menschen' [On the Meaning of Science in Our
   Time and on the Destiny of Man] (undated, but probably 1936 or 1937). The argument is the same, but 'the political' has been transformed into 'politics' throughout!
130 Morgenthau, *Politics Among Nations*, first edition, p. 391.
131 Interestingly, Morgenthau's conceptualization of conflicts as disputes and tensions
   was adopted by Charles de Visscher in his *Théories et Réalités en Droit International
   Public* (Paris: A. Pedone, 1953); translated into English by P. E. Corbett as *Theory
   and Reality in Public International Law* (Princeton University Press, 1957).
132 Morgenthau, *Politics Among Nations*, first edition, p. 346.

to be some of the central notions of what would become his 'realist theory of international politics'. But Lauterpacht would haunt him in more ways than one. In October 1948, Morgenthau published a review of three books in the journal *The Review of Politics*,[133] one of them being the sixth edition of Oppenheim's *International Law* (1940/1947),[134] a famous manual in two volumes (the first entitled 'Peace', the second 'War and Neutrality') first published in 1905 and 1906 (the second volume, for some reason, always came out first). Oppenheim's opus was posthumously published, from the fourth edition onwards, first by Arnold D. McNair and then by Hersch Lauterpacht.[135] In Volume I of the third and fourth editions of the textbook, there is a section entitled 'Seven Lessons of the History of the Law of Nations', of which the first reads:

> The first and principal moral is that a Law of Nations can only exist if there is an equilibrium, a balance of power, between the members of the Family of Nations. If the Powers cannot keep one another in check, no rules of law will have any force, since an over-powerful State will naturally try to act according to discretion and disobey the law.[136]

Paradoxically, although having cited the fourth edition of Lassa Oppenheim's *International Law* repeatedly in *Die Internationale Rechtspflege*,[137] Morgenthau seems to have forgotten to incorporate Oppenheim's assertion that international law could not exist without a balance of power – an argument that was indeed very much compatible with his distinction between disputes and tensions – until he re-read earlier editions of the text for the book review.[138] For a

---

133 H. J. Morgenthau, 'International Affairs', *The Review of Politics*, 10 (1948), pp. 493–7.

134 L. Oppenheim, *International Law: A Treatise*. Sixth edition, edited by Hersch Lauterpacht, 2 vols. (London, etc.: Longmans, Green & Co, 1940 and 1947).

135 For an overview of the evolution of the nine existing editions of Oppenheim's treatise, see M. W. Janis, 'The New *Oppenheim* and its Theory of International Law', *Oxford Journal of Legal Studies*, 16 (1996), pp. 329–36.

136 L. Oppenheim, *International Law: a Treatise*. Fourth edition, edited by Arnold D. McNair (London, etc.: Longmans, Green & Co, 1926 and 1928), pp. 99–103, at 99. In the first edition there were originally five lessons, a sixth was added in the second edition, and a seventh in the third.

137 Morgenthau, *Die Internationale Rechtspflege*, pp. 7, 12, 15, 83, 102, 113, 117 and 137.

138 I deliberately use the word 'forgotten' because the assertion that there is no international law without a balance of power is also found in Morgenthau, 'Positivism, Functionalism, and International Law', *American Journal of International Law*, 34 (1940), pp. 260–84, at 275, as well as in *Scientific Man vs. Power Politics*, p. 104, where he writes: 'A rule of law [in the international field] not supported by the mutual

proper appraisal of the new edition under review obviously entailed seeing what had been changed; and lo and behold, Lauterpacht, who inevitably did not take a liking to the claim that the balance of power was a prerequisite for international law, unceremoniously proceeded to scrap this first lesson of the Law of Nations altogether, in preparation for the fifth edition.[139] Ever since, Benedict Kingsbury writes, 'the notion that balance of power principles might be relevant to international law has been virtually unutterable among members of the "invisible college of international lawyers"'.[140]

Morgenthau did not fail to react to this act of sabotage by his critic of old. It must be regretted, he wrote,

that in § 51 Professor Oppenheim's reference to the balance of power has been omitted as one of the factors which has contributed to the development of international law. Since this reference is inconsistent with Professor Oppenheim's basic assumption of the self-sufficiency of international law, it might well be said that Professor Lauterpacht's omission of that reference constitutes an improvement of the original in view of that assumption. Yet it seems to this reviewer to be a tribute to Professor Oppenheim's critical realism [sic!] that the illusion of his legalistic philosophy could not completely blind him to the realities of international affairs. The recognition of the intimate relation between international law and international politics is indeed indispensable for the understanding of international law as it actually is.[141]

Indeed, as Kingsbury has pointed out,[142] Oppenheim considered the balance of power principle to be determinative of law: rather than being in itself a principle *of* international law, the distribution of power was one of the defining structural features of international

---

interest which the parties concerned have in its observance can be maintained as a valid rule of conduct only by an ever precarious balance of power.' Moreover, Morgenthau would surely have been confronted with Oppenheim's treatise again at the University of Chicago, where he began by teaching Quincy Wright's courses. Wright, very much attuned to international law debates, discussed Oppenheim's use of the balance of power in *A Study of War* (University of Chicago Press, 1942), pp. 268–9, 745, 765 and 905.

139 Indeed, the section in the fifth edition is now entitled 'Four Lessons of the History of the Law of Nations', instead of seven! L. Oppenheim, *International Law: A Treatise*. Fifth edition, edited by Hersch Lauterpacht, 2 vols. (London, etc.: Longmans, Green & Co., 1935 and 1937), pp. 80–2.

140 Kingsbury, Benedict, 'Legal Positivism as Normative Politics: International Society, Balance of Power and Lassa Oppenheim's Positive International Law', *European Journal of International Law*, 13 (2002), pp. 410–36, at 420.

141 Morgenthau, 'International Affairs', p. 494.

142 Kingsbury, 'Legal Positivism as Normative Politics', p. 417.

politics, and thus one of the fundamental conditions *for* international law. If states were to adhere to international legal rules, a balance of power had to be in place – hence Morgenthau's assertion that with the demise of the balance of power system in the first half of the twentieth century, the possibility of attaining peace through international law had disappeared as well. What is ironic, however, is that such a distinction between legal normativity and political/ethical normative structures came from the pen of someone like Oppenheim, whose positivist conception of international law was one of the reasons why principles such as the balance of power came to be erased from the substance of legal inquiry in the first place.[143]

Although too late to be included in the first edition of *Politics Among Nations*, Morgenthau did not fail to mention his newfound friend in the second edition. Already in the new Preface, one reads: 'The relationship between the balance of power and international law, which was known to many of the classical writers of international law and was still emphasized in the first editions of Oppenheim's treatise, has again found its deserved place in a theory of international politics.'[144] Turning to the index, one finds a new entry preceding the already existing 'Oppenheim–Lauterpacht' entry: 'Oppenheim, Lassa, 577; on balance of power as foundation for international law, 252'.[145] Indeed, Morgenthau had meanwhile added several paragraphs to the opening section of the chapter on international law. In international society, law had necessarily to be decentralized in nature, given that this society was made up of sovereign states that were not obliged to any supranational law-giving or law-enforcing authority. The fact that international law nonetheless existed, Morgenthau now argued, was the result of two 'objective social forces': complementary interests of states and a balance of power. That this was the case, he continued, was already recognized by 'one of the foremost modern teachers of international law', 'Professor Oppenheim', whose first of the 'six morals' of the second edition of *International Law* he subsequently cited in full. Surprisingly, Morgenthau decided not to mention Lauterpacht

143 *Ibid.*, pp. 419–20.
144 H. J. Morgenthau, *Politics Among Nations: The Struggle for Power and Peace*. Second edition (New York, NY: Alfred A. Knopf, 1954), p. viii.
145 *Ibid.*, p. xvi of the index.

explicitly, but merely added in a footnote that it was interesting that references to the balance of power 'have been eliminated by the editor from the later editions'.[146]

That Morgenthau decided not to go after Lauterpacht, however, is not the central issue.[147] Of far greater importance is the fact that in a book on power politics, one that espouses a 'theory' of political realism, the likes of Oppenheim are cited at length and openly praised. Given that the preface to a second edition of a well-received book is generally what readers will turn to first, one can suppose that it was written with care. Lassa Oppenheim did not make it into these pages by accident. Rather, it is a telling reminder of Morgenthau's intellectual heritage, and of his close relation to German legal theory.

Conclusion

This chapter has tried to show that a number of notions central to Morgenthau's realism – namely the struggle for power as the key manifestation of all politics, the balance of power as the basis for international cooperation, and the distinction between disputes and tensions as a way of explaining the inadequacy, or limited usefulness, of international dispute settlement mechanisms – were the result of a series of reflections on the way the justiciability of disputes was discussed in international legal scholarship. The reactions he received for the published version of his doctoral dissertation, notably from Hersch Lauterpacht, incited him to rephrase some of his core ideas in subsequent writings, particularly in *La notion du 'politique'*. The concepts and positions formulated during the early 1930s would serve as the basis for the approach to law and politics Morgenthau would continue to adhere to in the United States.

Unsurprisingly, the young Morgenthau reacted, often very emotionally, to criticisms that other, already more established colleagues

146 *Ibid.*, p. 252.
147 Indeed, the two men were on friendly terms: Lauterpacht and Morgenthau met up on a number of occasions in Geneva in the early 1930s, and Lauterpacht even wrote a favourable letter of recommendation to the Academic Assistance Council in Britain to further Morgenthau's (ultimately in vain) cause of acquiring a university position there. When Morgenthau finally managed to gain a foothold in the United States, Lauterpacht wrote, 'I was ... glad to see that you found a post, however modest. You went twice through a tragic experience, and it is time that you should be given some recognition for your work'. Letter from Lauterpacht to Morgenthau, 25 March 1939, HJM-Container 34.

presented him with. It is clear from Morgenthau's later writings that the fact that someone of the calibre of Lauterpacht discussed his work was very important to him. *La notion du 'politique'* bears testimony to Morgenthau's attempts to counter Lauterpacht's objections to his argument, and to clarify his position. As this chapter highlighted, he was not altogether successful in doing so. Yet his labours did lead him to formulate assertions that would continue to have a significant bearing later on in his career. Resorting to extra-legal concepts was Morgenthau's way of grappling with the tensions between arguments leaning either towards the apologist or the utopian in international legal discourse. For the practising international lawyer, Morgenthau's approach ultimately amounted to unfruitful rule-scepticism. For the foreign policy decision-maker, however, his reflections turned out to be welcome tools for making sense of inter-state relations.

3   Hans Kelsen and the reality of norms

The previous chapter took a closer look at some of Morgenthau's early writings on the justiciability of disputes in international law. Morgenthau had diagnosed the international system as suffering from the struggle for power in a static system of international law unable to cope with the dynamic element manifested in the underlying 'tensions' that characterize the aspirations of states. In works published in 1934 and 1935, he would now shift his attention away from the justiciability of disputes and towards the recognition that the only way to curb the will to power through law was by means of an effective system of sanctions. Most striking about this period in Morgenthau's career is his sudden turn towards Hans Kelsen's theory of norms, not at all an approach that marks his early writings. The fact that he came into direct contact with Kelsen, who lectured at the Graduate Institute of International Studies in 1932 and then moved there a year later, is perhaps the most obvious reason for this change of focus.

This chapter will outline Morgenthau's miserable attempt to find his ground in Geneva, and will briefly discuss the work of Hans Kelsen and Arthur Baumgarten, both of whom arguably feature prominently in any redescriptive reading of Morgenthau's writings. Indeed, Morgenthau's engagement with the 'reality' of norms left a lasting mark on the way he thought about the role of law in the international arena, the potentialities and limits of norms to rein in the pursuit of power, as well as the prospects of attaining a world state. Just as in Chapter 2, I will again seek to highlight how many of the issues Morgenthau addressed in these early works would continue to resonate in his later attempts in the United States to make his thoughts compatible with his new institutional settings.

La faculté de droit

Morgenthau did not have a good time of it in Geneva. As I out-lined in Chapter 1, he had managed to secure an opening in the Law Faculty thanks to the help of his mentor, the legal philosopher Arthur Baumgarten, who had been able to put in a good word with his former colleagues at the University of Geneva. But the celebra-tions were short-lived. Morgenthau and his wife were desperately short of cash, and the prospect of a bit of financial security through employment as lecturer was immediately jeopardized by the nega-tive reactions to his inaugural lecture.

A German draft of that lecture, which Morgenthau attempted to give in French, can be found in the archives. It runs under the title 'The Struggle of German Theory of the State over the Reality of the State'.[1] From our privileged contemporary perspective of the 'open horizon',[2] the lecture is quite an insightful piece of work. It outlines with a great degree of clarity the story that I sketched out at the beginning of Chapter 2: Jellinek's reaction to Laband, the crisis of German *Staatsrechtslehre* struggling to come to terms with increas-ing political transformation in the late-Wilhelmine political system, and the ultimate breakdown of that order with the establishment of the Weimar Republic following the disaster of the First World War. Perhaps Morgenthau could be faulted for not going into the details of the debates of the *Vereinigung der deutschen Staatsrechtslehrer* – this would undoubtedly have given him additional argumentative strength – but he does outline how Jellinek's system was overcome by Kelsen's move towards a pure normative theory on the one hand, and by the 'anti-normative' positions of Carl Schmitt and Rudolf Smend on the other. As may be expected, given its brevity, the text constitutes a rather simplified account of what is, in essence, a highly complex and at times also fragmented and incoherent debate – indeed, one need only think of certain 'great debates' in International Relations to realize that things were not always as

1 'Der Kampf der deutschen Staatslehre um die Wirklichkeit des Staates', in HJM-Container 110. The Law Faculty had asked Morgenthau to send the German text after the French lecture had failed to impress them; letter of Albert Richard, doyen of the Law Faculty, to Hans Morgenthau, dated 21 March 1932, HJM-Container 197.
2 M. Stolleis, *Geschichte des öffentlichen Rechts in Deutschland 3: Weimarer Republik und Nationalsozialismus* (Munich: C. H. Beck, 2002), p. 153.

clear-cut for the people involved in these academic altercations. But the lecture did depict the times in the way the debate continues to be characterized to this day.

Substantively, the lecture laid out a number of Morgenthau's central themes. Essential in these telling times, Morgenthau began, was a proper appraisal of the 'reality of the state', understood, following Jellinek, according to the 'ultimate psychological sources' pertaining to it. Kelsen's pure theory of law, Morgenthau asserted, was no longer tenable, not least after Erich Kaufmann's telling critique of its neo-Kantian premises.[3] Smend and Schmitt did recognize the need for reintroducing the political into conceptualizations of public law, Morgenthau charged, but both their attempts were inadequate because they were fragmentary and not part of a coherent theoretical framework or system. New formulations would thus have to return to the formalism of Jellinek and Kelsen, and begin to transcend it anew, in a quest for Jellinek's psychological sources that have their place in the 'human soul'. This is vintage Morgenthau, and contains significant traces of the rambling manuscript on the origins of the political in human nature mentioned in Chapter 2.[4]

Arthur Baumgarten congratulated Morgenthau for his inaugural lecture in a letter, adding that if there were those in the audience who did not understand it, then '*de se queri debet*'.[5] For Morgenthau, however, the fact that certain members of the faculty failed to be convinced by the lecture – be it by the (lack of) legal substance, or simply because Morgenthau's French appears to have been dreadfully poor – was a serious setback. He was duly informed that the lecture had not allowed the faculty to gain a clear picture of his abilities, and that he was requested to hold another one, this time in German, in order to alleviate the additional factor of insufficient

3 E. Kaufmann, *Kritik der neukantischen Rechtsphilosophie: Eine Betrachtung über die Beziehung zwischen Philosophie und Rechtswissenschaft* (Tübingen: Mohr (Siebeck), 1921). It is not the place to engage with Kaufmann's polemical yet quite remarkable text in this book, although its influence on subsequent law debates – as well as Kaufmann's overall status in the history of legal theory – would itself merit a redescription.

4 H. J. Morgenthau, 'Über die Herkunft des Politischen aus dem Wesen des Menschen' [On the Derivation of the Political from Human Nature], 1930, HJM-Container 151.

5 Letter from Arthur Baumgarten to Hans Morgenthau, 31 March 1932, HJM-Container 196.

linguistic capacity.[6] Following the second lecture, which ran under the title 'The Position of the Presidents of the Reich according to the Weimar Constitution',[7] Morgenthau was still not cleared. Another letter followed, telling him that he would be employed 'on probation', and that he would be allowed to teach one course per semester – in German, as Morgenthau had requested. Indeed, he would remain on probation until he finally passed his third qualifying lecture in 1935; when the news of his change of status finally reached him, however, Morgenthau had already moved on to Madrid.[8]

Yet the real sticking point was, of course, the issue of the habilitation, the second monograph that aspiring academics in the German university system had to produce after their doctoral dissertation in order to be eligible for a *venia legendi*, or the right to teach as a full faculty member. Morgenthau had begun thinking about his habilitation under the supervision of Arthur Baumgarten in Frankfurt, and part of the agreement with the University of Geneva had been, it appears, that he would be able to continue his work on it and be granted the degree there.

It is unclear from Morgenthau's correspondence with the Law Faculty in Geneva what the original title of the habilitation he had begun thinking about with Baumgarten had been. Whatever it was, Morgenthau asked permission in early 1932 from the Law Faculty to allow him to change the title: he now wished to write on *'La notion du droit fiscal international et l'imposition des bénéfices'*.[9] Morgenthau's flirtations with international economic law were short-lived, however. Exactly one year later, Morgenthau was granted permission to hand in a manuscript, the first part of which would run under the title *'La nature de la norme juridique, en particular la notion de capacité'*; there would moreover be a second part (*une 'partie spéciale'*) of as yet undefined title. Only six weeks later Morgenthau then handed in his habilitation manuscript! It ran under the above title of the first part, and the *'partie spéciale'* seemed to have been left out entirely.

6 See the letter from Albert Richard to Hans Morgenthau, 21 March 1932, HJM-Container 197.
7 'Die Stellung der deutschen Reichspräsidenten nach der Weimarer Verfassung'. See the announcement flyer of the University of Geneva Law Faculty, 5 April 1932, HJM-Container 197.
8 C. Frei, *Hans J. Morgenthau: An Intellectual Biography* (Baton Rouge, LA: Louisiana State University Press, 2001), p. 45.
9 Letter from Albert Richard to Hans Morgenthau, 7 May 1932, HJM-Container 197.

In November 1933, the ominous letter came: the commission had deemed the manuscript to be insufficient. Given the success with his previous publications on the justiciability of disputes, however, the new doyen of the Law Faculty, Paul Logoz (1888–1973), offered him a second chance: the possibility of handing in a new piece of work before the end of the 1933/1934 winter semester (i.e. within four months).

Morgenthau sulked. In a series of letters to Logoz, Morgenthau attacked the evaluations delivered by Professors Walther Burckhardt (1871–1939) and Paul Guggenheim, evaluations that were, indeed, anything but flattering.[10] Morgenthau was particularly distraught about Guggenheim's evaluation, as the two had been on rather friendly terms (by Morgenthau's standards, at least) since 1929. Yet Guggenheim, who had already been quite critical of Morgenthau's *Die internationale Rechtspflege*,[11] seemed to have been genuinely disappointed with the manuscript Morgenthau had submitted.[12] But Morgenthau refused to give in, and even contemplated suing Guggenheim for libel at one point, an idea that Hugo Sinzheimer wisely told him to drop.[13] In the end, a favourable change of circumstances saved him. For one, Morgenthau continued elaborating on the manuscript,[14] and eventually handed it in to Félix Alcan's reputed publishing house in Paris, the result of which is the book *La réalité des normes, en particulier des normes du droit international*.[15] Frei suggests that the publication of the book forced the faculty to act,

---

10 See Guggenheim's evaluation in HJM-Container 120; see also Frei, *Hans. J. Morgenthau*, p. 46.

11 H. J. Morgenthau, *Die internationale Rechtspflege, ihr Wesen und ihre Grenzen* (Leipzig: Noske, 1929). On Guggenheim's appraisal, see Chapter 2.

12 This is where I disagree with Frei, *Hans. J. Morgenthau*, pp. 46–8, who sides with Morgenthau and believes the allegation that Guggenheim, the 'fellow Jew', had double-crossed him. Substantively, Morgenthau's work on the reality of norms was indeed, as Guggenheim wrote in his evaluation, 'devoid of the least originality' and had 'nothing constructive to contribute' to the way international law was taught by Guggenheim and his colleagues at the time – and continues to be taught at the Graduate Institute to this day.

13 The way Morgenthau had handled the issue of his habilitation had been frowned upon by his peers throughout the process; see for instance the exchange of letters – already in the summer of 1929 – between Hugo Sinzheimer and Gustav Radbruch (1878–1949), found in HJM-Container 48.

14 This is evident from a letter to Baumgarten dated 7 February 1934, HJM-Container 196.

15 H. J. Morgenthau, *La réalité des normes, en particulier des normes du droit international: Fondements d'une théorie des normes* (Paris: Félix Alcan, 1934).

although the extent of this pressure is questionable. Undoubtedly the crucial factor was Kelsen's move to Geneva. Although attempting to be critical of Kelsen and his work, Morgenthau did, as will be elaborated below, develop a manuscript that was heavily indebted to Kelsen's theory of norms. In any event, Morgenthau found an ally in Kelsen. A new evaluation committee was formed, and Kelsen's positive appraisal carried the day, as Morgenthau himself would later acknowledge: 'If it had not been for Kelsen, my academic career would probably have come to a very premature end.'[16]

Turning the page to the first lines of the preface of *La réalité des normes*, it becomes immediately apparent that the habilitation debacle had left its mark. From the outset, Morgenthau is on the defensive, replying to 'two possible objections' before the reader even has an idea of what the book is about. And just like in *La notion du 'politique'*,[17] discussed in Chapter 2 above, Morgenthau began by asserting that he did not see the point of following the common method of developing the theory to be espoused in the book in light of existing works that may be opposed to it. This would simply mean, using the words of Arthur Schopenhauer (1788–1860), applying the academic practice of making nine books into a tenth. Moreover, most points of contention would lie in what Georg Simmel (1858–1918) called *'Grundgesinnungen'*, basic premises that it did not make sense to refute on logical grounds, as they fell into the realm of metaphysics:

> It is rather the *will to power* that pushes men towards the necessarily vain attempt to destroy, with the aid of logical arguments, all opposing conceptualizations, and that seeks to make the victory of a theory into the victory of a man.[18]

Moreover, Morgenthau continued, there would be those who would deem the work too theoretical, too a priori and removed from reality, but did not Aristotle say that it is in the nature of the thinker to know all that it is possible to know, without always knowing all the

---

16 H. J. Morgenthau, 'Interview with Bernhard Johnson', in K. W. Thompson and R. J. Meyers (eds.), *Truth and Tragedy. A Tribute to Hans J. Morgenthau*. Second edition with new Postscript (New Brunswick, NJ: Transaction Books, 1984), pp. 333–86, at 354.

17 H. J. Morgenthau, *La notion du 'politique' et la théorie des différends internationaux* (Paris: Sirey, 1933).

18 Morgenthau, *La réalité des normes*, pp. viii–ix; emphasis added.

details? All this makes for a by now typical start to a Morgenthau publication.

The reader is then informed that the book owed much – indeed, 'its very existence' – to two individuals, Arthur Baumgarten and Hans Kelsen. Before turning to the book's substantive chapters, it is necessary to dwell on these two scholars for a moment here. For in certain respects, Kelsen and Baumgarten could not be more different, both intellectually and in terms of renown in the field of legal theory. Yet a more careful reading of *La réalité des normes* shows that both had left their mark on Morgenthau: the one, Kelsen, very explicitly, in that an engagement with his writings constitutes the subject matter of the text, and the other, Baumgarten, in rather more subtle and thus also less demonstrable – but ultimately equally important – ways.

Hans Kelsen

Generally perceived as one of the most influential legal scholars of the twentieth century, who continues to fuel lively controversy and debate,[19] Hans Kelsen is by far the easier of the two to situate. We are well aware of his biographical data – already in 1968 one of his disciples, Rudolf A. Métall, published an (albeit rather biased) biography.[20] Born in Prague in 1881, Kelsen went on to attain his *Doctor juris* at the University of Vienna in 1906, and after receiving his habilitation for his opus *Hauptprobleme der Staatsrechtslehre*,[21] he became *Privatdozent* for public law and legal philosophy at the University of Vienna Law Faculty in the summer of 1911, and then professor after the war in 1918. Between 1921 and 1930 he also served as judge at the constitutional court. The details – Kelsen soon became a publicly known figure and found himself frequently in the papers (and not always for the most enviable reasons) – need not concern us here. Suffice it to say that in 1930 Kelsen decided to leave Vienna for an offer of a chair in public and international law at

---

19 See S. L. Paulson and B. Litschewski Paulson (eds.), *Normativity and Norms: Critical Perspectives on Kelsenian Themes* (Oxford: Clarendon Press, 1998); S. L. Paulson and M. Stolleis (eds.), *Hans Kelsen: Staatsrechtslehrer und Rechtstheoretiker des 20. Jahrhunderts* (Tübingen: Mohr Siebeck, 2005).

20 R. A. Métall, *Hans Kelsen: Leben und Werk* (Vienna: Franz Deuticke, 1969).

21 H. Kelsen, *Hauptprobleme der Staatsrechtslehre, entwickelt aus der Lehre vom Rechtssatze* [1911]. Second edition (Tübingen: Mohr, 1923).

the University of Cologne. After the National-Socialist takeover in 1933, Kelsen was informed (he found out about it one morning from the papers) that he had been suspended (*beurlaubt*), after which he opted for an offer from William E. Rappard (1883–1958) to come to the Graduate Institute of International Studies in Geneva, where he had already lectured in 1932.[22] In June 1940, at the age of sixty, Kelsen eventually emigrated to the United States, where he would first follow Roscoe Pound's invitation to come to the Harvard Law School (to hold the prestigious 'Oliver Wendell Holmes Lectureship') before joining the Political Science Department at the University of California (Berkeley) in 1942. Although Kelsen thus belongs to the group of scholars who, like Morgenthau, switched from Law to Political Science,[23] his age and reputation at this point meant that the move was of little consequence for the work he would continue to engage in until his death in 1967, nor for the way he would be remembered.

Together with his colleagues of the so-called Vienna School – in particular Joseph L. Kunz (1890–1970) and Alfred Verdross (1890–1980) – Kelsen is known in particular for his influential and controversial 'pure theory of law'. Yet the pure theory is only the culmination of a more general critical reaction to Jellinek, one that already characterizes his early work and in particular his voluminous *Hauptprobleme der Staatsrechtlehre*. Under the influence of neo-Kantian philosophy, which posited a strict separation of *Sein* and *Sollen*, Kelsen argued that it was methodological syncretism to try to blend legal with moral-political analysis.[24] Legal science should be a purely normative discipline based on the notion of imputation

---

22 It is sometimes asserted that Kelsen lost his professorship in Cologne to Carl Schmitt; this is not quite accurate. At the time, Schmitt had already accepted to come to Cologne to become the successor of Fritz Stier-Somlo (1873–1932), who had held a chair of public law there. When Kelsen was suspended, the faculty wrote a letter of complaint to Berlin, which everyone except Schmitt signed. Métall, *Hans Kelsen*, p. 61, may be right that Schmitt's signature would have swung the balance in Kelsen's favour, but given the way events would proceed to unfold the following years, it was perhaps thanks to Schmitt's involuntary and unwanted help that Kelsen was spared far worse than the mere loss of his position.

23 See A. Söllner, 'Vom Völkerrecht zum *science of international relations*. Vier typische Vertreter der politikwissenschaftlichen Emigration', in I. Srubar (ed.), *Exil, Wissenschaft, Identität: Die Emigration deutscher Sozialwissenschaftler 1933–1945* (Frankfurt a.M.: Suhrkamp, 1988), pp. 164–80.

24 H. Kelsen, *Das Problem der Souveränität und die Theorie des Völkerrechts. Beitrag zu einer reinen Rechtslehre* [1920]. Second edition (Tübingen: Mohr, 1928), p. 2.

(*Zurechnung*): to every (legal) norm is attached a coercive sanction that is the (legal) consequence of non-compliant behaviour.

An elaboration of this idea led Kelsen to postulate the identity of state and law (*Identitätsthese*), and the corollary that the dualistic conceptualization of considering international and domestic law to be separate normative systems was logically unsound. Instead, Kelsen formulated an 'objective' construction in which national and international law were conceived as forming a monistic system based on the principle of delegation: every norm can be ascribed to another norm that is superordinate to it, with the delegated norm deriving its validity from the latter. The result is the hierarchical structure of norms (*Stufenbaulehre*) Kelsen borrowed from his colleague Adolf Julius Merkl (1890–1970), which culminates in the basic norm (*Grundnorm*) that represents a hypothetical 'fiction' embodying the unity of the legal system.[25] In terms of the monistic conceptualization of state and international law, one is left with the non-legal (i.e. moral-political) choice between two epistemological hypotheses: either one considers state law to be the highest form of law (*der Primat der staatlichen Rechtsordnung*), or one takes international law to override it (*der Primat des Völkerrechts*). In each case, the relationship is one of delegation.

By itself, however, this did not yet entail a reply to those who denied that international law was 'law' because of the lack of an enforcing authority. In order to overcome this dilemma, Kelsen needed to show that the international legal order was a coercive one, i.e. that international law was law because its norms were still of the structure: if A (sanction-inducing behaviour), then B (sanction). From Kaltenborn von Stachau he took the idea that the difference between the domestic and the international was that the latter system was decentralized, because enforced by individual states. It was 'primitive' law, as the sanction was still based on the principle of self-help, but it was 'law' nonetheless, with its system of sanctions, understood within the framework of the *Primat des Völkerrechts*, comprised of reprisals (under customary law) and war.[26]

---

25 On Merkl's role in the formulation of Kelsen's '*Stufenbau*' see M. Borowski, 'Die Lehre vom Stufenbau des Rechts nach Adolf Julius Merkl', in Paulson and Stolleis (eds.), *Hans Kelsen*, pp. 122–59.
26 See H. Kelsen, *Unrecht und Unrechtsfolge im Völkerrecht* (Vienna and Berlin: Julius Springer, 1932); H. Kelsen, 'Théorie générale du droit international publique',

Arthur Baumgarten

Contrary to Kelsen, Arthur Baumgarten is a forgotten figure in the history of legal philosophy. Michael Stolleis' impressive three-volume history of German public law, for instance, mentions him exactly once, in a footnote,[27] while the majority of anthologies and edited volumes of German jurists ignore Baumgarten entirely.[28] Indeed, all who have previously studied Morgenthau's *La réalité des normes* have managed to work their way through the book without mentioning Baumgarten, at least not substantively.[29] And all this even though Morgenthau dedicated the book to him, mentions him at length in the preface, and makes extensive reference to his work throughout the monograph.

Baumgarten was born in Königsberg (Prussia) in 1884. After studying law in Tübingen, Geneva, Leipzig and Berlin, he completed his doctorate with the renowned professor of criminal law, Franz von Liszt (1851–1919). In 1909, he became professor at the University of Geneva, before moving on to Cologne in 1920, to Basel in 1923, and to Frankfurt am Main in 1930 (where Morgenthau was, for a time, his assistant). He emigrated to Switzerland in 1933 (acquiring Swiss nationality in the process), and spent time in the Soviet Union in 1935. Although professor of legal philosophy at the University of Basel, his increasing identification with Marxism and the Communist labour movement (he was co-founder of the Swiss labour party in 1944) made the authorities in Switzerland uneasy,

Recueil des Cours de l'Académie de Droit International (RCADI), 42 (1932/IV), pp. 117–352; and in particular J. von Bernstorff, *Der Glaube an das universale Recht: Zur Völkerrechtstheorie Hans Kelsens und seiner Schüler* (Baden-Baden: Nomos, 2001), pp. 69–95.

27 M. Stolleis, *Geschichte des öffentlichen Rechts in Deutschland 1: Reichspublizistik und Policeywissenschaft 1600–1800* (Munich: C. H. Beck, 1988); Stolleis, *Geschichte des öffentlichen Rechts in Deutschland 2: Staatsrechtslehre und Verwaltungswissenschaft 1800–1914* (Munich: C. H. Beck, 1992); and Stolleis, *Geschichte des öffentlichen Rechts in Deutschland 3*. Reference to Baumgarten is made in the third volume, p. 169.

28 See H. Klenner and G. Oberkofler, *Arthur Baumgarten (1884–1966). Rechtsphilosoph und Kommunist. Daten und Dokumente zu seiner Entwicklung* (Innsbruck: Studien-Verlag, 2003), p. 24.

29 Notably Frei, *Hans. J. Morgenthau*; M. Koskenniemi, *The Gentle Civilizer of Nations: The Rise and Fall of International Law 1870–1960* (Cambridge University Press, 2002); J. W. Honig, 'Totalitarianism and Realism: Hans Morgenthau's German Years', *Security Studies*, 5 (1995/6), 283–313; and A. Carty, 'The Continuing Influence of Kelsen on the General Perception of the Discipline of International Law', *European Journal of International Law*, 9 (1998), 344–54.

leading to him being constantly spied on by the Swiss Federal Police.[30] In 1946, he began lecturing in Leipzig, before finally moving to the Soviet occupation zone in 1949, where he would become professor at the Humboldt University in Berlin and enjoy an illustrious late career wholeheartedly supported by the East German bureaucratic machinery. Baumgarten died in 1966, aged eighty-two.

The secondary literature on Baumgarten is quite amusing, and boils down to a handful of statements and anecdotes with which a few East German disciples, who keep citing each other (as well as the same passages from Baumgarten's books), make it seem as if there is broad consensus over Baumgarten's merits. Yet even they are forced to back-pedal with every move. An entertaining instance of this is the article by Hermann Klenner marking the 100th birthday of Baumgarten. Klenner begins his article with the sentence, 'The most important legal philosopher the German bourgeoisie has produced in the first half of this [the twentieth] century is called Arthur Baumgarten'.[31] Yet he struggles to make good on this claim. 'In spectacular confrontations with the likes of Rudolf Stammler, Erich Kaufmann, Max Ernst Mayer, Hans Kelsen, Gustav Radbruch, Carl August Emge, Julius Binder, Hermann Kantarowicz, Carl Schmitt, Erik Wolf, Karl Larenz, Josef Kohler, Victor Cathrein, Leonard Nelson, Karl Petraschek, Wilhelm Sauer',[32] Klenner writes, 'Baumgarten was never involved'; 'he remained a foreign object (*Fremdkörper*) within the dominant legal ideology, a side issue (*Randerscheinung*), a legal philosopher on the move, one, for whom it was always easier to say what he was *not* than what he was'; 'essentially, he seems to have written all his major works past the requirements of his class'; 'they were all untimely meditations'; 'with his old-school legal-philosophical liberalism he was pursuing a lost cause'. One could go on.

---

30 See Klenner and Oberkofler, *Arthur Baumgarten*.
31 H. Klenner, 'Arthur Baumgarten und die deutsche Rechtsphilosophie in der ersten Hälfte dieses Jahrhunderts. Zum 100. Geburtstag des Rechtswissenschaftlers', *Staat und Recht*, 33 (1984), pp. 202–10.
32 Stammler (1856–1938), Mayer (1875–1923), Emge (1886–1970), Binder (1870–1939), Kantarowicz (1877–1940), Wolf (1902–77), Larenz (1903–93), Kohler (1849–1919), Cathrein (1845–1931), Nelson (1882–1927), Petraschek (1876–1950) and Sauer (1879–1962) were all prominent names in German legal philosophy.

Two of Baumgarten's major works, his three-volume *Die Wissenschaft vom Recht und ihre Methode*[33] and *Der Weg des Menschen: Eine Philosophie der Moral und des Rechts*,[34] were both cited extensively by Morgenthau in *La réalité des normes*. Baumgarten does not make for an easy read, especially since he managed to get through most of the 3,000 pages that make up his published monographs alone, with practically no references or citations. And Klenner is certainly right in pointing out that it is easier to determine what Baumgarten is not than to classify him. For a start, he is clearly opposed to the neo-Kantian split between the *Sein* and *Sollen*, and thus against the type of pure normative theory proposed by Hans Kelsen's Vienna School and the likes of Rudolf Stammler. Yet Baumgarten does not fit into the anti-normative camp either, even though, as I pointed out in Chapter 2, this is rather a broad church in itself. Albeit a proponent of empiricism, Baumgarten did not identify with the German legal realists of the German Free Law School (*Freirechtsschule*), or with other shades of the less radical *Interessenjurisprudenz*.[35] And although always tending towards metaphysical analysis, he was as far away from neo-Thomistic natural law approaches of a Victor Cathrein as he was from a legal metaphysics of the neo-Hegelian bent à la Josef Kohler.[36]

Baumgarten's own approach, which he termed 'legal-philosophical liberalism', was at once opposed to positivist, transcendental and socialist conceptions of law: the formalism that separates the legal 'ought' from the social 'is' is pernicious; the meaning of the human existence cannot be boiled down to a set of deontological duties towards a higher authority; and the free development of the individual has to be the primary aim of any legal system. Baumgarten was, in an intellectual sense at least, old-fashioned, and the fact that he failed to latch on to any of the contemporary legal debates of his time is perhaps the main reason why this undoubtedly highly gifted individual failed to create any sort of a following. Transcendental

---

33 A. Baumgarten, *Die Wissenschaft vom Recht und ihre Methode*. Three volumes (Tübingen: Mohr (Siebeck), 1920 and 1922).

34 A. Baumgarten, *Der Weg des Menschen. Eine Philosophie der Moral und des Rechts* (Tübingen: Mohr (Siebeck), 1933).

35 W. Weichelt, 'Unbeugsamer Humanist, Kommunist und Rechtsgelehrter', in E. Poppe and W. Weichelt (eds.), *Arthur Baumgarten zum 100. Geburtstag* (Berlin: Akademie Verlag, 1985), pp. 10–23, at 12.

36 See Klenner, 'Arthur Baumgarten und die deutsche Rechtsphilosophie', pp. 204–5.

evolutionism, social entelechies and a eudemonistic conception of morality were unlikely catchphrases with which to steal the show in the Weimar Republic.[37] As he himself admitted: 'At the beginning of the twentieth century I was an anachronism, and felt like one as well.'[38]

If, then, as Weichelt argues,[39] the likes of Carl Schmitt and Hans Kelsen did not take Baumgarten seriously 'because they failed to understand him', what can be said for Morgenthau who was, after all, Baumgarten's assistant? In fact, the influence may be more profound than one might ascertain at first sight. Morgenthau clearly took from him the conviction that the clear distinction between the 'is' and the 'ought', central to neo-Kantianism and the work of Kelsen, was a fruitless endeavour – and here, tellingly, Morgenthau does not follow the much more prominent line of critique of Erich Kaufmann,[40] whom he only mentions in the first inaugural lecture I discussed at the outset of this chapter, but not at all in *La réalité des normes*. As the next section of this chapter will highlight, the strategy of trying to 'save' Kelsen's theory from its neo-Kantian premises without situating or identifying himself with any alternative position is also a strategy Baumgarten (but not the likes of Guggenheim) would have favoured. Furthermore, Baumgarten was convinced at the time that the solution to the problems faced by international law the way it was framed in the inter-war period lay in the creation of a world state,[41] a position that Morgenthau would continue to explore in later periods of his career.

Nevertheless, these broader substantive issues were not unique to Baumgarten, and making a case for his impact on Morgenthau is arguably just as challenging as the one William Scheuerman has tried to make for Hugo Sinzheimer.[42] Indeed, Ernst Fraenkel (1898–1975) did claim in an 1958 article, and very rightly so, that Morgenthau

---

37 See W. Loose, 'Zum humanistischen Streben und philosophischen Denken Arthur Baumgartens', in U. Dähn (ed.), *Vom Liberalismus zum Sozialismus: Zum 100. Geburtstag von Prof. Dr. Dr. h. c. Arthur Baumgarten* (Potsdam-Babelsberg: Akademie für Staats- u. Rechtswissenschaft d. DDR, 1984), pp. 7–19, at 15.

38 Cited in Klenner and Oberkofler, *Arthur Baumgarten*, p. 14.

39 Weichelt, 'Unbeugsamer Humanist', p. 10.

40 Kaufmann, *Kritik der neukantischen Rechtsphilosophie*.

41 U.-J. Heuer, 'Zum Verhältnis von Rechtswissenschaft und Philosophie', in Poppe and Weichelt, *Arthur Baumgarten zum 100. Geburtstag*, pp. 33–9, at 35.

42 See in particular W. E. Scheuerman, 'Realism and the Left: The Case of Hans J. Morgenthau', *Review of International Studies*, 34 (2008), pp. 29–51.

learnt from Hugo Sinzheimer what one probably would not have had the opportunity to learn in a comparable manner anywhere else in Germany at the time: to understand law as a factor and product of the social process, embedded in the stream of social and economic forces, but ennobled through the ethos, indeed the pathos of a universal idea of justice.[43]

Given that Morgenthau rarely cited the work of Sinzheimer, such a case is based on the big-picture approach of comparing the entirety of Sinzheimer's intellectual legacy, to the greatest extent possible, with Morgenthau's writings. The same, I would argue, needs to be done for the case of Baumgarten. Morgenthau was not alone in criticizing Kelsen's work and its neo-Kantian premises, but the *way* he went about doing so has a definite Baumgartenian ring to it.

Baumgarten was an old-school thinker who operated with a very large and sweeping brushstroke, and a rereading of both *La notion du 'politique'* and *La réalité des normes* on this account shows that Morgenthau attempted to emulate the rather eclectic style of his mentor. Baumgarten quite explicitly maintained that too many citations in academic writing may be evidence of the studiousness of the author but not necessarily of a surplus of original ideas,[44] and Morgenthau seemed to have taken this to heart. Gone is the meticulous way in which he went about writing his doctoral dissertation, *Die internationale Rechtspflege*, which had been praised by both Guggenheim and Lauterpacht for demonstrating an astonishing familiarity with the relevant literature. Now, Morgenthau was far more inclined towards much sparser referencing and the tendency for plenty of hand-waving instead of concrete legal argumentation. This is also why, I believe, Guggenheim was so disappointed with the manuscript that Morgenthau tried to hand in for his habilitation.

In any event, none of this makes *La réalité des normes* any less indebted to Hans Kelsen and his work, as most of the book's reviewers clearly recognized.[45] More importantly, perhaps, many of them

43 E. Fraenkel, 'Hugo Sinzheimer (1958)', in *Reformismus und Pluralismus: Materialien zu einer ungeschriebenen politischen Autobiographie* (Hamburg: Hoffmann and Campe, 1973), pp. 131–42, at 137.
44 Related in H. Wünsche, 'Das Völkerrecht als Instrument zur Sicherung des Friedens und des Selbstbestimmungsrechts der Völker in den Auffassungen Arthur Baumgartens', in Dähn, *Vom Liberalismus zum Sozialismus*, pp. 51–64, at 51.
45 See for instance J. L. Kunz, 'Review of Morgenthau, *La réalité des normes*', *Zeitschrift für öffentliches Recht*, 15 (1935), pp. 671–2; and G. Chklaver, 'Review of Morgenthau, *La réalité des normes*', *L'Esprit International* (April 1935), p. 265.

were indeed as sceptical as Guggenheim was about Morgenthau's text. Yves de la Brière (1877–1941) was perhaps the most explicit when he wrote:

Let us simply admit our perplexity with regard to this volume. We are not sure to have understood what the author is trying to signify and demonstrate. Not only is the French deficient, but the clarity of language and of thought seem insufficient ... But again, we undoubtedly have not understood anything and blush at our lack of perspicacity.[46]

Such negative reviews, however, did not prevent Kelsen from backing his newfound disciple in the second evaluation committee that ultimately earned Morgenthau his habilitation, complimenting him for having chosen to tackle 'what may be the most difficult problem in normative theory'.[47]

The reality of norms

So what precisely was this 'most difficult problem in normative theory', as Kelsen had called it? The study of norms, Morgenthau claimed at the outset of *La réalité des normes*, can be broken down into four fundamental categories: the logical structure of norms, the reality of norms, the content of norms, and the realization of norms.[48] The Vienna School generally dealt with the first of these, the logical structure of norms, as it was the only issue that it considered truly scientific and normative by nature. The content of norms

---

46 [*Avouons très simplement notre embarras devant ce volume. Nous ne sommes par sûr de comprendre ce que veut signifier et démontrer l'auteur. Non seulement la rédaction française est défectueuse, mais la clarté du langage et de la pensée paraît insuffisante ... Mais encore une fois, nous redoutons de n'y avoir rien compris et nous rougissons de notre manque de pénétration.*] Y. de la Brière, 'Review of Morgenthau, *La réalité des normes*', *Etudes* (1935); fragment located in HJM-Container 145. Highly amusing is also the physical presence, in HJM-Container 145, of the first page of the book, which someone had torn out of the copy held by the Law Faculty in Paris. Handwritten on it is the following: 'The author of this little work is a loafer, ignorant of all aspects of philosophy, pretentious like all loafers. He understands nothing of the philosophical problem he is treating.' [*L'auteur de cet opuscule est un fumiste, ignorant tout de la philosophie, prétentieux comme tous les ignorants. Il ne comprend rien au problème philosophique dont il traite.*] Perhaps the most positive review was written by Frederick S. Dunn, 'Review of Morgenthau, *La réalité des normes*', *American Journal of International Law*, 28 (1935), p. 834.
47 Kelsen's evaluation can be found in HJM-Container 65. See also Frei, *Hans J. Morgenthau*, p. 48.
48 Morgenthau, *La réalité des normes*, p. 2.

was the subject matter of traditional, positivist jurisprudence, and the realization of norms was sociological by nature, and dealt with the relation between norms and that part of reality they are supposed to form – Morgenthau's own concept of 'tensions' was a relation of this sort. The reality of norms, however, had yet to be treated, and was thus to be the focus of the work.

The book is essentially a highly theoretical and at times cumbersome effort to save Kelsen's 'immense theoretical progress'[49] from the hollow conceptualizations of neo-Kantianism – to save the Vienna School from the Marburg School, so to speak. It was Edmund Husserl who had distinguished normative disciplines from theoretical ones, and Kelsen made use of this insight for his normative theory of law. However, under the influence of the neo-Kantian School, Morgenthau charged, Kelsen misunderstood the relative nature of the 'is' and the 'ought', in the sense that he did not admit the possibility of conceiving of the reality of the 'ought', of the '*Da-Sein*' of the '*Sollen*'. As Baumgarten had written, those who always and with everything attempt to bring the *Sein* into strict opposition to the *Sollen* will inevitably fall with the *Sollen* into absolute nothingness – *Rechtsleere* instead of *Rechtslehre*.[50]

What did Morgenthau mean by 'reality of norms', 'considered as the empirical manifestation of the category of the ought'?[51] The issue of reality, he wrote, contained three aspects: the first was epistemological (the relation between the content of our ideas and the content of empirical being); the second, ontological (the nature of being as such); and the third, the phenomenological relation between the idea as such and being as such. The reality of norms thus does not deal with the idea ('I have to walk'), but rather with the psycho-physical act through which this 'ought' is expressed ('I walk', 'I think about walking', etc.). It is this third aspect that Morgenthau sought to engage with: following Husserl's distinction between real and imaginary definitions,[52] Morgenthau argued that

---

49 *Ibid.*, p. 1.
50 Baumgarten, *Die Wissenschaft vom Recht und ihre Methode*, p. 224. This play on words is based on the fact that *Lehre* (the study of) and *Leere* (emptiness) are pronounced identically in German.
51 Morgenthau, *La réalité des normes*, p. 8.
52 See E. Husserl, *Logische Untersuchungen; 1. Band: Prolegomena zur reinen Logik* (Husserliana XVIII) (The Hague: Nijhoff, 1984), p. 241.

'reality' in such a pure phenomenological approach signified abstract (as opposed to normative) 'validity'. It is here that Morgenthau attempted to contrast his own to the work of Kelsen, who would have asserted that there is a third, ideal reality of the *Sollen* that is outside of the realm of the psychological-physical altogether[53] – this is also where Morgenthau begins to slide away from the rule approach in Koskenniemi's framework,[54] and starts to take up the sceptical position. Yet for all his efforts, Morgenthau's entire book is dependent upon and shaped by the theory and terminology of Kelsen, to whom he is indebted for being able to pose the question that he does in the first place. Moreover, the critique of Kelsen that he offers on this subject of 'ideal reality' is far from being highly original, and actually comes quite close to the position of Max Weber, who Kelsen engages with extensively on precisely this issue[55] – the closer one looks, the more Guggenheim's negative appraisal of the *Habilitationsschrift* seems to have been on the mark.

Morgenthau began with Wilhelm M. Wundt (1832–1920) – a prominent German experimental psychologist – and his definition of a norm as 'a prescription of will that designates, from among the set of possible actions, the one that must be chosen':[56] what distinguishes a norm from other types of rules is the fact that it is derived from human will, a will that wishes to maintain or change a facet of reality. Paralleling Kant's distinction between autonomous and heteronomous will,[57] Morgenthau asserted that depending on whether or not the will that establishes the norm is identical to the will for which it is destined, one can distinguish between autonomous and heteronomous norms, with legal norms falling into the latter group. For in order to distinguish one category of norms from another – Morgenthau treated three types of norms: morals, mores and legal norms – it did not suffice to look at the content alone. Rather, it had to be remembered, according to Morgenthau, that a norm has two constitutive elements: the first is its normative

53 Morgenthau, *La réalité des normes*, p. 11.
54 See Chapter 1, pp. 34–6 above.
55 Kelsen, *Das Problem der Souveränität*, pp. 162–3.
56 Morgenthau, *La réalité des normes*, p. 22; W. Wundt, *Ethik: Eine Untersuchung der Tatsachen und Gesetze des sittlichen Lebens*, Vol. 1 [1886]. Third edition (Stuttgart: Ferdinand Enke, 1903), p. 167.
57 I. Kant, 'Grundlegung zur Metaphysik der Sitten' [1785], in Kant, *Werke*, Vol. IV (Berlin: Akademieausgabe, 1911), pp. 385–463, at 440–1.

disposition (the expression of a will intending to realize something, either by itself, or by another will – in other words, its content); the second, its validity. Validity here signified what Léon Duguit (1859–1928) called 'the intensity of the social reaction brought about by its violation':[58] a norm is only valid, is only 'real', if it is backed up by an enforceable sanction. The reality of a norm lies in the abstract ability of a particular will to determine the content of its own or another's will for the realization of what the norm was destined to bring about.[59]

Norms, Morgenthau continued, could thus be categorized according to the type of validity pertaining to them. Norms of morality are autonomous (the author of the norm and the recipient constitute the same will) and their validity is derived from human conscience. Mores and legal norms, by contrast, are heteronomous. The distinction between the two lies in the fact that for the case of mores, validity is derived, in the realm of social psychology, from the spontaneous and arbitrary reaction by a large or key part of the community that supports the realization of a certain normative order. The validity of a legal norm, by contrast, is itself based on another system of norms, i.e. is normatively determined. A legal system thus has various superimposed layers of norms, with the validity of one norm resting on another norm, which in turn also has to be valid. This is Kelsen's conceptualization of a hierarchical structure of norms, whose ultimate level is the basic norm, or a group of norms forming a constitution.[60] The ultimate issue was thus how to validate the basic norm, which led into the famous debate, between Kelsen and Schmitt, on the guardian of the constitution.[61] Morgenthau

---

58 L. Duguit, *Traité de droit constitutionnel, Vol. 1* [1911]. Second edition (Paris: E. de Boccard, 1921), p. 25.

59 Morgenthau, *La réalité des normes*, p. 46.

60 Again, Morgenthau failed to distance himself effectively from Kelsen. In the introduction (Morgenthau, *La réalité des normes*, p. 7), he asserted in a lengthy footnote that the 'profound difference' between his own 'fundamental point of view' and that of Kelsen was the fact that he wanted to derive a theory of norms that was not a theory of state law – when he finally came round to discussing legal norms, however, he did so through recourse to the concepts of 'constitution' and 'head of state', again explicitly drawing on the work of Kelsen.

61 This debate has often been used to (over-)emphasize the essential differences in the positions of Kelsen and Schmitt; on the many parallels between the work of Kelsen and the early work of Schmitt, however, see H. Hofmann, *Legitimität gegen Legalität: Der Weg der politischen Philosophie Carl Schmitts* [1964]. Fourth edition with a new Introduction (Berlin: Duncker & Humblot, 2002), p. 34 et seq.; also A.

concurred with Kelsen – and indeed Baumgarten – on this point: the basic norm was necessarily not legal, but had to be, '*en dernière analyse*', a norm of morality.[62]

Morgenthau, however, was interested in international law. And whereas in his earlier work the focus was on the absence of a legislative mechanism that was able to cope with the 'tensions' international dispute settlement bodies had to deal with, the attention was now turned to the nature of sanctions, and to the absence of a centralized enforcement mechanism. Following Kelsen, international law is no different from state law, in that it is an order of constraint, with each rule consisting of an illegal act (*Unrecht*) and a sanction (*Unrechtsfolge*).[63] An international delinquency is only a special case of unlawful action, and if there is a key difference between the international and domestic spheres, then it lies in the fact that international law is a primitive type of law because it is decentralized. The consequence of this is the identity of the holders of validity and the subjects of the international legal order: the normative reality of international law depends almost exclusively and most often directly on the will of the states and their representatives who are at the same time the subjects of international law.[64]

Sanctions

Morgenthau drew out the logical consequences of these reflections in a subsequent article, published in French, after having moved to the *Instituto de Estudios Internacionales y Económicos* in Madrid. In a laborious two-part essay spanning fifty-eight pages, Morgenthau attempted to build on the theoretical framework of *La réalité des normes* by elaborating on what he called a 'theory of sanctions', but that in effect is more of a conceptual typology. Defining a sanction as 'the measure of constraint that intervenes in the case of a

Carty, 'Interwar German Theories of International Law: The Psychoanalytical and Phenomenological Perspectives of Hans Kelsen and Carl Schmitt', *Cardozo Law Review*, 16 (1995), pp. 1235–90, who shows how both Kelsen and Schmitt followed Sigmund Freud's meta-psychoanalytical work in order to escape the 'menace of the masses' and reject any theory of law based on the idea that the populations of modern European states formed concrete communities.

62 Morgenthau, *La réalité des normes*, p. 78.
63 See Kelsen, *Unrecht und Unrechtsfolge im Völkerrecht*; and Kelsen, 'Théorie générale du droit international publique'.
64 Morgenthau, *La réalité des normes*, p. 242.

violation of a norm',[65] Morgenthau argued that the only distinction that enriches our understanding of the structure of norms is
that between by nature pacifist sanctions (public opinion and moral
sanctions), and those that realize themselves through physical force
(vendettas, capital punishment and war).

This distinction raised the issue of proportionality. Morgenthau
reminded his readers of the difference between the validity and the
effectiveness of a norm: what he called *'l'efficacité de la norme'* was
of no importance for the norm as such – i.e. for its validity, deriving
from the fact that it is 'willed' by the legal order – but only touched
on the practical question of whether the norm is 'realizable' against
the will of those towards which it is addressed. This is where the
notion of proportionality comes into play: the norm is only effective if the sanction that results from its infringement is such that the
potential benefits accrued from not adhering to the norm are less
than the credible threat of the impending sanction: no community,
for Morgenthau, could do without coercive – and thus inherently
violent – sanctions.

Yet the situation just described is only the first in a series of possible scenarios, Morgenthau continued. Another would be if an actor
or group of actors does not simply oppose the realization of a norm,
but its actual existence: i.e. if it is not merely the norm's effectiveness that is questioned, but its very validity. Not only do such groups
work against the enforcement of the norm through the realization
of the sanction it entails, but they do not want anyone else to have
to adhere to the sanction-inducing norm either. Such aspirations
of replacing a system of norms A with some other system B are
thus not simply 'illicit', but rather have a 'political' or 'revolutionary' character.[66] Three possible situations present themselves: either
the sanctions of system A suppress those of B, or group B manages to overthrow system A – in both cases, the 'proportionality'
of either sanctions A or B is realized. More interesting, according
to Morgenthau, is the third possible case, where neither normative
order manages to attain superiority over the other, and both systems

65 H. J. Morgenthau, 'Théorie des sanctions internationales', *Revue de droit international
    et de législation comparée*, 36 (1935), pp. 474–503 and 809–36, at 482–3.
66 *Ibid.*, pp. 492–3.

coexist in a fragile balance of their respective sanctions, a balance that is, in itself, the '*norme vitale*' of the order thus created.

This last scenario characterized the international system, Morgenthau asserted. Here one finds a number of legal systems of norms that exist simultaneously and together make up the international community. Each system of sanctions attains its highest degree of effectiveness on its respective territory, and this empirical superiority constitutes the state: 'the state is the domain of validity of norm-sanctions that attain the highest degree of empirically observable effectiveness on a given territory'.[67] Sovereignty is thus the exclusive disposition of physical force as a sanction of norms.

Morgenthau continued by taking issue with the Anglo-American 'anti-sanction school', arguing that there is no such thing as an international morality or an international system of mores, as that school asserted. If state A infringes upon the rights of state B, Morgenthau claimed, then the public in states C, D and E will not react 'spontaneously', but will only form a 'public opinion' if state C, D or E deems it to be in its interest to shape, through propaganda, such an opinion: 'What we call the public opinion of the international community is thus, as a general rule, nothing other than the sum of the different national opinions of artificial origin, opinions that could, given their origin, just as easily be identical as they could be diverging.'[68] 'International public opinion' could never be an effective sanction in the international community – at best, the public opinion in state C could question the actions of C, at which point you would be back with the scenario discussed above, in which such a group is either suppressed by the existing order or manages to overthrow it.

The real dilemma, however, Morgenthau pointed out, was not so much the settling of international legal disputes, disputes which could be adjudicated by international courts through an interpretation of existing international law, but rather underlying tensions between the status quo of the current order and the 'necessities' or interests of the disputing parties. And it is here that the real nature of the international system presented itself. For if, indeed,

---

67 [*L'Etat est le domaine de validité des normes-sanctions qui atteignent sur un territoire déterminé au plus haut degré d'efficacité empiriquement constatable.*] *Ibid.*, p. 810. See also Morgenthau, *La réalité des normes*, p. 215.
68 Morgenthau, 'Théorie des sanctions internationales', p. 813.

the international hierarchical system of norms is akin to that of the domestic order, i.e. if it is made up of an hierarchical structure of legal norms whose ultimate guarantee, or basic norm, is not legal but moral in nature, then the problem in international law is that the pyramid is extremely flat: the norm prescribing the application of sanctions against a violator of the international legal order rests immediately on the moral foundation of the international community, because the executive organs of individual states are the only executive organs in the international sphere. In the domestic system, between the moral foundation of the legal order and the norms prescribing the use of physical force, there is a whole series of hierarchically structured norms that have the function of guaranteeing the execution of these primary norm-sanctions. In international law, however, as Morgenthau already pointed out in *La réalité des normes*, the holders of validity are also the subject of the international legal order. This is the reason why Morgenthau, just like Kelsen, deemed international law to be 'primitive'.

The resulting situation, for Morgenthau, was obvious: every state defends its juridical position against every other state, and coercive reprisals served the function of sanctions. Hence, Morgenthau's proportionality principle also finds itself realized: the most powerful state, i.e. the state whose sanctions are the most effective relative to the system of sanctions of other states, will generally have the greatest chance of realizing the order it aspired to through the norms of international law. The only way to maintain the juridical spheres of two rival states is thus by attaining a certain '*équilibre*' or 'balance of power' (Morgenthau uses the English expression here for the first time) between the coercive means of each. It is on such a balance of power that the very existence of general international law depends.[69]

The 'tragic task' of the jurist, Morgenthau concluded, was to accept this state of affairs. Taking to task the legitimacy of an existing domestic or international legal order would raise moral and political questions that lay beyond the scope of a scientific study of the law. The aspirations of many a pacifist to incorporate the issue of justice assumed that it was possible to attain a 'harmony of interests', which, for Morgenthau, was an unrealizable dream:[70] striving

69 *Ibid.*, p. 827.   70 *Ibid.*, p. 831.

for absolute justice would be 'to wait for the millennium' while in the meantime losing the relative justice realized in an existing legal order, and thus also peace. As it would later, rather cynically, be expressed in *Scientific Man vs. Power Politics*:

The rule of law has come to be regarded as a kind of miraculous panacea which, wherever applied, would heal, by virtue of its intrinsic reasonableness and justice, the ills of the body politic, transform insecurity and disorder into the calculability of a well-ordered society, and put in the place of violence and bloodshed the peaceful and reasonable settlement of social conflicts. The rule of law had accomplished this in the domestic field, and the rule of law would accomplish it again in the international sphere, provided it was given a chance. Transfer the rule of law to international affairs and 'order under law' will reign supreme there, too. How to effect this transfer remains, then, the only problem to be solved. Persuasion, propaganda, education, scientific proof, and democratization of foreign affairs are the means by which governments and peoples shall be induced to put international relations under the dominance of the rule of law.[71]

Kelsen's legacy

Morgenthau's *La réalité des normes* and his lengthy article on sanctions are key in any exploration of Morgenthau's legal heritage. Both are written in dreadful French, and engaging with them in detail is not an altogether pleasant exercise – which is probably one of the reasons why many have shied away from the task. But these two publications do represent the foundation for many of Morgenthau's subsequent views, including his all-pervasive struggle to come to terms with what he would go on to call the 'dominant doctrine' of formalist legal positivism.

Arthur Baumgarten supplied Morgenthau with an angle on Kelsen's theory of norms that would dominate his research agenda well into the 1940s. Morgenthau's obsession with the 'reality' of the ought, with 'social forces' that are determinative of normativity – an issue that was also high on the agenda of his previous mentor, Hugo Sinzheimer – stem directly from Baumgarten's critique of Kelsen's neo-Kantian premises. Morgenthau's unease with legal

---

71 H. J. Morgenthau, *Scientific Man vs. Power Politics* (University of Chicago Press, 1946), p. 100.

formalism is precisely his persuasion that this formalism ignores the *Da-Sein* of the *Sollen* to produce a *Rechtsleere* that Morgenthau would later refer to under the heading of 'legalism'. I will return to this in Chapter 5.

It will be remembered from the previous chapter that Morgenthau discussed two devices in *Politics Among Nations* through which peace could be maintained: one is 'the self-regulatory mechanism of the social forces which manifests itself in the struggle for power on the international scene, that is the balance of power'; the other consists of 'normative limitations upon that struggle in the form of international law, international morality, and world public opinion'.[72] This being said, however, Morgenthau was keen to point out that we should not fall prey to the 'basic misconception' that there was a choice 'between power politics and its necessary outgrowth, the balance of power, on the one hand, and a different, better kind of international relations, on the other'.[73] For power is 'a crude and unreliable method of limiting the aspirations', Morgenthau argued, and although a system based solely on such Machiavellian notions of political expediency would indeed resemble Hobbes' state of nature as a war of all against all, such a scenario would not be part of political reality. This is where the normative aspect inherent in Morgenthau's thought becomes clear, for he elaborates: 'Actually, however, the very threat of such a world where power reigns not only supreme, but without rival, engenders that revolt against power, which is as universal as the aspiration for power itself.'[74] And the substance of this revolt, though often taking on ideological connotations by those trying to conceal their aims of power, is to be found in the normative orders of morals, mores and law – the three types of norms that were the focus of *La réalité des normes*. The argument is the same: every rule of conduct, Morgenthau tells his readers, entails two elements, the command and the sanction. 'No particular command is peculiar to any type of norm ... It is the sanction that differentiates these different types of rules of conduct'.[75]

72 H. J. Morgenthau, *Politics Among Nations: The Struggle for Power and Peace* (New York, NY: Alfred A. Knopf, 1948), pp. 8–9.
73 *Ibid.*, p. 125.   74 *Ibid.*, p. 169.
75 *Ibid.*, p. 170.

Morgenthau continued *Politics Among Nations* with chapters on international morality, world public opinion, and then international law. Just as in the 1935 article on sanctions, it is pointed out that the use of the notions of 'international' morality and 'world' public opinion seek to hide the realities of international affairs. So-called world public opinion is in effect 'moulded by the agencies of national policies', and it is also these same agencies that seek to construct an 'international' morality by claiming that their 'national conceptions of morality [enjoy] supranational, that is, universal recognition'. As I will argue in Chapter 5, this is a theme that will remain central to Morgenthau's understanding of the dynamics of international politics, and that comes across quite clearly in publications throughout the 1950s and 1960s.[76]

In *Politics Among Nations*, Morgenthau then focuses the attention on international law. He begins by warning against the extreme views of exaggerating the importance of international law, on the one hand, and denying its existence, on the other.[77] And contrary to what one might expect from the 'theoretician of power', one soon reads that '[i]t is also worth mentioning, in view of a widespread misconception in this respect, that during the four hundred years of its existence international law has in most instances been scrupulously observed'.[78] Nevertheless, just as in his works of 1934 and 1935, Morgenthau asserted, in true Kelsenian fashion, that international law was 'a primitive type of law' because it was almost completely decentralized law with respect to its three basic functions of legislation, adjudication and enforcement. As Morgenthau wrote in *Scientific Man vs. Power Politics*, 'the mores and laws of society endeavour to strengthen through positive sanctions the moral condemnation of individual aspirations for power, to limit their modes and sphere of action, and to suppress them altogether'. Above the state, however, 'there is no centralized authority beyond the mechanics of the balance of power, which

---

76 See in particular H. J. Morgenthau, *In Defense of the National Interest: A Critical Examination of American Foreign Policy* (New York, NY: Alfred A. Knopf, 1951); Morgenthau, *The Purpose of American Politics* (New York, NY: Vintage Books, 1960); Morgenthau, *A New Foreign Policy for the United States* (New York, NY: Praeger, 1969).
77 Morgenthau, *Politics Among Nations*, p. 209.
78 *Ibid.*, p. 211.

could impose actual limits upon the manifestations of its collective desire for domination'.[79]

In sum, Morgenthau debunks international law as simply fulfilling the ideological function for policies of the status quo. 'Law in general', he writes, 'and, especially, international law is primarily a static social force'[80] – this is again the Morgenthau of the writings on the justiciability of disputes. And whereas in the domestic context the presence of legislative, judicial and enforcement mechanisms enabled law to influence the distribution of power, in the international sphere it was dependent on a stable equilibrium to exist at all. Nevertheless, Morgenthau concluded, the creation of such mechanisms remains the only way to attain a lasting peace, and this, he speculated, required the establishment of a world state, although current conditions made this creation 'unattainable'. He nonetheless remained optimistic on this point: 'If the world state is unattainable in our world, yet indispensable for the survival of that world, it is necessary to create the conditions under which it will not be impossible from the outset to establish a world state.'[81] The foundations for such a position clearly lie in the convictions of Arthur Baumgarten, as well as in the cosmopolitan project of Kelsen and the Vienna School, based on the monistic notion of a hierarchically structured, unified system of law in which state law is only a part. Only then does one come to the conclusion that the current system is primitive, and that the teleological 'ideal' is the *civitas maxima*, or Morgenthau's world state.[82]

At the time of writing *Politics Among Nations*, Morgenthau appears reluctant to make the extent of his indebtedness to Kelsen explicit; I will discuss some of the reasons for this reluctance to identify with his mentors of old in Chapter 4. But Morgenthau did manage to have Kelsen invited to Chicago for a series of 'handsomely paid'

---

79 Morgenthau, *Scientific Man vs. Power Politics*, p. 169.
80 *Ibid.*, p. 64.   81 *Ibid.*, p. 539.
82 For extensive examinations of Morgenthau's use of the term 'world state' that completely miss Kelsen's influence, see J. P. Speer II, 'Hans Morgenthau and the World State', *World Politics*, 20 (1968), pp. 207–27; and C. Craig, 'Hans Morgenthau and the World State Revisited', in M. C. Williams (ed.), *Realism Reconsidered: The Legacy of Hans J. Morgenthau in International Relations* (Oxford University Press, 2007), pp. 195–215.

guest lectures in 1954,[83] and would go on to dedicate his anthology, *Truth and Power*, to him.[84] And on Kelsen's ninetieth birthday, Morgenthau wrote a letter to him, which read:

Your life has meant one thing for me: the consistent fearless pursuit of truth regardless of where it may lead to. Your example has taught me what it means to be a scholar. For that lesson I owe you a debt of gratitude which can only be discharged by following your example.[85]

Morgenthau will not have failed to notice the steady decline in the influence of Kelsen and the Vienna School after the Second World War. The 'stateless' theoretical construction of international law advocated by proponents of that school was simply not compatible with the realities of the Cold War, nor with the intellectual climate of the post-war United States. Just like Morgenthau, Kelsen was grappling with the new cultural and institutional setting he now found himself in, a setting that was not congenial – if not outright hostile – to his style of German philosophizing. By the time he wrote the preface to his critical analysis of the law of the United Nations in 1950, the elderly scholar had all but capitulated:

'Juristic' in contradistinction to 'political' has the connotation of 'technical'. It is not superfluous to remind the lawyer that as a 'jurist' he is but a technician whose most important task is to assist the law-maker in the adequate formulation of the legal norms ... [C]oncerning the separation of law and politics ... the former, as a means, is subordinate to the latter, as an end, and ... political ends may be achieved by other means than by imposing obligations and conferring rights upon persons subjected to a strict law.[86]

Throughout the commentary, Kelsen's dilemma of trying to maintain the strict separation between law and politics that characterizes the rule approach, while at the same time still grappling to uphold his own cosmopolitan project, becomes strikingly apparent.[87] Morgenthau, by contrast, did not seem to be conscious of

---

83 Frei, *Hans J. Morgenthau*, p. 49.

84 H. J. Morgenthau, *Truth and Power: Essays of a Decade, 1960–1970* (New York, NY: Praeger, 1970).

85 Letter from Morgenthau to Kelsen, 4 October 1971, HJM-Container 33.

86 H. Kelsen, *The Law of the United Nations: A Critical Analysis of its Fundamental Problems. With Supplement* (New York, NY: F.A. Praeger, 1950), pp. xiii and xvii.

87 See also J. von Bernstorff, *Der Glaube an das universale Recht*, pp. 199–201.

the paradox involved in advocating both a rule-scepticist position and the aspiration of attaining a world state. Nonetheless, he confined any reference to Kelsen in *Politics Among Nations* to the list of further readings, and chose to end the book with an appeal to diplomacy rather than law – here again, we witness Morgenthau's discursive grey zone in which he uses the building blocks of international legal theory, but makes himself the external critic. The underlying logic, however, is unmistakably Kelsenian.

Conclusion

The reception of Hans Kelsen in International Relations is negligible, and is mainly confined to (mostly superficial) negative portrayals of the way the Vienna School approached the issue of norms (and sanctions) in the international sphere. Hedley Bull (1932–85), for instance, would later write in *The Anarchical Society* that '[t]he idea of international law as a coercive order based on a system of sanctions which is decentralized is a fiction which, when applied to reality, strains against the facts'.[88] And John H. Herz, another German-Jewish émigré who was actually a student of Kelsen before becoming another 'classical realist',[89] argued that the overall binding force of a legal order lay not, as argued by Kelsen (and Morgenthau), in the effectiveness of sanctions, but rather in the 'establishment of legal liability through the constatation of non-norm-conforming conduct'.[90] Kelsen's attempt to convey 'an aura of legality to extra-legal fact', Herz charged, only made it 'the most sophisticated natural law theory which has been developed this [the

---

88 H. Bull, *The Anarchical Society: A Study of Order in World Politics* [1977]. Second edition (Basingstoke: Macmillan, 1995), p. 127.

89 Born in Düsseldorf in 1908 as Hans Hermann Herz, Herz would complete his doctorate under Kelsen's supervision at the University of Cologne before following his professor to the Graduate Institute of International Studies, Geneva, in 1935. In 1938, Herz emigrated to the United States. The International Relations scene remembers him as the author of two successful monographs, *Political Realism and Political Idealism: A Study in Theories and Realities* (University of Chicago Press, 1951) and *International Politics in the Atomic Age* (New York, NY: Columbia University Press, 1959), as well as for having established the term 'security dilemma' in the literature.

90 J. H. Herz, 'The Pure Theory of Law Revisited: Kelsen's Doctrine in the Nuclear Age', in S. Engel (ed.), *Law, State and International Legal Order: Essays in Honour of Hans Kelsen* (Knoxville, TN: University of Tennessee Press, 1964), pp. 107–18, at 114.

twentieth] century'.[91] And that characterization was not meant to be a compliment.

Contemporary International Relations theory's take on norms is in stark contrast to the theory of norms espoused by Kelsen, and adopted by the likes of Morgenthau. The study of norms in neo-liberal institutionalist and social constructivist approaches prioritizes the 'diffusion', 'projection' and 'internalization' of norms by actors on the international scene – exemplary is some of the work by Martha Finnemore, Peter J. Katzenstein and in particular Gary Goertz,[92] whose 'typology of international norms' is the perfect example of the one-sided focus on what Morgenthau called the realization of norms, as opposed to the reality of norms. The focus is on processes, and on the system as a whole; in other words, on how the norm interacts with its environment. This realization is not the way a formalist such as Kelsen would have conceived of the study of norms. He, by contrast, would seek to look inside the norm itself, to assess factors affecting the validity of a norm, its structure and its content. Mainstream International Relations theory does not harbour such ambitions, which would quickly lead one into the fields of moral philosophy, psychology, and today even neuroscience. Instead, contemporary regime theory, based on the work of the likes of Stephen D. Krasner and Robert Keohane,[93] couples realist premises with a notion of informal norms generating collaborative regimes in a world of interdependent states. The result is the shift from what Martti Koskenniemi calls a 'culture of formalism' to a 'culture of dynamism', in which the realist mantra over the irrelevance of international law, understood in formalistic terms, is transcended by a focus on 'the technical language of optimisation, effectiveness, and compliance': 'conflicting participant interpretations about what might count as breach [in the legal sense] are set aside by technical measurements that are able to give a direct answer to questions about compliance irrespective of normative disagreements – but of

91 *Ibid.*, p. 108.
92 M. Finnemore, *National Interests in International Society* (Ithaca, NY: Cornell University Press, 1996); P. J. Katzenstein (ed.), *The Culture of National Security: Norms and Identity in World Politics* (New York, NY: Columbia University Press, 1996); G. Goertz, *Contexts of International Politics* (Cambridge University Press, 1994).
93 See in particular S. D. Krasner (ed.), *International Regimes* (Ithaca, NY: Cornell University Press, 1983); R. Keohane, *After Hegemony: Cooperation and Discord in the World Political Economy* (Princeton University Press, 1984).

course only under the assumption that the rule is *known* independently of such agreements'.[94] The likes of Kelsen, Lauterpacht and Morgenthau, who were troubled by precisely the types of normative ambiguities that the language of regime theory now occludes, have no place in such a discourse.

94 Koskenniemi, *The Gentle Civilizer of Nations*, pp. 496–7.

4   Legal realism and behaviouralist social science

'Every intellectual in emigration', Theodor Adorno (1903–69) wrote in *Minima Moralia*, 'is, without exception, mutilated in some way, and does well to recognize this if he wishes to avoid being taught a cruel lesson behind the tightly-closed doors of his self-esteem'.[1] Morgenthau certainly did recognize it and, perhaps better than most, was able to secure a niche for himself by identifying and taking up a twofold compromise position – between his fundamentally 'Kelsenian' convictions and US legal theory, and between the thought-styles of International Law and those of Political Science. How successful he was in doing so is reflected in the fact that we, the International Relations heirs of his 'classical realism', do not recognize it as a compromise at all. Yet a compromise it was, attained largely through bouts of improvisation and a few strokes of good fortune. The circumstances surrounding these events, and the way Morgenthau went about his academic transformation, is the subject of this chapter.

In order to join Morgenthau on his journey across the Atlantic, we need to set the scene by outlining the intellectual milieu that awaited him. Of course, just as in Chapter 2, no attempt will be made to provide a comprehensive account of the history of US legal theory.[2] The following pages will thus merely flag a series of 'events' and turning points that are relevant to the task of situating Morgenthau in the US law scene. It will then be shown how Morgenthau tried to make his own research agenda compatible with this new setting, and how his efforts were ultimately in vain. The chapter outlines the

1 T.W. Adorno, *Minima Moralia: Reflexionen aus dem beschädigten Leben* [1951] (Frankfurt a.M.: Suhrkamp, 2003), p. 35 (my translation, OJ).
2 For a very readable and nuanced account since the 1870s, see N. Duxbury, *Patterns of American Jurisprudence* (Oxford: Clarendon Press, 1995).

institutional realities with which he was confronted in Chicago, and how his failure to grapple with the behaviouralist methodologies of his new colleagues in Political Science ultimately led him to distance himself from his legal research agenda as well.

Legal realism

With hindsight, developments in jurisprudence may be seen as components of ideological responses to social change[3] – such linkages seem particularly clear in the case of the United States. The common law, transported across by the British to their colonies, had to be adapted to the complex circumstances of a heterogeneous system with a multiplicity of jurisdictions subsumed under the constitution of 1787. It then had to be modernized to accommodate the industrial and technical revolution that commenced in earnest after 1870 and, with an ever-growing amount of new legislation and cases, the sources of law also had to be simplified in order to be practically manageable.[4] These challenges were at the forefront of a transformation that went from 'classical' legal thought to 'progressivism' and the 'legal realism' of the early 1930s.[5]

Late nineteenth-century US legal reasoning, enshrined in the constitution of 1787 with the words 'a government of laws and not of men', was embodied in the outlook of Christopher Columbus Langdell (1826–1906), appointed Dean of the Harvard Law School in 1870. For Langdell, law was a 'science', consisting of 'certain principles or doctrines',[6] with 'all the available materials of that

---

3 G. E. White, 'From Sociological Jurisprudence to Realism: Jurisprudence and Social Change in Early Twentieth-Century America', *Virginia Law Review*, 58 (1972), pp. 999–1028, at 1028.

4 See W. Twining, *Karl Llewellyn and the Realist Movement*. Reprinted with a Postscript (London: Weidenfeld and Nicolson, 1985), pp. 3–4.

5 As Neil Duxbury rightly points out, however, one needs to be wary of the typical portrayal of US legal theory as a 'pendulum-swing vision' going from formalism to the legal realist 'revolt' against such formalism, back to the formalism of process jurisprudence and the 'law and economics' movement, before again swinging to the realism of Critical Legal Studies. Such readings tend to over-dramatize distinctions between supposedly contrary theoretical positions and schools of thought, when the differences were actually everything other but clear – neither for those supposedly taking up such positions at the time, nor for those who subsequently tried to attach labels to them. Duxbury, *Patterns of American Jurisprudence*, pp. 1–7.

6 C. C. Langdell, *A Selection of Cases on the Law of Contracts* (Union, NJ: The Lawbook Exchange, 1871).

science ... contained in printed books'.[7] His conception of law was court-centred, focused on the case method, and made no attempt to distinguish between descriptive and normative propositions.[8] Indeed, in his concern for deducing general principles from concrete cases, Langdell was not far from the image of law propagated in 'stable' nineteenth-century Europe,[9] where a legal conservatism determined to consolidate the existing order finally enticed Rudolf von Jhering (1818–1892) to formulate his famous critique of the 'heaven of legal concepts' (*juristischer Begriffshimmel*) in which lawyers used a 'dialectic-hydraulic interpretation press' to squeeze any desired meaning into a legal text or concept, as well as a 'hair-splitting machine' with which the applicant to this heaven for legal theoreticians had to divide a single hair into 999,999 equal parts during the entrance examination.[10]

Enter Justice Oliver Wendell Holmes, Jr (1841–1935), 'the most important and influential legal thinker America has had'[11] and – although this is a tendentious generalization[12] – the intellectual inspiration for the coming generation of legal realists. 'It is the merit of the common law', he proclaimed in 1870, 'that it decides the case first and determines the principle afterwards'.[13] It was not long before he also began to take serious issue with Langdell:

7 C. C. Langdell, Address to Harvard's alumni association in 1886, reprinted in *Harvard University 1636–1886: A Record of the Commemoration, November Fifth to Eighth, 1886, on the Two Hundred and Fiftieth Anniversary of the Founding of Harvard College* (Cambridge, MA: John Wilson and Son, 1887).

8 Twining, *Karl Llewellyn and the Realist Movement*, p. 12.

9 See Chapter 2.

10 R. von Jhering, *Scherz und Ernst in der Jurisprudenz: Eine Weihnachtsgabe für das juristische Publikum* [1891] (Darmstadt: Wissenschaftliche Buchgesellschaft, 1988), pp. 257 and 262–3.

11 M. J. Horwitz, *The Transformation of American Law 1870–1960: The Crisis of Legal Orthodoxy* (New York, NY and Oxford: Oxford University Press, 1992), p. 109.

12 Not least because the later generation of legal realists, while conceiving of Holmes as the forerunner to the general attack against formalism, completely ignored Holmes' opposition to judicial activism, which was, after all, a central characteristic of legal realism; see L. Menand, *The Metaphysical Club: A Story of Ideas in America* (New York, NY: Farrar, Straus and Giroux, 2001), pp. 421 and 438; also Duxbury, *Patterns of American Jurisprudence*, p. 46, who rightly points out that it is a convenient, but ultimately 'oversimplified intellectual history' to label Holmes as an unequivocal anti-formalist.

13 O. W. Holmes, 'Codes, and the Arrangement of the Law' [1870], in *The Collected Works of Justice Holmes: Complete Public Writings and Selected Judicial Opinions of Oliver Wendell Holmes*. Volume 1, edited by Sheldon M. Novick (University of Chicago Press, 1995); cited in Menand, *The Metaphysical Club*, p. 217.

Mr Langdell's ideal in the law, the end of all his striving, is the *elegentia juris* or *logical* integrity of the system as a system. He is, perhaps, the greatest living legal theologian. But as a theologian he is less concerned with his postulates than to show that the conclusions from them hang together.[14]

Holmes, a true Civil War veteran (he had been shot through the chest, through the neck and in the foot on three different occasions[15]) and, together with the likes of William James (1842–1910) and Charles Sanders Peirce (1839–1914), a member of the Metaphysical Club,[16] followed up his critique with the publication of the monograph *The Common Law*,[17] 'the first cannon shot in his fifty-year battle against the armies of legalistic formalism'.[18] 'The life of the law has not been logic: it has been experience', Holmes told his readers. 'The felt necessities of the time, the prevalent moral and political theories, intuitions of public policy, avowed or unconscious, even the prejudices which judges share with their fellow-men, have had a good deal more to do than the syllogism in determining the rules by which men should be governed'.[19] Influenced by the general move towards Darwinism that characterized most academic fields in the later decades of the nineteenth century, Holmes argued that the common law had also developed according to a process of natural selection.

The flirtation of the social sciences and law with Darwinism subsided towards the turn of the century, however, and Holmes himself

14 O. W. Holmes, Review of Langdell, *A Selection of Cases on the Law of Contracts* (1879), *American Law Review*, 14 (1880), pp. 233–5, at 233; cited in Twining, *Karl Llewellyn and the Realist Movement*, p. 15.

15 See G. E. White, *Oliver Wendell Holmes, Jr.* (Oxford University Press, 2006), pp. 17–26.

16 Much has been made of this so-called Metaphysical Club, although, as Louis Menand shows in his impressive and very readable book of the same name, nobody of the group except Peirce ever mentioned a 'metaphysical club' in any letters, notes or diaries. But an informal group of sorts was formed in Cambridge, MA, in 1872, although its exact name, makeup and duration remain unclear.

17 O. W. Holmes, *The Common Law* (Boston, MA: Little, Brown and Co., 1881).

18 E. A. Purcell, Jr, 'American Jurisprudence between the Wars: Legal Realism and the Crisis of Democratic Theory', *The American Historical Review*, 75 (1969), pp. 424–46, at 426. In the same year, 1881, Holmes was appointed to the Supreme Judicial Court of Massachusetts, where he would serve for twenty years before being appointed to the US Supreme Court, where he would act as judge for another thirty years. He died in 1935, two days before his ninety-fourth birthday.

19 Holmes, *The Common Law*, p. 1; also in W. W. Fischer III, M. J. Horowitz and T. A. Reed (eds.), *American Legal Realism* (New York, NY: Oxford University Press, 1993), p. 9.

changed his views somewhat – leading Horwitz[20] to rightly point out that one should indeed speak of the early Holmes of *The Common Law* and then the later Holmes of his famous article, 'The Path of the Law'[21] and his dissenting opinion in *Lochner* v. *New York* (1905). Central to 'The Path of the Law' is the so-called 'prediction theory'. In order to know 'the law and nothing else', Holmes argued, 'you must look at it as a bad man, who cares only for the material consequences which such knowledge enables him to predict, not as a good one, who finds his reasons for conduct, whether inside the law or outside of it, in the vaguer sanctions of conscience'. The bad man 'does not care two straws for the axioms or deductions', yet what he does want to know is how the courts will ultimately act: 'The prophecies of what the courts will do in fact, and nothing more pretentious, are what I mean by the law.'[22] Holmes' conception of predictivist jurisprudence effectively constituted 'a first, tentative step outside Langdell's laboratory ... Whereas, for Langdell, everything about the law could be fitted between the covers of a book, Holmes introduced a totally new element into the jurisprudential framework: namely, people'.[23]

Holmes' sharp distinction between law and morality was, according to Morton J. Horwitz,[24] the first clear articulation of legal positivism by any US legal thinker; it was also an implicit rejection of the Darwinian belief that fact and value could be merged. But contrary to *The Common Law*, Holmes' article 'The Path of the Law' now went against the Langdellian tradition, arguing that law was a social creation: whereas 'for the rational study of the law the black-letter man may be the man of the present', 'the man of the future is the man of statistics and the master of economics', Holmes asserted. 'It is revolting to have no better reason for a rule of law than that ... it was laid down in the time of Henry IV'.[25] As Horwitz sums up:

With 'The Path of the Law' Holmes pushed American legal thought into the twentieth century. It is the moment at which advanced legal thinkers renounced the belief in a conception of legal thought independent of

20 Horwitz, *The Transformation of American Law 1870–1960*, p. 110.
21 O. W. Holmes, 'The Path of the Law', *Harvard Law Review*, 10 (1897), pp. 457–78.
22 *Ibid.*, pp. 459–61.
23 Duxbury, *Patterns of American Jurisprudence*, p. 36.
24 Horwitz, *The Transformation of American Law 1870–1960*, p. 140.
25 Holmes, 'The Path of the Law', p. 469.

politics and separate from social reality. From this moment on, the late-nineteenth-century ideal of an internally self-consistent and autonomous system of legal ideals, free from the corrupting influence of politics, was brought constantly under attack.[26]

In practice, 'progressive' legal thought came into being largely through the decision of the US Supreme Court in *Lochner* v. *New York*, commonly known as the Sugar-Baker's Case. Section 110 of the New York labour law stipulated that employees working in a 'biscuit, bread or cake bakery or confectionary establishment' should not be permitted or required to work more than sixty hours a week, or ten hours on any particular day. When a baker was sentenced and convicted for letting one of his employees do just that, the Supreme Court reversed the decision as an unconstitutional interference with freedom of contract, according to the prohibition of the Fourteenth Amendment 'to deprive any person of life, liberty or property, without due process of law'. Holmes did not agree: 'The Fourteenth Amendment does not enact Mr Herbert Spencer's Social Statics', he charged. *Social Statics: or, The Conditions Essential to Human Happiness Specified, and the First of Them Developed*, published by Spencer (1820–1903) in 1851, advocated the laissez-faire principle that '[e]very man has freedom to do all that he wills, provided he infringes not the equal freedom of any other man'.[27] Such ideas had no place in a state constitution, Holmes rumbled:

a Constitution is not intended to embody a particular economic theory, whether of paternalism and the organic relation of the citizen to the State or of *laissez faire* ... It is made for people of fundamentally differing views, and our accident of finding certain opinions natural and familiar, or novel, and even shocking, ought not to conclude our judgement upon the question whether the statues embodying them conflict with the Constitution of the United States ... General propositions do not decide concrete cases.[28]

The advent of pragmatism at the end of the nineteenth century had led to a questioning of the prevalent process-oriented conception of

---

26 Horwitz, *The Transformation of American Law 1870–1960*, p. 142.

27 H. Spencer, *Social Statics: or, The Conditions Essential to Human Happiness Specified, and the First of Them Developed* (London: John Chapman, 1851), p. 103; cited in Menand, *The Metaphysical Club*, p. 422.

28 An extract of Holmes' dissenting opinion is reprinted in W. W. Fischer III, M. J. Horwitz and T. A. Reed (eds.), *American Legal Realism* (New York, NY and Oxford: Oxford University Press, 1993), pp. 25–6.

justice and an overall turn to consequentialism in social thought.[29] Just as this led to scepticism about the functioning of an 'invisible hand' in a neutral and just market economy – leading to the anti-naturalist polemics of Thorstein Veblen (1857–1929) and then later by the work of institutional economists such as Robert Lee Hale (1884–1969) – so too did it lead to scepticism, as witnessed in Holmes' call for judicial self-restraint in the *Lochner* case, about how realistic an orthodox legal doctrine was that conceived of the law as simply reflecting or facilitating such a self-regulating market.[30]

Roscoe Pound, at the time Dean of the University of Nebraska College of Law, hailed Holmes' *Lochner* dissent as the first real exposition in the United States of what he termed 'sociological jurisprudence':

The sociological movement in jurisprudence, the movement for pragmatism as a philosophy of law, the movement for the adjustment of principles and doctrines to the human conditions they are to govern rather than to assumed first principles, the movement for putting the human factor in the central place and relegating logic to its true position as an instrument, has scarcely shown itself as yet in America. Perhaps the dissenting opinion of Mr. Justice Holmes in *Lochner v. New York*, is the best exposition of it we have.[31]

Instead of the artificial process of reasoning that had hitherto been prevalent in the form of what Pound called 'mechanical jurisprudence',[32] it was now time for a philosophy of law that made use of insights from economics, as well as the social and political sciences[33] – it was time for 'law in action', rather than 'law in books'.[34] This trend was particularly evident in the famous 'Brandeis Brief' submitted by Louis D. Brandeis (1856–1941) to the Supreme Court in the case of *Muller v. Oregon* (1908), over whether maximum hours laws for women were unconstitutional under the *Lochner v. New York* ruling. The Brandeis Brief contained two pages of legal reasoning

---

29 Horwitz, *The Transformation of American Law 1870–1960*, p. 194.
30 *Ibid.*, p. 197.
31 R. Pound, 'Contract of Law', *Yale Law Journal*, 8 (1909), pp. 454–87, at 464; see also R. Pound, 'The Scope and Purpose of Sociological Jurisprudence', *Harvard Law Review*, 24 (1911), pp. 591–619 and 25 (1911), pp. 140–68.
32 R. Pound, 'Mechanical Jurisprudence', *Columbia Law Review*, 8 (1908), pp. 605–23.
33 See White, 'From Sociological Jurisprudence to Realism', p. 1004.
34 R. Pound, 'Law in Books and Law in Action', *American Law Review*, 44 (1910), pp. 12–36.

and ninety-five pages of sociological and economic data on the living conditions of women working in factories.[35]

The progressivist attack on classical legal thought culminated in a movement that ran under the label of 'legal realism' – it was, however, far from being a coherent school, as the majority of those who came to be associated with it had no say in the establishment of the label, nor were many of them particularly inclined to identify with it subsequently. Already in 1931, Max Radin (1880–1950) had warned that '[a] word like "realism" is so likely to become a mere incantation, a word to bless or ban, that unless progressives and traditionalists, realists and conceptionalists all alike are careful, they may find themselves tripping over their terms to the no small damage of their intelligibility and intellectual integrity'.[36] Yet a new generation of scholars did emerge in the post-First World War years, mostly at Yale, Columbia, and the new Johns Hopkins Institute. This generation was much more conscious of the effort to strive for social reform and engineering through 'realistic' legislation that included insights from behaviouralist social science and economics. Including the likes of Walter Wheeler Cook (1873–1943), Charles E. Clark (1889–1963), William Underhill Moore (1879–1949), Herman Oliphant (1884–1939), Hessel E. Yntema (1891–1966) and William O. Douglas (1898–1980), these jurists upheld the progressivist rule-scepticism and were wary of the artificial distinction between law and politics; but to this many added an element of value-scepticism that the older generation of Roscoe Pound, Benjamin Cardozo (1870–1938) and John Chipman Gray (1839–1915) did not share. 'The present wave of nominalism in juristic science', Morris R. Cohen (1880–1947) wrote, 'is a reaction by younger men against the *abuse* of abstract principles by an older generation that neglected the adequate factual analysis necessary to make principles properly applicable'.[37] The Great Depression had only strengthened convictions that market processes were social constructs, and that the law was out of sync with a complex social reality. The artificiality of the law–politics distinction of classical legal thought, conceptualized

---

35 See Horwitz, *The Transformation of American Law 1870–1960*, p. 209.

36 M. Radin, 'Legal Realism', *Columbia Law Review*, 31 (1931), pp. 824–8, at 824.

37 M. R. Cohen, 'Justice Holmes and the Nature of Law', *Columbia Law Review*, 31 (1931), pp. 352–67, at 363; cited in Horwitz, *The Transformation of American Law 1870–1960*, p. 201; emphasis in the original.

in deductive legal reasoning that was neutral and thus apolitical – and hence also distinct from moral reasoning – had finally to be overcome.

The systematic use of the term 'realism' originated in a brief exchange of views in 1930 between the young Karl N. Llewellyn (1893–1962) and the grey eminence of Roscoe Pound, now Dean of the Harvard Law School and judge on the Supreme Court – although the catalyst for the exchange was actually the publication of the extremely controversial *Law and the Modern Mind* by Llewellyn's collaborator, Jerome Frank (1889–1957).[38] The details of the debate (some of which are highly entertaining) need not concern us here. Suffice it to say that Llewellyn published an article in 1930 entitled 'A Realistic Jurisprudence – The Next Step', in which one of things he wrote was that Pound's work amounted to nothing more than 'bedtime stories for a tired bar'.[39] Pound reacted promptly with an article 'The Call for a Realist Jurisprudence',[40] to which Llewellyn wrote 'Some Realism About Realism: Responding To Dean Pound',[41] a paper that included the famous (but highly unrepresentative) list of twenty so-called realists that have been taken as the basis for the bulk of historical scholarship on legal realism ever since – until the likes of Morton Horwitz and Neil Duxbury finally began to rewrite this chapter of the US history of ideas in the 1990s.

As intimated above, the label 'legal realism' was itself first used by Jerome Frank in *Law and the Modern Mind*, a book that seems to have been the actual reason, rather than Llewellyn's article, for why Pound sat down to write a response in the first place.[42] Frank, who had arguably read one book on psychoanalysis too many (and who, indeed, had himself been psychoanalysed[43]), steeped his book in Jean Piaget's (1896–1980) work on child psychology, arguing that the quest for certainty in the law was the result of the father–child pattern, of the subconscious desire to have the law play the role of

38 J. Frank, *Law and the Modern Mind* [1930] (London: Stevens & Sons Ltd, 1949).
39 K. N. Llewellyn, 'A Realistic Jurisprudence – The Next Step', *Columbia Law Review*, 30 (1930), pp. 431–65, at 435.
40 R. Pound, 'The Call for a Realist Jurisprudence', *Harvard Law Review*, 44 (1931), pp. 697–711.
41 K. N. Llewellyn, 'Some Realism about Realism: Responding to Dean Pound', *Harvard Law Review*, 44 (1931), pp. 1222–64.
42 Horwitz, *The Transformation of American Law 1870–1960*, p. 175.
43 See N. Duxbury, 'Jerome Frank and the Legacy of Legal Realism', *Journal of Law and Society*, 18 (1991), pp. 175 205.

the 'Father-As-Infallible-Judge': 'The essence of the basic legal myth or illusion is that law can be entirely predictable. Back of this illusion is the childish desire to have a fixed father-controlled universe, free of chance and error due to human fallibility.'[44] The 'Completely Adult Jurist', by contrast, embodied in 'Mr. Justice Holmes', was the one who is able to throw off this irrational desire for certainty and accept law's indeterminacy – soon, popular legend had boiled down his argument to the assertion that a judge's decision depended on what he had eaten for breakfast.

Of course, were it not for these more radical elements, legal realism would perhaps never have created the stir that it did. As Hermann Kontorowicz (1877–1940) pointed out, such exaggerations 'had the wholesome effect of giving a sensational touch to the movement which perhaps was necessary in order to arouse general attention'.[45] Yet because of the exchange between Llewellyn and Pound, too much emphasis has since been placed on the distinction between sociological jurisprudence and legal realism; in a sense, the latter is only a slightly less general – and certainly more radical in its (over-) emphasis on judicial decisions – version of the former.[46] Although running the risk of exchanging one vague label for another, legal realism may well be called 'legal pragmatism', in the way pragmatism was understood by Charles Peirce and William James. According to the realists, the law was not simply a body of rules that was applied, and under which cases were subsumed. It was far more than that, for it was also a means of social control – 'the law is what it does', as one commentator put it.[47] Laws were seen to regulate social life, and in order to do so effectively, jurists had to incorporate insights from economics, sociology, political science, anthropology and social psychology. It was all about experience, rather than logic, about facts, rather than general propositions – indeed, it was the law's

---

44 Frank, *Law and the Modern Mind*, p. 34.
45 H. Kontorowicz, 'Some Rationalism About Realism', *Yale Law Journal*, 43 (1934), pp. 1240–53, at 1252.
46 For a useful discussion of the similarities between legal realism and both US and European variations of sociological jurisprudence see A. Auburtin, 'Amerikanische Rechtsauffassung und die neueren amerikanischen Theorien der Rechtssoziologie und des Rechtsrealismus', *Zeitschrift für ausländisches öffentliches Recht und Völkerrecht*, 3 (1933), pp. 529–67.
47 G. H. Sabine, 'The Pragmatic Approach to Politics', *American Political Science Review*, 24 (1930), pp. 865–85, at 878.

indeterminacy that was at the core of the legal realist agenda.[48] Law was not a static structure the application of which students could acquire by learning the methods of inductive reasoning, and *stare decisis*, the theory of precedent, was 'simply a gimmick by which clever judges fool other people and stupid judges occasionally fool themselves', as Grant Gilmore caricatured it.[49] Law was, in a word, a 'technology', and the behaviouralist social-scientific methods that were increasingly in vogue were not what Morgenthau, for one, had bargained for.

Morgenthau's 'radical legal realism'

From a substantive point of view, one might be inclined to suppose that the conditions in the United States were favourable for Morgenthau. For, as I tried to outline in Chapters 2 and 3, he too was critical of the law–politics distinction, and with the way legal discourse tried to ignore the inherent tensions in its formalist doctrine. What is more, Morgenthau had, since the publication of *La réalité des normes*[50] and whilst working in Madrid, gone on to outline his critique further in a pamphlet, published in French, entitled *Positivisme mal compris et théorie réaliste du Droit international*.[51] In it, Morgenthau called for a 'radical legal realism' that would rise out of the ashes of the disqualified 'dominant doctrine' of traditional legal positivism – a doctrine that had been thoroughly debunked, according to Morgenthau, by Hans Kelsen, James L. Brierly (1881–1955), and a certain Roscoe Pound.[52]

This dominant doctrine, Morgenthau began the pamphlet, took on the label 'positivism' because it distinguished itself, first, from metaphysics: the 'science' of law only concerned itself with empirically observable norms and not with imaginary creations associated with 'natural law'. Second, and as a logical corollary of the first

---

48 See A. Altman, 'Legal Realism, Critical Legal Studies, and Dworkin', *Philosophy and Public Affairs*, 15 (1986), pp. 205–35.

49 G. Gilmore, 'Legal Realism: Its Cause and Cure', *Yale Law Journal*, 70 (1961), pp. 1037–48, at 1038.

50 H. J. Morgenthau, *La réalité des normes, en particulier des normes du droit international: Fondements d'une théorie des normes* (Paris: Félix Alcan, 1934).

51 H. J. Morgenthau, *Positivisme mal compris et théorie réaliste du Droit international* (Madrid: Mélanges Altamira, 1936).

52 *Ibid.*, p. 2.

point, the positivism of the dominant doctrine only considered those norms as 'valid' that were '*posées*', as Brierly expressed it[53] – '*gesatzt*', in German – by legislative organs, thereby excluding all morals and mores from the analysis, and thus also rejecting all 'non-juridical' (i.e. moral and political) reasoning.

Both of these elements led to the '*positivisme mal compris*', to a dominant doctrine that was a long way from being properly positivist not only because it missed a large part of reality, but also because it incorporated into its analysis elements that were empirically unverifiable, and thus inadmissible to and against the core principles of positivism as the term was understood in the philosophy of science.[54] Its a priori attack on anything resembling natural law, without empirical observation of valid law that may well have natural law premises, did not lead to a scientific study of law, but rather to a type of 'negative metaphysics' that failed to take into account the empirically determined structure of reality, Morgenthau charged. Moreover, the apologist nature of the legal monism on which the dominant doctrine was based forced it to resort to a variety of fictions, grouped under the heading of 'customary law', in order to explain away the fact that a whole host of valid norms did not stem from state legislation. In line with the US progressivists, Morgenthau also argued that by removing all non-juridical elements from its field of analysis, the doctrine thus came to forget the purely hypothetical character of the separation between the legal sphere and other normative domains, a separation that was crucial for the analysis of norms to correspond with reality.

Kelsen's brand of positivism was superior to this dominant doctrine on several accounts, Morgenthau continued. It provided clarity, gave formal structure to the legal domain, drew out the final logical consequences of the antagonism between natural law and legal positivism, and constituted a bridging device between traditional positivism and a new, scientific approach.[55] Of course, Kelsen's system was not without its weaknesses, especially with regard to its problematic neo-Kantian premises and its reductionist state monism; yet through its construction of an internally coherent system of norms

53 J. L. Brierly, 'Le fondement du charactère obligatoire du droit international', *Recueil des cours de l'Académie de droit international*, 23 (1928-III), pp. 463–552, at 486.
54 Morgenthau, *Positivisme mal compris*, p. 7.   55 *Ibid.*, pp. 10–11.

that hierarchically culminated in the extra-legal basic norm, it nonetheless provided, Morgenthau enthusiastically proclaimed, the necessary toolbox to break through the walls of the dominant doctrine and make way for a 'radical legal realism' that re-establishes the link between the science of law and juridical realities.[56]

Morgenthau's legal realism moreover assumed that international law, just as every legal order, was an autonomous system of norms culminating in a basic norm that was of necessity in the realm of morals or mores – here he repeated his position elaborated in *La réalité des normes* and in his article on sanctions, which I outlined in Chapter 3. Moreover, empirically there is both a vertical and a horizontal link between the legal and other normative spheres: a particular norm of international law could be upheld by a juridical sanction and at the same time by a moral one. Recognizing the cumulative nature of these sanctions also meant, Morgenthau argued, revisiting – and rewriting – the theory of sources of international law: the bundle of heterogeneous norms running under the notion of 'customary law' had to be unpacked. Laying claim to a true positivism also meant distinguishing between all those norms of international law listed in various treatises and manuals, and those that were actually valid and thus '*en vigeur*' because backed by an effective sanction.[57]

Yet this was only the first step. A truly realist theory of international law would then also analyse the content of the norms of international law according to 'realist principles'.[58] The Covenant of the League of Nations cannot be interpreted using the methods of the civil code, and it is not possible to conceive of a political treaty such as a colonial agreement in the same way as a sales contract: interpretation that contents itself with the superficial appearance of diplomatic language inevitably fails to capture the real normative function of norms of international law. A realist theory of law, and in particular international law, would thus also have to engage with '*son substratum social*': the political. And here, contrary to the way the literature on Morgenthau (and Schmitt) usually frames the issue, Morgenthau very explicitly claimed, in the last paragraph of his pamphlet, that the political is an intrinsic element

56 *Ibid.*, p. 14.   57 *Ibid.*, pp. 15–17.
58 *Ibid.*, p. 18.

of international law itself. While the dominant doctrine showed a constant aversion to 'the political' and attempted to eliminate and expel it from its field of analysis, 'the realist theory finds precisely here the preferred field for its investigations'.[59] It is this aversion to the political that is at the heart of what Morgenthau would later call 'legalism', an issue that I will discuss in Chapter 5.

Sobering realities

When Morgenthau stepped off the *SS Königstein* in New York Harbour on 28 July 1937, he could have been forgiven for a sense of hope and expectation. After all, he was not too badly positioned. He was neither too old and set in his ways like Ernst Rabel (1874–1955),[60] for instance, nor too young and inexperienced to be of little interest to academic establishments.[61] And as the previous section attempted to demonstrate, his research interests and overall outlook were not, at first sight, all that different from the main themes addressed by progressivism and the legal realists. Moreover, the late 1920s and early 1930s had been the heyday of exchange between US and continental European legal scholars, who were recognized

59 [*la théorie réaliste, toutefois, trouve précisément ici le champ préféré de ses investigations*] *Ibid.*, pp. 19–20.
60 Originally a Romanist and papyrologist, Rabel was founder and director of the Kaiser Wilhelm Institute of Foreign and International Private Law in Berlin, and the pioneer of modern comparative law in Germany. Between 1935 and 1938, the University of Chicago spent three years dragging its feet contemplating whether to invite him; he finally managed to obtain a temporary, month-by-month allowance at the University of Michigan Law School. In 1945, at the age of 71, Rabel returned to Germany to teach as an honorary professor at his old institute, which had meanwhile moved to Tübingen. See R. Zimmermann, '"Was Heimat hieß, nun heißt es Hölle": The Emigration of Lawyers from Hitler's Germany: Political Background, Legal Framework, and Cultural Context', in J. Beatson and R. Zimmermann (eds.), *Jurists Uprooted: German-speaking Émigré Lawyers in Twentieth-century Britain* (Oxford University Press, 2004), pp. 1–71; also K. Graham, 'The Refugee Jurist and American Law Schools, 1933–1941', *American Journal of Comparative Law*, 50 (2002), pp. 777–818. The Dean of Michigan Law School would later admit his school's ignorance regarding the importance of Rabel in legal scholarship: 'We did not know who he was'; see the Preface by the editors in M. Lutter, E. C. Stiefel and M. H. Hoeflich (eds.), *Der Einfluß deutscher Emigranten auf die Rechtsentwicklung in den USA und in Deutschland: Vorträge und Referate des Bonner Symposiums im September 1991* (Tübingen: Mohr (Siebeck), 1993), pp. iii–v, at v.
61 For a useful discussion of this see H. A. Strauss, 'Wissenschaftsemigration als Forschungsproblem', in H. A. Strauss, K. Fischer, C. Hoffmann and A. Söllner (eds.), *Die Emigration der Wissenschaften nach 1933: Disziplingeschichtliche Studien* (Munich, etc.: K. G. Saur, 1991), pp. 7–23.

as the leading minds in the field. Given the difference between the US and German legal systems, this exchange was never very intense and, indeed, rather one-sided: US philosophical trends towards empiricism and pragmatism were frowned upon by German philosophy professors, and as Franz Neumann recounts, the likes of John Dewey were practically never taught in continental Europe.[62] But comparative legal studies nonetheless flourished for a time, and law professors continuously set sail across the Atlantic for lectures and conferences – Llewellyn, for instance, taught at the University of Leipzig in 1928–9, and again in 1931–2.[63] All this also meant that when things turned sour in Germany, legal scholars fleeing the regime were hopeful of being positively received in the United States.

Yet by the late 1930s, circumstances had changed quite significantly. The rise of totalitarian regimes across Europe had led to a far-reaching 'crisis of democratic theory'[64] in the United States, one that went well beyond the elements and measures that are usually associated with McCarthyism. The inward reflection over US ideals and values resulted in a much broader reaction entailing the trend to restore the blurred distinction between law and politics, and to rethink the relation between democratic political culture and legal theory.[65] The most immediate consequence of these reflections was an ardent attack on the legal realists, the tone of which 'grew in bitterness in proportion to the spread of fear and uncertainty created by the success of the totalitarian governments of Europe' until, by the time Morgenthau arrived on the scene, this criticism had 'turned into a direct frontal assault on realism as a form of scepticism, nihilism, and moral relativism that was helping to destroy American civilization'.[66]

The assault had both an academic and a public component to it, as Neil Duxbury has showcased.[67] The public one focused primarily

62 F. L. Neumann, 'Intellektuelle Emigration und Sozialwissenschaft (1952)', in Neumann, *Wirtschaft, Staat, Demokratie: Aufsätze 1930–1954.* Edited by Alfons Söllner (Frankfurt a.M.: Suhrkamp, 1978), pp. 402–23, at 416.
63 See Graham, 'The Refugee Jurist'.
64 E. A. Purcell, Jr, *The Crisis of Democratic Theory: Scientific Naturalism and the Problem of Value* (Lexington, KY: The University of Kentucky Press, 1973).
65 Horwitz, *The Transformation of American Law 1870–1960*, p. 247.
66 Purcell, Jr, *The Crisis of Democratic Theory*, pp. 159–60.
67 N. Duxbury, 'The Reinvention of American Legal Realism', *Legal Studies*, 12 (1992), pp. 137–77.

on Holmes, as the dangerous precursor of ideas that were now proving to be the ultimate threat to the United States, pronounced by none other than a prominent judge – indeed, *the* prominent judge – of the US Supreme Court. For was it not Holmes' prediction theory of law, his focus on the person, rather than the principle, the contextualization of law, rather than the adherence to legal rules, that marked the beginning of law's navigation into dangerous waters? Suddenly, it was as if a dark side to Holmes had been uncovered. Summarizing the 'fundamentals of Holmes' juristic philosophy', one critic, for instance, wrote:

The essence of law is physical force. Might makes legal right. The law is to be divorced from all morality. There is no such thing as a moral ought – it is a mere fiction. Ultimately there is only the physical necessity of behaving or being killed. There is no absolute truth. Man is a cosmic ganglion. His ideas probably have no more cosmic value than his bowels. He himself has no more cosmic significance than a baboon or a grain of sand. There is too much fuss about the sanctity of human life. To the state man is a means to be sacrificed if necessary in the interest of the state. The ultimate arbiter of all life is physical force. The ultimate ratio decidendi when men disagree is this, in Holmes' words: 'We don't like it and shall kill you if we can'.[68]

From there it was but a small step to articles with crude titles such as 'Hobbes, Holmes and Hitler'.[69]

There was, however, also an academic assault on the brand of legal realism, and the likes of Karl Llewellyn soon found themselves on the back foot. In his influential book for the aspiring law student, entitled *The Bramble Bush: On Our Law and Its Study*,[70] Llewellyn had proclaimed the infamous thirteen words, 'What these officials do about disputes is, to my mind, the law itself'. These were, he later acknowledged, 'unhappy words when not more fully developed', for he should not have forgotten that 'one inherent drive which is a living part of even the most wrongheaded and arbitrary legal system' was to make that system 'more closely realize an ideal of justice'.[71]

---

68 J. C. Ford, 'The Fundamentals of Holmes' Juristic Philosophy', *Fordham Law Review*, 11 (1942), pp. 255–78, at 275; emphasis in the original.

69 B. W. Palmer, 'Hobbes, Holmes and Hitler', *American Bar Association Journal*, 31 (1945), pp. 569–73; see also Duxbury, 'The Reinvention of American Legal Realism', pp. 159–64.

70 K. N. Llewellyn, *The Bramble Bush: On Our Law and Its Study* [1930] (Dobbs Ferry, NY: Oceana, 1960).

71 *Ibid.*, p. 9; see also Horwitz, *The Transformation of American Law 1870–1960*, p. 248.

Yet in a time when the country sought reassurance and conviction in its democratic institutions, it was precisely these kinds of assertions that critics of legal realism jumped upon. For Hitler himself was being quoted as arguing that

it was the fundamental error of the jurists and lawmakers to think that they could create life by means of a constitution and a code of law … Constitutions can only conclude real developments; they can never precede them. Artificial construction violates life.[72]

Was this not exactly what US legal realism was preaching? And were some of its proponents not in close contact with Germany and even the Nazi regime? Roscoe Pound's acceptance in October 1934 of an honorary degree from Germany's ambassador to the United States on the steps of Harvard's Langdell Hall only made matters worse.[73] The US legal establishment found itself in disarray.

Perhaps the most intense attack on legal realism came from the Catholic Thomists, a neo-scholastic legal movement that was on the resurgence in the United States at the time. Walter B. Kennedy (1885–1945), professor of law at Fordham University and arguably the most renowned advocate of this position at the time, expressed his dismay over legal realism in a way that typifies the critique:

The old order of legal principles and rules, precedents and authorities, is being supplanted by strange and technical discussions of background, function, lump behaviour, environment, institutions, and law-law.

I sometimes suspect that those who would remove all concepts and all ideals from the field of law, fail to think through the results and consequences of their goose-step philosophy. I wonder if they realize just where this logic leads when it is carried out to the last degree. This act-first-and-explain-later formula is certainly the dominant objective both in pragmatic and realist philosophies of law. It is likewise a dominant factor in the jurisprudence of the dictator nations. 'Law,' says a German jurist, 'is that which is *useful* to the German nation.' 'Law,' says another Nazi interpreter of law, 'is what Aryan men *consider* as law'.

72 Cited in H. Kohn *et al.*, *The City of Man: A Declaration of World Democracy* (New York, NY: Viking Press, 1941), p. 75.
73 Felix Frankfurter (1882–1965) tried boycotting the event, Harold Laski (1893–1950) called it a 'tragic lapse', and *The New Republic* wrote that 'Dean Pound's action will be interpreted by German propagandists around the world as an answer to Nazi critics'; all cited in Graham, 'The Refugee Jurist', p. 790.

When we hear jurists in high station in this country announce that American law should be tested solely in terms of pragmatic utility or timely opportunism or fortuitous results, it seems to me that these formulas could be lifted out of the realist setting without the change of a word and tendered to the European dictators as an accurate definition of their own objectives in the totalitarian states.[74]

If legal realism and ethical relativism were leading to totalitarianism, Thomistic rationalism, the likes of Kennedy contended, led straight to democracy via its justification of natural law. '[T]he essential tenets of Realism contradict all the fundamental principles of Democracy', Francis E. Lucey (1891–1970), regent of the Georgetown University School of Law, bluntly put it: 'Democracy *versus* the Absolute State means Natural Law *versus* Realism.'[75] And whereas Thomism was certainly not the only legal theory available as an alternative to realism, and although, as Duxbury writes, the assault on legal realism 'amounted to little more than crude attempts at proselytisation',[76] the legal realists, by now in full retreat, did indeed shift in that direction: Max Radin, Walter Wheeler Cook, and even Jerome Frank and Karl Llewellyn all moved closer to incorporating elements of natural law into their theoretical frameworks.[77] The details of these debates and academic trends need not concern us here (although they do bear some of the seeds for understanding post-war US legal scholarship[78]). For present purposes, it suffices to conclude that by the time Morgenthau arrived on the scene, his concoction of a 'radical legal realism' founded on Kelsen's 'German goose-step philosophy' was no longer the best marketing device.[79]

---

74 W. B. Kennedy, 'Walter B. Kennedy', in Julius Rosenthal Foundation for General Law (ed.), *My Philosophy of Law: Credos of Sixteen American Scholars* (Boston Law Book Co., 1941), pp. 143–60, at 151–2; emphasis in the original.

75 F. E. Lucey, 'Natural Law and American Legal Realism: Their Respective Contributions to a Theory of Law in a Democratic Society', *Georgetown Law Journal*, 30 (1942), pp. 493–533, at 523 and 533; emphasis in the original. See also Purcell, 'American Jurisprudence between the Wars', p. 439; Purcell *The Crisis of Democratic Theory*, p. 168; and Duxbury, 'The Reinvention of American Legal Realism', pp. 168–9.

76 *Ibid.*, p. 170.

77 Purcell, *The Crisis of Democratic Theory*, pp. 168–75. Nonetheless, making 'encouraging noises' in the direction of natural law ultimately did not constitute 'conceding any ground', Duxbury, 'The Reinvention of American Legal Realism', p. 174.

78 See also Horwitz, *The Transformation of American Law 1870–1960*, pp. 150–68.

79 The fact that Kelsen was a Jew and soon-to-be-émigré to the United States made little difference there. Morgenthau was well aware of this, which is probably the main reason why he also did not make his indebtedness to Kelsen explicit in *Politics Among*

Yet the substance of Morgenthau's work and its German foundations were only part of the problem. A further dilemma was quite simply the sheer number of young lawyers and aspiring legal scholars trying to find their way around in the land of plenty, a land that was moreover no longer doing so well after the Great Depression – Yale Law School, for instance, cut its research budget from over $18,000 in 1929–30 to under $4,000 in 1936–7.[80] The exodus from Germany, Austria and the Czech territories had become serious with the infamous Law for the Reconstitution of the Professional Civil Service of 7 April 1933, which spelt out the desire of the National-Socialist regime to rid the German academic landscape of its Jewish and otherwise un-German (i.e. radically leftist and social democratic) influence. In the winter semester of 1932/3, there were a total of 496 persons teaching in German law faculties. Of these, 132 were expelled, 88 because they were Jewish, 44 for political reasons. Of these 132, 69 went into exile (73 if Austria and the German University of Prague are included), of which 24 settled in the United States, and 15 in Britain.[81]

With many US law schools taking years to decide whether they should accept a single German legal scholar into their ranks – be it for budgetary reasons, or for acknowledged anti-Semitic tendencies[82] – the situation was dismal, and the statistics just cited only

---

Nations, but only once his career had taken off in the right direction and he was firmly established as professor at the University of Chicago (see Chapter 3, pp. 97–102).

80 Graham, 'The Refugee Jurist', p. 783. Karl Löwenstein (1891–1973), one of the first displaced scholars to arrive in the United States, had warned Morgenthau in 1935 that New York was already teeming with young German jurists, and advised him not to come. Letter from Löwenstein to Morgenthau, dated 28 March 1935, HJM-Container 196.

81 The figures are from Zimmermann, '"Was Heimat hieß, nun heißt es Hölle"', pp. 53–4. Overall, the numbers were obviously much higher, although it took a number of years before the trickle became a torrent. Many of those who were the target of Nazi legislation, in particular those categorized as Jewish, took Germany to be their homeland, and even once persecution was underway, the majority were determined to stay in the hope that things would again take a turn for the better. Hence 'only' 37,000 Jews left Germany in 1933, and 23,000 in 1934. Yet things did not improve, for the Nazi regime, realizing their lack of success in inducing Jews to leave, gradually tightened the screws. 1938 and 1939 saw a further 120,000 Jews leave Germany, and another 130,000 from Austria. A further 30,000 were exiled for political reasons, reasons which included the refusal to divorce from a non-Aryan spouse. Most of those who left ended up in the United States (130,000), Latin America (between 75,000 and 90,000) and Palestine (around 60,000). The figures for those who settled in Britain were lower, although many refugees passed through the country as trans-migrants on their way to their final destinations.

82 See Graham, 'The Refugee Jurist', p. 783.

tell part of the story. For one, the likes of Morgenthau or Herz are not even part of these figures. Morgenthau left Germany for Geneva before the National Socialists came to power, a fact that the Academic Assistance Council in Britain was quick to point out when Morgenthau tried applying for such support. He simply did not classify as a refugee. Of course, Morgenthau would have had a case arguing that had it not been for the way those of German-Jewish descent were discriminated against already long before the regime change occurred, he would not have left in the first place. He would, moreover, probably have argued that once in Geneva, the coming to power of the Nazis made returning to Germany impossible and thus the end result was, for all practical purposes, the same. But Morgenthau's case does show the limitations of the oft-cited statistics.

What is more, the literature on émigré scholars is also significantly biased in the direction of a 'winner's history'. As Kyle Graham correctly points out, surveys of the intellectual migration to the United States have generally painted a somewhat rosy picture of 'illustrious immigrants' being welcomed with open arms in US law schools.[83] One of the obvious reasons for this bias is quite simply the fact that the majority of these surveys focus on the few that did emigrate successfully, or indeed have actually been written by them. The result is that '[f]ew of these reflections capture the hesitance and, in some quarters, hostility that greeted the displaced scholars. Most bend over backwards to paint the opposite picture'.[84]

Of course, there certainly were a few success stories – Arthur Nussbaum (1877–1964), Friedrich Kessler (1901–98) and Max Rheinstein (1899–1977) are among them. But the bulk of the émigré scholars could not stay in the field of law; the lucky ones moved to Political Science and, in particular those with a grounding in International Law, to the new field of International Relations. Morgenthau falls into this category. However, his transition was not at all as straightforward as the literature generally assumes it to have

---

83 *Ibid.*, pp. 778–9.
84 *Ibid.*, p. 779. The same is true for those scholars who emigrated to Britain, where the majority was classified as enemy aliens and ended up being detained for much of the war in camps on the Isle of Man and elsewhere; see Beatson and Zimmermann, *Jurists Uprooted*; also O. Jütersonke, 'Book Review of Beatson and Zimmermann (eds.), *Jurists Uprooted*', *Journal of the History of International Law*, 9 (2007), pp. 163–9.

been, and is a far cry from constituting a clear and conscious choice on the part of Morgenthau.

A functionalist approach to international law

Morgenthau thus found himself cornered on several fronts – and as I outlined in Chapter 1, the difficulties he faced in finding an academic opening are a reflection of this barren state of affairs. Yet it is quite remarkable with what speed and lucidity he went about coming to terms with his new environment. Already in Brooklyn College, but then more intensely at the University of Kansas City, Morgenthau had to teach 'just about everything under the sun', from contracts, family laws, wills, torts and jurisprudence to criminal law, administrative law, constitutional law, US government, political theory and comparative government.[85] Numerous book reviews and review articles published in the period 1939 to 1943 attest to his efforts. The émigré scholar was quickly acquiring the new toolkit he needed to fit in with his new surroundings.

Nowhere are Morgenthau's efforts more obvious than in this 1940 article in the *American Journal of International Law*. Entitled 'Positivism, Functionalism and International Law', the paper is an elaborate attempt to reconcile his Kelsenian formalism with the US law scene of the late 1930s.[86] The article is based on a slightly reformulated statement of the critique of the dominant, positivist doctrine that Morgenthau had already espoused in the *Positivisme mal compris* pamphlet. This he now used to call for a 'functional theory of international law' that would overcome the inadequacies of the positivist doctrine and depict international law 'as it really is'.

Legal positivism, Morgenthau began, delimited its subject matter by, on the one hand, separating the legal sphere from morality and mores, and thus also from the other sciences such as sociology or psychology; on the other hand, it confined its attention to those legal rules that were enacted by the state, thereby excluding all

85 H. J. Morgenthau, 'Interview with Bernhard Johnson', in K. W. Thompson and R. J. Meyers (eds.), *Truth and Tragedy. A Tribute to Hans J. Morgenthau*. Second edition with new Postscript (New Brunswick, NJ: Transaction Books, 1984), pp. 333–86, at 366–7.
86 H. J. Morgenthau, 'Positivism, Functionalism, and International Law', *American Journal of International Law*, 34 (1940), pp. 260–84.

norms the existence of which cannot be traced to the statute books or to court decisions. These legal rules were accepted without passing judgment on either their ethical value or their practical appropriateness, and were taken to form a logically coherent system. These four characteristics – legalism, state monism, agnosticism and dogmatic conceptualism – formed the positivist 'fiction' that had now come under increasing attack by various forms of sociological and realist jurisprudence, by Kelsen's pure theory, and by a resurgent natural law movement following the rise of totalitarianism in Europe.[87]

While increasingly being questioned in domestic law, in international law the positivist doctrine was still in full swing, Morgenthau continued. This was because international law was 'primitive', as Kelsen had called it, or 'in a retarded stage of scientific development', as Morgenthau now framed it – a development, moreover, that was not always following a linear progression:

As represented by its sanest elements, the science of international law still stands where the science of municipal law stood in 1910; in terms of its post-World War development, its most spectacular branches, invaded by the political ideology of Geneva, have gone back at least to the point from which positivism started in the last decades of the nineteenth century.[88]

The reasons for this cyclical pattern (if not regression) lay in the fact that international law lacked the criteria for distinguishing between 'seemingly' and 'actually' valid rules of international law, Morgenthau argued. Whereas the legal monism of the domestic system provided a problematic but nonetheless workable criterion for the validity of a legal norm, the positivist doctrine of international law was faced with the dilemma of being at once too narrow and too broad: not all rules embodied in written documents and treaties were valid international law, while there were also valid rules of international law that were not enshrined in written documents.[89] This was particularly worrying with regard to the developments of the inter-war period: did the Kellogg–Briand Pact, for instance, still constitute valid international law after years of being violated?

87 *Ibid.*, pp. 261–2.
88 *Ibid.*, 264. This 'political ideology of Geneva' will be discussed in more detail in Chapter 5.
89 In contemporary terminology, legal theorists would call this the over- and under-inclusiveness of rules and doctrines.

Here, the shortcomings of positivist 'legal self-sufficiency', of the assumption that law could be understood without recourse to the other normative and social spheres, were strikingly apparent, Morgenthau continued. The result of all this was 'a threefold misconception of what international law actually is'; again, Morgenthau repeated the arguments already expressed in *Positivisme mal compris*. First, positivist doctrine was unable to recognize that the normative spheres of law, mores and morality support one another and were, indeed, part of one integral normative system – the practice of the positivist jurist of repudiating both natural law and ethics as irrelevant metaphysics was thus in itself a type of 'negative metaphysics', as it stemmed from preconceived reasoning rather than the type of empirical observation that was advocated. Second, its state monism forced it to regroup all valid norms of international law that could not be traced back to written documents of states under the heading of 'customary law', 'a veritable panacea for its theoretical troubles'. Third, positivism became dominant in municipal law only because the sociological context (social and economic interests and tensions, conflicting aspirations of power, and so on) had been incorporated into legal reasoning:

In the domestic field, it [positivist jurisprudence] became instrumental in distorting the legal reality and originating that positivist conceptualism with which a decadent legal science attempted to adapt the old legal rules to new economic and social needs, but at the same time maintained the fictitious assumption that the written law already contained, logically, all the rules necessary for the solution of those new problems. Thus the juridical pseudo-logic became the artificial makeshift by which a stationary law could be reconciled with a moving social reality.[90]

Yet in the international sphere, Morgenthau asserted, there never had been (and never could have been) any sort of correspondence between legal concepts and sociological context in the first place: 'The identical text of an arbitration treaty or non-aggression pact may have quite different legal meanings, according to the political situation existing between different contracting parties.'[91] Rather, an 'individual situation' requires an 'individual interpretation' of the legal rule.

90 *Ibid.*, p. 270.   91 *Ibid.*, p. 272.

A 'truly scientific theory of international law', therefore, had to avoid these mistakes in order to come closer to reality, Morgenthau claimed. Moreover, '[i]t seems to be a logical choice to call such a theory by the name of realist'.[92] Yet there were two reasons not to use the term, he continued. The first was the (somewhat trivial) observation that a whole host of household names of the 'traditional doctrine' in international law, from Erich Kaufmann to Georges Scelle to Alfred Verdross, had, at one point or another in their writings, called themselves 'realists' or 'realistic'. They had thus 'misused' the term and 'deprived it of its distinctive character in the international field'. The second, and undoubtedly more significant, reason was that realism had become 'a collective designation for several tendencies in modern jurisprudence ... [that] search for the psychological, social, political and economic forces which determine the actual content and working of legal rules and which, in turn, are determined by them'.[93] These 'tendencies' were, of course, sociological jurisprudence in general and legal realism in particular. And then comes Morgenthau's quick-fix solution: what these 'tendencies' had in common was their 'scientific goal' of formulating functional relationships between these forces and legal rules: '[h]ence, "realist" jurisprudence is, in truth, "functional" jurisprudence'.[94]

Morgenthau's attempt to slide from realism to functionalism was nothing short of being horribly unoriginal. The two terms were used interchangeably by most of the so-called legal realists[95] – a fact that Morgenthau seemed to have been well aware of given the references he chose to include in a lengthy footnote. Moreover, as Felix S. Cohen (1907–53) had pointed out, use of the term 'functionalism' did not necessarily render greater precision nor was it a label any less misused than 'realism'.[96] And even Llewellyn himself, for instance, had written in 'Some Realism About Realism – Responding to Dean Pound' that realism could also be called the 'functional approach', because that label 'stresses the interest in, and valuation by, effects'.[97]

92 *Ibid.*, p. 273.   93 *Ibid.*, pp. 273–4.
94 *Ibid.*, p. 274.
95 On this point, see L. Kalman, *Legal Realism at Yale, 1927–1960* (Chapel Hill, NC: University of North Carolina Press, 1986).
96 F. S. Cohen, 'Transcendental Nonsense and the Functional Approach', *Columbia Law Review*, 35 (1935), pp. 809–49, at 821–2.
97 Llewellyn, 'Some Realism About Realism', p. 1234.

But all these antics do bear testimony to Morgenthau's recognition of just how problematic it had become to identify oneself with legal realism, and how he hoped that by hiding behind the less chastised term 'functionalism', he would be able to make his own research agenda more compatible with his new US environment.

The article ends on a few preliminary reflections, similar to the ones Morgenthau expressed in *Positivisme mal compris*, on what such a functionalist theory of international law might entail. First and foremost, a functionalist theory had to recognize that in the absence of a group holding the monopoly of organized physical force, as was the case in the domestic sphere, legal rules could not be imposed without there being complementary interests or a balance of power: 'Where there is neither community of interests nor balance of power, there is no international law', Morgenthau bluntly put it.[98] And when these social forces and the legal rules are no longer compatible, the resulting transformational conflict is precisely the 'tension' that Morgenthau had already conceptualized in his 1929 dissertation. From this Morgenthau also derived the complementary requirement of a 'functional concept of validity', because rules of international law did not receive their validity through their enactment into a legal instrument (such as a treaty), but through the existence of a credible (i.e. enforceable) sanction – here again, Morgenthau borrowed large chunks of his analysis from the 1935 article in the *Revue de droit international et de législation comparée*.[99]

As in *Positivisme mal compris*, Morgenthau ended on the contention that the political was an intrinsic part of international law. In his view, there were two types of international law: the first derived from municipal law and was founded on the 'permanent and stable interests of states', the second expressed 'in terms of rights and duties, temporary interests ever given to change'.[100] The first type represented 'the bulk' of international legal rules and principles, and entailed diplomatic privileges, territorial jurisdiction, extradition, maritime law and arbitral procedure – agreement on such issues being in the interests of all states. Into the second category

---

98 Morgenthau, 'Positivism, Functionalism, and International Law', p. 275.
99 See Chapter 3, pp. 93–7.
100 Morgenthau, 'Positivism, Functionalism, and International Law', pp. 278–9.

fell 'political agreements, especially treaties of alliance and their modern substitutes, which, under the legalistic guise of treaties of general arbitration, consultation, or friendship, frequently pursued aims at least preparatory to close political ties'.[101] The dominant positivist doctrine failed to distinguish between these two types of international law, Morgenthau charged. By attempting to apply the methods of municipal civil law to all issues at hand, international legal doctrine failed to come to terms with the norms of 'political international law' whose validity was completely dependent on underlying social forces. It was thus necessary to 'develop systematically concepts and methods capable of conveying the legal characteristics, as well as the functional dependence on political factors, of political international law'.[102] It was such a functional theory of law, Morgenthau finally declared, that would 'prepare the ground for satisfying the greater ethical and political desire to improve international relations by means of the law'.[103]

'Improving international relations by means of the law' – this is not a statement that, according to the mainstream interpretation in both International Relations and International Law, one would necessarily associate with Morgenthau, the advocate of power politics. But in 1940 Morgenthau was still attempting to engage with his peers in the legal profession by trying to find a way of formulating a more 'realistic' conceptualization of international law, one that would capture the inherent social forces at work in producing the 'tensions' that characterized relations among states. The 1940 article was, indeed, the last time Morgenthau engaged in such an attempt, inducing Martti Koskenniemi to call it his 'legal swansong'.[104] But as I will try to flesh out in the remaining pages of this chapter, the fact that Morgenthau would increasingly turn his back on international law was not so much due to a change in his convictions, but rather due to an unwillingness to come to terms with the newer social scientific methodologies that were being developed to do precisely what he was calling for.

---

101 *Ibid.*, p. 279.   102 *Ibid.*, p. 280.
103 *Ibid.*, p. 284.
104 M. Koskenniemi, *The Gentle Civilizer of Nations: The Rise and Fall of International Law 1870–1960* (Cambridge University Press, 2002), p. 459.

Trouble in Chicago

In 1943, Morgenthau accepted an offer from the University of Chicago to replace Quincy Wright for a period of six months. This opportunity is generally interpreted as the real breakthrough in Morgenthau's career, as the stepping stone that would lead to the highly successful decades in which he excelled both as a prolific author and as an indefatigable lecturer. Yet these accounts from the perspective of a 'winner's history' fail to capture the adversity Morgenthau faced in Chicago, and it was – once again – a series of lucky breaks that made Morgenthau stand out as having been so much more successful than many of his émigré peers. For while the battles in law and jurisprudence were fought in Yale and Harvard, the *Hochburg* of the fledgling 'new science of politics' was undoubtedly Chicago: quite unawares, it seems, Morgenthau had walked straight into the lion's den.

In the first decades of the twentieth century, the field of Political Science had undergone a period of change and upheaval comparable to the move to legal realism in jurisprudence. Just as in Law, the distinction was being made between formalist and realist approaches to social inquiry: realistic, i.e. empirical, studies were believed to be the way through which to cope with the profound challenges posed by the onset of the industrial age.[105] One of the key figures in this transformation was the 'grandfather' of behaviouralism, Charles E. Merriam (1874–1953). Department chair at the University of Chicago from 1923 to 1940, Merriam persuaded a generation of political scientists that academic professionalism entailed the search for the causes of political behaviour using rigorous research methods. Politics was, for Merriam, a 'policy science' – he originally called it 'political prudence'[106] – and it was in large part due to his influence that a rapport was established between professional social science and New Deal policy-makers.[107] As Albert

---

105 Duxbury, *Patterns of American Jurisprudence*, p. 95; see also D. Ross, *The Origins of American Social Science* (Cambridge University Press), p. 64.

106 C. E. Merriam, 'The Present State of the Study of Politics', *American Political Science Review*, 15 (1921), pp. 173–85, at 176.

107 See R. Seidelman (with Edward J. Harpham), *Disenchanted Realists: Political Science and the American Crisis, 1884–1984* (Albany, NY: State University of New York Press, 1984), p. 111.

Somit and Joseph Tanenhaus write: 'His extraordinarily influential essay on "The Present State of the Study of Politics," led to the appointment of an Association Committee on Political Research, to three National Conferences on the Science of Politics, and eventually, it is only a slight exaggeration to say, to the creation of the Social Science Research Council.'[108] The earlier generation of progressivist academics, according to Merriam, had failed to realize the influence of technology on politics and society – the impending 'crisis of democratic theory' was in large part due to antiquated political perceptions, practices and structures that were out of sync with a rapidly changing social and economic environment.

The call for a new science of politics steeped in statistics and insights from psychology was never fully realized by Merriam himself, however. Although possessing a 'shrewd sense of the lay of the land', Dorothy Ross writes, he seemed to have had 'little analytical depth'.[109] It was thus up to a group of veritable disciples at the University of Chicago to bring Merriam's agenda to fruition. The most prolific of these was undoubtedly Harold D. Lasswell. As Raymond Seidelman writes, '[m]ore than any of the other young recruits to Merriam's University of Chicago department, Lasswell took his chairman's homilies about methodological sophistication to heart'[110] – indeed, Ross goes as far as claiming that in Lasswell, 'Merriam found the psychological and scientific capacity he himself lacked and perhaps also found a voice for the disappointment in politics he could not quite express'.[111] Lasswell agreed with Merriam that politics was about understanding the functional relationships between small groups vying for control in and ultimately domination over society;[112] the study of politics thus entailed focusing on human cause–effect relationships, on the dynamics of organized pressure groups, and on the overall processes of social action through which power was attained and exercised. One of

---

108 A. Somit and J. Tanenhaus, *The Development of American Political Science: From Burgess to Behavioralism* (New York, NY: Irvington Publishers, 1982), p. 110. Merriam would then go on to elaborate on the substance of his article in the book *New Aspects of Politics* (University of Chicago Press, 1925).
109 Ross, *The Origins of American Social Science*, p. 395.
110 Seidelman, *Disenchanted Realists*, p. 133.
111 Ross, *The Origins of American Social Science*, p. 457.
112 See C. E. Merriam, *Political Power: Its Composition and Incidence* (New York, NY: Wittlesey House, 1934).

Lasswell's books was aptly called *Politics: Who Gets What, When, How*.[113]

Although Merriam and his group dominated the Political Science department, they did not always get their own way, leading to serious friction between the department and the university's administration. In 1929, Robert Maynard Hutchins (1899–1977), until then Dean at Yale Law School, came to Chicago to be inaugurated as the university's new president – aged only thirty. Hutchins, an ardent legal realist, seemed the perfect choice for science-oriented Chicago. A legal empiricist, Hutchins had over the previous decade advocated new approaches to the social sciences, and had himself published a series of monographs with the likes of Mortimer J. Adler (1902–2001) and Jerome Michael (1890–1953) on ways of incorporating insights from psychology into the study of law.[114] Merriam, for his part, had throughout the late 1920s been working actively for the creation of a 'School of Politics' that 'would have a dramatic quality in that it would emphasize the scientific aspects of politics, and express with the utmost clearness the idea of the relationship between science and government'.[115] Given Hutchins' scientific orientation, Merriam may have been hopeful of finding a new ally in his quest for the new school. But he would soon be bitterly disappointed.

The Hutchins of the early 1930s was, to the surprise of many, a far different kettle of fish than had originally been supposed. Like most of his legal realist colleagues, the Depression and the rise of totalitarianism induced Hutchins to have second thoughts about his intellectual convictions, and soon he joined in the fray attacking scientific naturalism from his newly adopted neo-Aristotelian premises.[116] Now in the position of president of one of the most prominent universities in the United States, Hutchins tried putting his 'intellectual conversion'[117] into action by calling for drastic changes in the curriculum and pushing for comprehensive

---

113 H. D. Lasswell, *Politics: Who Gets What, When, How* (New York, NY: McGraw-Hill, 1936).
114 Purcell, *The Crisis of Democratic Theory*, p. 141.
115 Cited in M. T. Hearney, 'The Chicago School That Never Was', *PS: Political Science and Politics*, 40 (2007), pp. 753–8, at 754.
116 See Purcell, *The Crisis of Democratic Theory*, pp. 141–2.
117 M. A. Dzuback, 'Hutchins, Adler, and the University of Chicago: A Critical Juncture', *American Journal of Education*, 99 (1990), pp. 57–76, at 57.

education reforms – to the horror, it seems, of not just Merriam and his group, but of a large proportion of the faculty. Spurred on by his friend Mortimer J. Adler, whom Hutchins had offered a position at Chicago in 1930 against the objections of many members of the faculty, Hutchins set about focusing on what Adler referred to as the 'great books': Aristotle, Plato, Aquinas. As Purcell writes: 'As he [Hutchins] began to question his old pragmatic ideas under the pressure of events, the Aristotelian–Thomistic synthesis came to seem the answer to many of his intellectual problems.'[118] The Depression, according to Hutchins, had once again emphasized that education in the United States had failed; what was now needed was 'intellectual leadership'. Practical and vocational training was to be scrapped, and the focus shifted back to the humanities and the 'pure' sciences. Undoubtedly having Merriam's newly published *Political Power* in mind,[119] as well as the legal realists, Hutchins would soon dismiss not only Merriam's idea of a School of Politics but also his entire research agenda, which was distracting the university from what he deemed to be its true mission:

Power becomes the great word in political science; and the prediction of what the courts will do takes the place of justice as the object of the lawyer and the legal scholar. The scientific spirit leads us to accumulate vast masses of data about crime, poverty, and unemployment, political corruption, taxation, and the League of Nations in our quest for what is known as social control. A substantial part of what we call the social sciences is large chunks of data, undigested, unrelated, and meaningless.[120]

By the time Morgenthau arrived on the scene, Merriam had retired and been replaced for all practical purposes by Leonard D. White (1891–1958), Merriam's 'stand-in and front man', as Morgenthau called him, 'an expert in public administration but not a particularly powerful intellectual force'.[121] But the replacement of Merriam with White did not have much of a bearing on the sour relations between the university's president and the Political Science department – indeed, the antagonism between Hutchins and White was

---

118 Purcell, *The Crisis of Democratic Theory*, p. 145.
119 C. E. Merriam, *Political Power: Its Composition and Incidence* (New York, NY: Wittlesey House, 1934).
120 R. M. Hutchins, *The Higher Learning in America* (New Haven, CT: Yale University Press, 1936), p. 101; cited in Hearney, 'The Chicago School That Never Was', p. 755.
121 Morgenthau, 'Interview with Bernhard Johnson', p. 370.

such that White only officially replaced Merriam as the chairman of the Department of Political Science after Hutchins had retired. For Morgenthau, however, Hutchins appears to have contributed to his resilience against the Merriam clan, which did not take long to figure out that the new recruit was not one of their own: 'Very quickly there developed a certain tension between myself and Mr. White especially, and with the Merriam faction generally', Morgenthau recalls.[122] Just as for the intellectually re-born Hutchins, the new science of politics being advocated at Chicago was not Morgenthau's cup of tea. Teaching the 'great books' and preaching the need for 'intellectual leadership' was far more to his liking as well.[123]

Academic apostasy

Morgenthau's move to Chicago and his confrontation with behaviouralist social science was a key moment in his career. On the one hand, it resulted in his complete abandonment of what he had termed the 'functional approach' in the 1940 article, but what was in essence his continued attempt, since his 1929 dissertation, of inserting Sinzheimer's 'social realities' or 'social forces' into conceptualizations of international law. On the other, it led to his polemical reaction against all forms of 'scientism' and his eventual withdrawal from 'cutting-edge' academic debates in both International Law and Political Science, in favour of a more 'common sense' approach to US foreign policy and international politics.

It would not have taken Morgenthau long to discover that the functionalist research agenda he was advocating in International Law circles was already being followed by no other than Harold Lasswell (who had meanwhile resigned from his post as associate professor in Chicago and had moved to Washington, DC), together with Myers McDougal, professor at Yale Law School and in some respects the

---

122 *Ibid.*, pp. 370–1.
123 Indeed, Morgenthau would go on to give a regular course on Aristotle throughout much of his time at the University of Chicago. Transcripts of some of these lectures have recently been edited and published by Anthony F. Lang Jr: H. J. Morgenthau, *Political Theory and International Affairs: Hans J. Morgenthau on Aristotle's The Politics.* Edited by A. F. Lang Jr; foreword by J. H. Rosenthal (Westport, CT and London: Praeger, 2004); see also O. Jütersonke, 'Book Review Essay: Morgenthau and the Return to Ethics in a Realist Theory of Power Politics', *Cooperation and Conflict*, 41 (2006), pp. 463–9.

heir apparent of the legal realists.[124] No longer concerned with New Deal policies but with a post-war order based on US democratic values, Lasswell and McDougal called for a novel direction in legal education, one that would constitute 'conscious, efficient, and systematic *training for policy-making*'.[125] And while their lasting impact on US jurisprudence and legal education is arguably rather negligible, their focus on foreign policy meant that they did generate a post-realist conception of international law that is representative of the 'policy approach' in Martti Koskenniemi's framework and that continues to have a bearing on international legal scholarship.

This framework, it will be recalled from Chapter 1, concerned the four positions of modern legal scholarship in terms of degrees of normativity and concreteness in international law. The graphic representation of this framework is reprinted here, as Figure 4.1, for convenience. Just like the sceptical position, the policy approach begins by calling into question the rule approach as having too narrow a conception of binding force as being simply about the binary legal/illegal distinction with regard to formally neutral rules. Yet such a narrow focus on general doctrines and the formal validity of rules, McDougal argued, only nurtured law's indeterminacy and the artificial distinction between law and policy, between formulations *de lege lata* and *de lege ferenda*.[126] International law would only be relevant if it did not focus on formal authority, but rather on effective control established through value-dependent policies and processes. Unlike the sceptical position, therefore, the policy approach does posit the law's scope to be wide, incorporating a variety of 'prescriptions' that makes for a more realistic account of normative discourse in the international realm.[127]

Armed with the new behaviouralist techniques of the Merriam School, Lasswell and McDougal would begin to formulate a

---

124 See G. Casper, *Juristischer Realismus und politische Theorie im amerikanischen Rechtsdenken* (Berlin: Duncker & Humblot, 1967).

125 H. D. Lasswell and M. S. McDougal, 'Legal Education and Public Policy: Professional Training in the Public Interest', *Yale Law Journal*, 52 (1943), pp. 203–95, at 206; emphasis in the original.

126 M. McDougal, 'International Law, Power and Policy: A Contemporary Conception', *Recueil des cours de l'Académie de droit international*, 82 (1953-I), pp. 133–259, at 144; see also M. Koskenniemi, *From Apology to Utopia: The Structure of International Legal Argument* [1989]. Reissue with a new Epilogue (Cambridge University Press, 2005), p. 144.

127 *Ibid.*, pp. 201–9; also Duxbury, *Patterns of American Jurisprudence*, pp. 191–9.

binding force

		strong	weak
		Idealism (Alvarez)	Policy approach (McDougal)
material scope	wide		
	restricted	Rule approach (Schwarzenberger)	Scepticism (Morgenthau)

Figure 4.1 The structure of international legal argument

functionalist approach to legal processes that was essentially not far off from what Morgenthau had proposed in his 1940 article. Indeed, in a collaboration that would span forty-one years,[128] Lasswell and McDougal would go on to develop an elaborate legal 'policy science', based on democratic values and incorporating the methods of the social sciences into the study of law, that took up much of the intellectual space of Morgenthau's sketchy research agenda. And while Morgenthau never grappled with McDougal's legal work in his writings, McDougal would soon use Morgenthau as exemplary for the 'over-emphasis of naked power' as a factor on decision-making processes,[129] as 'one who would put the sword of power to law',[130] with no mention of Morgenthau's earlier aspirations. Already in their 1943 article on legal education, Lasswell and McDougal seem to have Morgenthau in mind when they write that 'neither a vague and amorphous emphasis on social "forces", "mores", and "purposes", nor a functionalism that dissolves legal absolutism for the benefit of random and poorly defined ends' could effect the fundamental changes in legal education that were required.[131] Not only did the sociological behaviouralism of Chicago prevent Morgenthau from

128 See H. D. Lasswell and M. S. McDougal, *Jurisprudence for a Free Society: Studies in Law, Science and Policy* (New Haven, CT: New Haven Press, 1992); also Kalman, *Legal Realism at Yale*, p. 178.

129 McDougal, 'International Law, Power and Policy, pp. 157–9.

130 M. McDougal, 'Law and Power', *American Journal of International Law*, 46 (1952), pp. 102–14, at 103.

131 Lasswell and McDougal, 'Legal Education and Public Policy', p. 207.

being assimilated by his new field of Political Science, but it also seemed to have dashed his hopes of pursing a functionalist approach to international law the way he had still envisaged in 1940.

Morgenthau's obvious aversion to the behaviouralist methods he encountered at Chicago is already apparent in his 1946 monograph, *Scientific Man vs. Power Politics*. Originally based on a lecture he gave at the New School for Social Research in New York in 1940, the book argued that the great mistake of the late nineteenth and early twentieth centuries had been to assume that the social world was susceptible to rational control conceived after the model of the natural sciences (a model, moreover, that the natural sciences themselves no longer adhered to), while domestic and international experiences told a different story.[132] Under the influence of John Dewey and others, it had been endeavoured to replace politics with science such that political manoeuvring became the scientific 'plan', the political decision the scientific 'solution', the politician the 'expert', the statesman the 'brain-truster' and the legislator the 'legal engineer'.[133] Yet politics was an art, and not a science, Morgenthau insisted, and what was needed was the 'wisdom and moral strength of the statesman' rather than the rationality of the engineer: 'Contemptuous of power politics and incapable of the statesmanship which alone is able to master it, the age has tried to make politics a science. By doing so, it has demonstrated its intellectual confusion, moral blindness, and political decay.'[134]

Undoubtedly disturbed by the way the Political Science department at Chicago was treating him, Morgenthau proceeded to throw all social scientific thought under the rubric of 'rationalism', and derogatorily label the academic spirit of the time 'scientism'. Schools of thought had become 'religious sects, fighting each other in the name of the full social truth which each claims to possess',[135] and no political thinker could 'expect to be heard who would not, at least in his terminology, pay tribute to the spirit of science and, by claiming his propositions to be "realistic," "technical," or "experimental," assume their compliance with scientific standards'.[136] This, Morgenthau complained, was nonsense, for there was 'no indication

132 H. J. Morgenthau, *Scientific Man vs. Power Politics* (University of Chicago Press, 1946), pp. 10 and 107.
133 *Ibid.*, pp. 31–2.   134 *Ibid.*, p. 16.
135 *Ibid.*, p. 144.   136 *Ibid.*, p. 33.

that the trained social scientist as actor on the social scene is more competent than the layman to solve social problems, with the exception of technical problems of limited scope'.[137]

Morgenthau was well aware that the book would not go down well with his colleagues in Chicago and, to make matters worse, it proceeded to receive terrible reviews, as he himself later admitted.[138] One reviewer pertinently pointed out that, 'scientific man having been determined upon as the scapegoat, the author flays about in every direction, associating with scientific man everything of which he disapproves at least since the dawn of the modern era'.[139] Another asserted that it was

not so much rationalism which Morgenthau criticizes so severely but an atrophied form of it which he has cut down and compressed to fit the scientific mind. Common English usage already has mutilated our concept of science to such an extent that we are forced to use a prefix whenever we refer to any science but natural science, and now Morgenthau comes along performing a like operation on reason and rationalism![140]

According to Morgenthau's own admission, it was more luck than anything else that prevented the publication from having any immediate consequences: 'I was fortunate that I had already received tenure a few weeks before that book [*Scientific Man vs. Power Politics*] came out, because I am certain that if the book had come out first, either I would not have received it at all, or else it would have been a very difficult task to obtain it.'[141] And in a letter to Michael Oakeshott (1901–90), Morgenthau wrote:

I can now see clearly that my attempts to make clear the distinctions between rationalism and rational inquiry, scientism and science, were in vain. I think I was fully aware of the importance and the difficulty of these distinctions when I wrote the book, and it is now obvious to me that I have failed in the task to make my meaning clear.[142]

---

137 *Ibid.*, p. 179.
138 'When it [*Scientific Man vs. Power Politics*] came out, it received the most disastrous reviews one can imagine'. Morgenthau, 'Interview with Bernhard Johnson', p. 371.
139 R. K. Gooch, 'Review of Morgenthau, *Scientific Man vs. Power Politics*', *American Political Science Review*, 41 (1947), pp. 335–6, at 336.
140 R. De Visme Williamson, 'Review of Morgenthau, *Scientific Man vs. Power Politics*', *Journal of Politics*, 9 (1947), pp. 115–17, at 116.
141 Morgenthau, 'Interview with Bernhard Johnson', p. 371.
142 Letter from H. J. Morgenthau to M. Oakeshott, 22 May 1948, HJM-Container 44.

As it so happened, luck was on Morgenthau's side, and with the success of *Politics Among Nations* in 1948, coupled with support from Hutchins, his place in the Political Science faculty at Chicago was secured.[143] And the more established he became, the more explicit was the critique he would voice against all these incomprehensible political scientists around him. One instance was a review article, published in the *American Political Science Review*, of Lasswell and Abraham Kaplan's well-known work *Power and Society: A Framework for Political Inquiry*.[144] Though written by 'the most eminent disciple of the Chicago school of political science and one of the most promising younger adherents of logical positivism', Morgenthau began by taking issue with the very first sentence of the book, which asserted that it was a book of 'political theory, not an analysis of the contemporary or impending political situation'.[145] For was it not rather a by-product of a research project on wartime communication with an immediate practical purpose? And how could a study centred on a quantitative content analysis based on 'either platitudinous, circular, or tautological' definitions and propositions deem itself to be a work of political theory, when it at best conveys 'information which Aristotle would have taken for granted'? Conceiving of political science as a purely empirical endeavour, with no attempt to articulate a political philosophy or link it with empirical enquiry, Morgenthau fumed, was both 'a contradiction in terms and a monstrosity':

There is an element of tragedy in the spectacle of two superbly endowed minds failing so thoroughly in spite of great ability and great effort. Yet that tragedy is not so much the tragedy of two men as the tragedy of political science and philosophy in America ... Our authors are among the most gifted representatives of schools which at present ride the crest of the wave. Yet in truth they represent an obsolescent point of view. The book perhaps constitutes the most extreme, and therefore self-defeating, product of the fundamental errors of those schools. It may well contribute to their demise

143 Indeed, Morgenthau had found a lasting friend in Hutchins. A letter from Hutchins to Morgenthau, dated 28 September 1971, reads: 'Dear Hans: I am very grateful for your kindness – a quality that has characterized you in all your relations with me for many years. I think I'm going to make it [to an event he had been invited to by Morgenthau], and one of the reasons I hope so is that I want to see you and sit at your feet again as I have often in the past', HJM-Container 28.
144 H. J. Morgenthau, 'Review of H. D. Lasswell and A. Kaplan, *Power and Society: A Framework for Political Inquiry* (New Haven, CT: Yale University Press, 1950)', *American Political Science Review*, 46 (1952), pp. 230–4.
145 Lasswell and Kaplan, *Power and Society*, p. ix.

by virtue of its own absurdity. There is already at work – in Chicago as elsewhere – a strong reaction to the 'straightforward empirical standpoint' of our authors. It is true that Mr. Lasswell and Mr. Kaplan don't know it yet. The research foundations don't know it yet. The professional organizations don't know it yet. But an ever-increasing number of able and vigorous thinkers do know it.[146]

Like many of those uncomfortable with the new methods at work in Political Science in the 1940s and 1950s, Morgenthau hoped that behaviouralism was simply a passing trend. Yet it was nonetheless rare – if not unique – to hear from someone endowed with a chair in Political Science at a leading US university that politics was an art, and not an empirical science, and that, as he declared in *Scientific Man vs. Power Politics*, '[n]o quantitative extension of scientific knowledge can solve those perennial problems which art, religion, and philosophy intend to answer'.[147]

While never engaging substantively with Political Science, Morgenthau continued to publish and speak about the 'state of the discipline' throughout the 1950s and beyond. It was clear that the institutional surroundings in Chicago were troubling him: a large majority of the Political Science department was pursuing a type of research that was completely foreign to his *Denkstil* of German *Staatslehre*, while others, notably the newcomer Leo Strauss, would soon attract a considerable following with an emphasis on the classics and the study of 'true' political theory. Morgenthau, somewhat left out in the cold, proceeded to deprecate both. '[M]uch of quantitative political science has become a pretentious collection of trivialities', he asserted, while political theory

has remained an indispensable part of the curriculum not because of the vital influence it has been able to exert upon our thinking, but rather because of a vague conviction that there is something venerable and respectable in this otherwise useless exercise. Thus the academic concern with political theory has tended to become an intellectually and practically meaningless ritual which one had to engage in for reasons of tradition and prestige before one would occupy oneself with the things that really mattered.[148]

---

146 Morgenthau, 'Review of Lasswell and Kaplan, *Power and Society*', pp. 233–4.
147 Morgenthau, *Scientific Man vs. Power Politics*, p. 109.
148 H. J. Morgenthau, 'Reflections on the State of Political Science', *Review of Politics*, 17 (1955), pp. 431–60, at 442 and 444.

Ultimately, what really mattered was 'the distinction between what is worth knowing intellectually and what is useful for practice',[149] and this was precisely what Political Science was lacking. The reason for this, according to Morgenthau, was the fact that the creation of departments of Political Science in the United States 'reflected the negative attitude of other academic disciplines, especially law, towards certain aspects of the political world'.[150] Political Science was a random collection of subject matters tied together through a 'vague orientation towards the nature and activities of the state and toward activities which have in turn a direct bearing upon the state'; the result, Morgenthau charged, was that Political Science 'has no unity of outlook, method, and purpose'.[151]

The methodological disenchantment of German-Jewish legal scholars who came to populate US Political Science departments is a defining feature of the way International Relations developed as an independent sphere of study. It is also an underdeveloped element in recent attempts to write the 'disciplinary history' of the field. John H. Herz, Morgenthau's émigré colleague who had also been under the wing of Hans Kelsen, wrote in a similar way about Political Science, and went even so far as to label himself and the likes of Morgenthau as 'traditionalists'. In a 1971 article entitled 'Relevancies and Irrelevancies in the Study of International Relations', Herz, going after the work of James N. Rosenau in particular, argued that they, the traditionalists,

have been able to predict outcomes on the basis of common sense analysis for which no gaming or computer-feeding was necessary. Hans Morgenthau's prediction that nothing will come of the Paris peace negotiations as long as we permit the present South Vietnamese government to be a copartner because no government will negotiate its own demise is a simple conclusion for which no ever-so-sophisticated analysis of the decision-making process, of alliances, of coalition, or of conflict resolution is required.[152]

Similarly, Strauss argued that the 'new science of politics' had come into being 'through an attempted break with common sense'. They,

---

149 *Ibid.*, p. 440.
150 H. J. Morgenthau, manuscript of a paper delivered at a conference at Northwestern University, June 1954, p. 1, HJM-Container 169.
151 Morgenthau, 'Reflections on the State of Political Science', p. 439.
152 J. H. Herz, 'Relevancies and Irrelevancies in the Study of International Relations', *Polity*, 5 (1971), pp. 25–47, at 36–7.

the 'old-fashioned political scientists', who had little concern with methodological questions, continued their 'old-fashioned practice' of adhering to 'Aristotelian political science', albeit with 'a somewhat uneasy conscience'.[153]

Herein lies the paradox in what Morgenthau was trying to accomplish: he had called for the incorporation of an empirical element into the study of international law, but by empirical he did not mean the type of analysis that one associates with modern social science. This is what his biographer Christoph Frei fails to appreciate fully when he identifies a 'remarkable change in Morgenthau's position' from the 'active and outspoken advocate of empirical research, in opposition to the prevailing trend in German public and constitutional law', to being 'no less emphatic in attacking an exaggerated enthusiasm for empirical research' in the United States.[154] Morgenthau's idea of empirical research, according to his *Denkstil* of German *Staatslehre*, was quite different from what has been developed and applied to this day in Political Science, as he would himself soon discover in Chicago. His subsequent attack on anything 'scientific' is more a reaction to the failure to come to terms with the methods he would have needed to engage with – both in Political Science *and* Law – rather than a rejection of his previous research agenda.[155] Nevertheless, he would never return to that agenda, instead using his newly acquired tenure track position to consolidate his role as an illustrious commentator on international affairs talking 'common sense' to a broader public. Once and for all, the juridical analyst *in* the field of International Law had turned into an external commentator *of* law.

153 L. Strauss, 'An Epilogue', in H. J. Storing (ed.), *Essays on the Scientific Study of Politics* (NewYork, NY: Holt, Rinehart andWinston, 1962), pp. 307–27, at 316 and 308.

154 C. Frei, *Hans J. Morgenthau: An Intellectual Biography* (Baton Rouge, LA: Louisiana State University Press, 2001), p. 194.

155 Morgenthau did engage with the functionalist approach of David Mitrany (1888–1975) in *Politics Among Nations*, third edition, pp. 525–36, and even wrote the Introduction to the 1966 edition of Mitrany's *A Working Peace System: An Argument for the Functional Development of International Organization* [1943] (Chicago, IL: Quadrangle Books, 1966), pp. 7–11. Yet Mitrany's notion of functionalism was altogether different to the way the term was used by Morgenthau and the legal realists – or, indeed, the way it was has since been employed by Luhmann in his impressive work on law in society: N. Luhmann, *Das Recht der Gesellschaft* (Frankfurt a.M.: Suhrkamp, 1995).

Conclusion

Morgenthau's combination of legal heritage and subsequent 'founding father' of the realist school in International Relations earned him the status of representative of the rule-sceptical position in some of the International Law literature.[156] That status is to a large extent merited, for here was someone who, unlike E. H. Carr or Raymond Aron (1905–83), for instance, was actually not an external critic but one of their own, a scholar versed in international legal theory who had consciously decided to focus on the lust for power and the underlying social forces determining the normative scope and bindingness of the law. It is precisely out of the disillusionment with the way the dominant doctrine of legal formalism was thinking about 'politics in terms of law' – rather than like the Ancient Greeks, who had still 'thought of law in terms of politics'[157] – that Morgenthau would develop his critique of what he called 'decadent legalistic statecraft' operating under the motto of *fiat justitia, pereat mundus*.[158]

As the previous three chapters have tried to demonstrate, it is not as if Morgenthau had turned to the rule-sceptical position overnight, or that his views on the matter were singularly coherent. With reference to our conceptual matrix it is possible to highlight the steps in the development of his thought. The attempt in his doctoral dissertation to explain away the empirical ineffectiveness of legal dispute settlement mechanisms by distinguishing between disputes and tensions situates him with the rule approach and opens him up to the charge of being an apologist; his reaction to the resulting criticism from Hersch Lauterpacht then saw him move back into the quadrant of the indelible sceptic. His subsequent engagement with the work of Hans Kelsen sees him back with the rule approach, but his notion of sanctions differs from that of Kelsen because validity, according to Morgenthau, lies not in the mere existence of a sanction-rule, but in the context-dependent reality of its enforcement. This is

---

156 See, for instance, B. S. Chimni, *International Law and World Order: A Critique of Contemporary Approaches* (New Delhi: Sage Publications, 1993); also A. Fischer-Lescano and P. Liste. 'Völkerrechtspolitik: Zu Trennung und Verknüpfung von Politik und Recht der Weltgesellschaft', *Zeitschrift für Internationale Beziehungen*, 12 (2005), pp. 209–49.

157 Morgenthau, *Scientific Man vs. Power Politics*, p. 98.

158 *Ibid.*, p. 107.

where Kelsen and Morgenthau part ways, and where Morgenthau inevitably slides back towards the sceptics. Thereafter, his call for a functionalist understanding of international law upon his arrival in the United States sees him move towards the policy-approach position, although his analysis, for reasons discussed above, did not go beyond the preliminary musings in his 1940 article in the *American Journal of International Law,* and ultimately leave him open to the critique of being utopian. Upon his arrival in Chicago, Morgenthau continued teaching introductory courses in public international law, but ceased to identify with the 'invisible college of international lawyers'. Once we reach *Scientific Man vs. Power Politics* and his idiosyncratic views on statecraft as a form of art, Morgenthau is no longer part of the international legal discourse and, for analytical purposes, at least, falls out of the matrix altogether.

5   Legalism, romanticism and irresponsible statecraft

As the preceding three chapters showed, Morgenthau was very much a Kelsenian formalist worried about the dangers posed by adherence to the dominant doctrine of legal positivism. This doctrine not only occluded a large part of reality, but also incorporated into its analysis empirically unverifiable elements. By contrast, a truly realist theory of international law, Morgenthau contended, would acknowledge and engage with its social substratum: the political. Anything else would be 'legalism', the artificial separation of the juridical sphere from not just the other normative spheres of mores and morals, but also of all insights from the social sciences and psychology. The result was a culture of irresponsible statecraft and the identification of 'the moral aspirations of a particular state' with 'the moral laws that govern the universe', an identification the fifth principle of political realism explicitly warned against in later editions of *Politics Among Nations*.[1]

In his 1940 call for a functionalist approach,[2] in *Scientific Man vs. Power Politics*,[3] in various versions of *Politics Among Nations* and then also in *In Defense of the National Interest*,[4] Morgenthau continuously spoke of this 'legalism', of the 'political ideology of Geneva', or of the 'legalistic-moralistic approach' to international politics. Such language has often been interpreted as meaning that Morgenthau deemed international law to be irrelevant, 'idealistic' or 'utopian',

---

1 H. J. Morgenthau, *Politics Among Nations: The Struggle for Power and Peace.* Third edition (New York, NY: Alfred A. Knopf, 1960), p. 11.
2 H. J. Morgenthau, 'Positivism, Functionalism, and International Law', *American Journal of International Law*, 34 (1940), pp. 260–84.
3 H. J. Morgenthau, *Scientific Man vs. Power Politics* (University of Chicago Press, 1946).
4 H. J. Morgenthau, *In Defense of the National Interest: A Critical Examination of American Foreign Policy* (New York, NY: Alfred A. Knopf, 1951).

and taken as a justification for focusing on material capabilities and the distribution of power instead. Yet as Morgenthau was eager to point out from the early 1950s onwards, this was not at all what he was trying to argue.

By 1951, Morgenthau had reached a public prominence that he himself could hardly have envisaged, particularly after the negative reactions to *Scientific Man vs. Power Politics*. But the success of his textbook *Politics Among Nations*, his appearance on the radar screen of policy circles through his stint as a consultant to George Kennan's Policy Planning Staff of the US State Department between 1949 and 1951, and finally his publication of *In Defense of the National Interest*, changed all that. Ever since his call for a realist theory of international law had fallen on deaf ears in 1940, Morgenthau had been distancing himself from the label 'realism', as the first edition of *Politics Among Nations*, which does not yet include the six principles of a realist theory of international politics, strikingly attests to. But as William Scheuerman neatly outlines in his recent book,[5] Morgenthau's stance shifted dramatically following an 'atomic flash somewhere in Asiatic Russia in 1949'.[6] Armed with his new central concept of the national interest, Morgenthau went on the offensive against all those, the Truman administration included, who conceived of the Soviet threat in legalistic and moralistic terms as one of 'good versus evil', rather than as a *political* problem of achieving a negotiated settlement.

This chapter will seek to unpack Morgenthau's (re)formulation of political realism, focusing in particular on the image of law propagated therein. I will do so by building on Morgenthau's 1949 critique of the work of E. H. Carr, a critique that will help to shed light on the concept of the 'national interest', the distinction between realism and utopianism, and the vocabulary of legalism, moralism and sentimentalism. What will emerge is a political realism that is far from being devoid of legal or moral considerations, but rather one that warns against the instrumentalization of a formalistic conception

---

5 W. E. Scheuerman, *Hans Morgenthau: Realism and Beyond* (Cambridge: Polity Press, 2009), pp. 70–100.

6 H. J. Morgenthau, 'The Conquest of the United States of Germany', *Bulletin of the Atomic Scientists*, 6 (1950), pp. 21–6, at 25. See also Scheuerman, *Hans Morgenthau*, p. 75.

of law by political powers that seek to clothe their aspirations in the language of universality.

E. H. Carr, the utopian of power

It is curious that E. H. Carr holds such a central position among the modern classics of International Relations given that most of his long life's work was spent doing and writing other things. Indeed, were it not for *The Twenty Years' Crisis 1919–1939*,[7] one would be at pains to find anything resembling a theoretical or conceptual contribution to international politics in the many books he wrote. Instead, one would remember Carr in one of his many other guises, as the philosopher of history for the high-school classroom (in the form of another classic and standard textbook, *What is History?*[8]), as the author of the mind-boggling and controversial *History of Soviet Russia* in fourteen volumes,[9] as the writer of remarkable but totally forgotten books on Dostoyevsky, Marx, the Russian revolutionary exiles and – arguably his best book – Bakunin,[10] or as one of the leading figures of *The Times* newspaper during the Second World War. We now have Jonathan Haslam's impressive biography to tell us all about the various stages of Carr's fascinating career.[11] Yet be that as it may, the field of International Relations did not hesitate long before singling out *The Twenty Years' Crisis* as the 'representative text', and labelling its author a 'classical realist' who, as the common story is succinctly summarized by Peter Wilson,

launched a devastating attack on 'utopian' thinking of the inter-war period; who rectified the most glaring omission in that body of thought, the almost total neglect of the factor of power; who reasserted the 'three essential tenets in Machiavelli's doctrine', that history is a process of cause and effect that can be analysed and understood by intellectual effort, but not guided by 'imagination', that practice creates theory and not theory, practice, and that morality is a product of power, not power of morality; and who, not without a certain diabolical relish, reasserted Count Walewski's dictum

7 E. H. Carr, *The Twenty Years' Crisis, 1919–1939: An Introduction to the Study of International Relations* [1939]. Reissued with a New Introduction and additional material by Michael Cox (Basingstoke: Palgrave, 2001).
8 E. H. Carr, *What is History?* (London: Macmillan, 1961).
9 E. H. Carr, *A History of Soviet Russia*. 14 volumes (London: Macmillan, 1950–78).
10 E. H. Carr, *Michael Bakunin* (London: Macmillan, 1937).
11 J. Haslam, *The Vices of Integrity. E. H. Carr, 1892–1982* (London: Verso, 1999).

that it was the business of the diplomat to cloak the interest of his country in the language of universal justice.[12]

Just as with Morgenthau, a one-sided interpretation of a small part of Carr's work was appropriated as part of the realist canon, and much of what was original and potentially interesting in his writings was occluded from view. If Morgenthau's contribution to International Relations theory was boiled down to his six principles of realism in the second edition of *Politics Among Nations*, the fifth chapter of *The Twenty Years' Crisis*, entitled 'The Realist Critique', was generally deemed sufficient to convey the position of yet another key realist. Indeed, the average undergraduate will most likely not even get to parts three and four of the book, on morality and law respectively.

Until recently, that is. For just as with Morgenthau, though on a much smaller scale and generally confined to 'English School' International Relations in the United Kingdom, a group of scholars have been rehabilitating E. H. Carr's thought in a way resembling the 'reclaiming texts' strategy Richard Ned Lebow referred to in the case of Morgenthau.[13] The likes of Ken Booth,[14] Paul Howe,[15] Charles Jones[16] and Michael Cox[17] have all sought to save Carr from the grip of the realists and show that his work was not as one-sided as it was generally made out to be, and that there was, after all, a certain degree of continuity and coherence among the various hats Carr wore. They argue that Carr's argument was not simply a realist attack on utopianism, but that Carr was striving to find a synthesis between the two; that it was impossible to establish international order on power alone; and that law and morality did play a central role in international politics. The result was dubbed 'utopian realism': *The Twenty Years' Crisis* is said to fluctuate between pessimistic realism and utopian optimism, and the synthetic interplay between

---

12 P. Wilson, 'Radicalism for a Conservative Purpose: The Peculiar Realism of E. H. Carr', *Millennium*, 30 (2001), pp. 123–36, at 123; notes omitted.
13 See Chapter 1.
14 K. Booth, 'Security in Anarchy: Utopian Realism in Theory and Practice', *International Affairs*, 67 (1991), pp. 527–45.
15 P. Howe, 'The Utopian Realism of E. H. Carr', *Review of International Studies*, 20 (1994), pp. 277–97.
16 C. Jones, 'Carr, Mannheim, and a Post-positivist Science of International Relations', *Political Studies*, XLV (1997), pp. 232–46; C. Jones, *E. H. Carr and International Relations. A Duty to Lie* (Cambridge University Press, 1998).
17 M. Cox (ed.), *E. H. Carr: A Critical Appraisal* (Basingstoke: Palgrave, 2000).

the two only comes to light when one looks beyond the usual passages and begins to construct a vision of E. H. Carr that sees him slide towards the ranks of those who, in loose International Relations terminology, go under the label of 'critical theory'.

Morgenthau held Carr in high esteem, and was even instrumental in getting some of his books, including *The Twenty Years' Crisis*, published in the United States. Yet this did not prevent him from writing an extremely critical review article of some of Carr's major works in the first issue of the new journal *World Politics*.[18] While calling Carr's work 'a contribution to political thought of the highest order', asserting that no contemporary thinker, with the exception of Reinhold Niebuhr, had 'seen more clearly and exposed with more acute brilliance the essential defects of Western political thought',[19] Morgenthau was soon finding fault with some of Carr's basic contentions, and this, in typically Morgenthauian fashion, in no uncertain terms. Carr's overall endeavour of finding a new synthesis between 'realism and utopia, theory and practice, ethics and politics', was ultimately a 'failure' because of a lack of sufficient philosophical foundations on which his views were based: 'Mr. Carr sets out to discover a new morality in the political world with only the vaguest notion of what morality is.' The last paragraph of the review was damning:

Mr. Carr, philosophically so ill-equipped, has no transcendent point of view from which to survey the political scene and to appraise the phenomenon of power. Thus the political moralist transforms himself into a utopian of power. Whoever holds seeming superiority of power becomes of necessity the repository of superior morality as well. Power thus corrupts not only the actor on the political scene, but even the observer, unfortified by a transcendent standard of ethics. Mr. Carr might have learned that lesson from the fate of the political romantics of whom the outstanding representatives are Adam Müller and Carl Schmitt. It is a dangerous thing to be a Machiavelli. It is a disastrous thing to be a Machiavelli without *virtù*.[20]

The above passage is in itself quite remarkable. Indeed, it was much appreciated by no other than Leo Strauss, who writes in a letter to Morgenthau, who had sent him a copy of the review:

18 H. J. Morgenthau, 'The Political Science of E. H. Carr', *World Politics*, 1 (1948), pp. 127–34.
19 *Ibid.*, p. 133.   20 *Ibid.*, p. 134.

It was very good of you to let me have this excellent and well-written paper. I was particularly pleased by the observation that we are so much in agreement with each other, and indeed, if one may judge from the necessarily sketchy and cryptic remarks in the last paragraph, that we are in complete agreement.[21]

Cryptic the last sentences of the review certainly are, and well worth unpacking. For one, they highlight the way in which Morgenthau saw the relationship between power politics and morality as being one of intricate interdependence: not only is it impossible, Morgenthau appears to suggest, to reflect about power from an amoral point of view (as many of his readers often supposed), but he also asserts that the political actor is prone to let her power aspirations move her towards a discourse in which power superiority is equated with taking the moral high ground as well. Moreover, if this is not recognized, the political analyst himself will enter into this apologist discourse of legitimizing the will to power of states. Finally, Morgenthau's powerful concluding remarks that make reference to Carl Schmitt's work on romanticism and Machiavelli's complex notion of *virtù* also tell us much about the way in which he conceived of his own realist position.

Ideology and utopia

Key to our exploration of Morgenthau's legalism critique is the concept of ideology, the way it was developed by Karl Mannheim in his opus *Ideology and Utopia*.[22] Morgenthau met Mannheim in the 1920s at the *Frankfurt Institut für Sozialforschung* (the famous 'Red Castle'), before leaving for Geneva, and Mannheim's book had a significant impact on the way Morgenthau conceived of the ways in which political actors 'refer to their policies' in terms of ethical and

21 Letter from L. Strauss to H. J. Morgenthau, dated 11 December 1948, HJM-Container 52.
22 K. Mannheim, *Ideology and Utopia: An Introduction to the Sociology of Knowledge* [1936] (London: Routledge & Kegan Paul, 1968). Mannheim's book is a difficult one to cite. It was first published in German in 1929; after emigrating to the United Kingdom, Mannheim then published an English version in 1936 (translated by Peter Maus) to which he added substantial sections. The English version was then used to create a third, enlarged and reworked German edition in 1952, and then a fourth edition in 1965 – again with more additions. The 1968 reprint of the 1936 English edition will be referred to throughout this chapter, as it is the one that Carr will have read and Morgenthau cites in *Politics Among Nations*.

legal principles in order to conceal 'the element of power, inherent in all politics'.[23] Since Carr also mentions *Ideology and Utopia* in the preface to the first edition of *The Twenty Years' Crisis* as being, alongside Reinhold Niebuhr's *Moral Man and Immoral Society*,[24] one of the books he was 'specially indebted' to,[25] it is worthwhile dwelling on Mannheim's text briefly. It will allow us to shed light on Morgenthau's legalism critique by juxtaposing it to Carr's arguments which Morgenthau had so vehemently criticized.

The title of Mannheim's book, *Ideology and Utopia*, is rather misleading, because the two concepts do not receive equal attention, and are, moreover, far from constituting clearly delineated (not to mention contrasting) terms, as some commentators continue to suggest. Central to the text is Mannheim's conceptualization of ideology, and in particular his distinction between a 'particular' and a 'total' conception of ideology – both denote phenomena of 'false consciousness', but with differing scope and radicalness. The particular conception remains on the psychological level and refers to the ideas, opinions, statements and propositions of an individual subject that are deemed to be 'more or less conscious disguises of the real nature of a situation, the true recognition of which would not be in accord with his interests'.[26] The total conception, by contrast, moves up to a more radical scepticism on the ontological and noological level of thought, and refers to 'the ideology of an age or of a concrete historico-social group, e.g. a class, when we are concerned with the characteristics and composition of the total structure of the mind of this epoch or of this group'.[27] Both conceptualizations make a subject's ideas and statements a function of the social conditions of that subject, but the total conception questions the actual worldview (*Weltbild* or *Weltanschauung*) of the individual or the group as such. Total ideology is when a certain thought style (*Denkstil*) is functionally related to the entire system of presuppositions on which it is founded; a statement by

23 Morgenthau, *Politics Among Nations: The Struggle for Power and Peace*. First edition (New York, NY: Alfred A. Knopf, 1948), p. 61.
24 R. Niebuhr, *Moral Man and Immoral Society: A Study in Ethics and Politics* (New York, NY: Scribner, 1932).
25 Carr, *The Twenty Years' Crisis*, p. cvii; *Hans J. Morgenthau: An Intellectual Biography* (Baton Rouge, LA: Louisiana State University Press, 2001).
26 Manheim, *Ideology and Utopia*, p. 49.   27 *Ibid.*, pp. 49–50.

an individual of a group can thus be decoupled from the disposition or intention of the individual and directly attributed to the collective subject.[28]

At the outset of Chapter 5 of *Politics Among Nations*, entitled 'The Ideological Element in International Policies', Morgenthau added a lengthy footnote in which he specified that 'The concept of ideology used in this chapter corresponds to what Karl Mannheim has called "particular ideology".'[29] And it is certainly not without bearing that he chose to focus on the 'particular' meaning; and not just in the pages of *Politics Among Nations*, but throughout much of what he wrote. Indeed, Morgenthau and Mannheim inevitably shared some of the same inspiration, while at Frankfurt, from the social-psychological theories of Freud and Alfred Adler (1870–1937) that were gaining momentum at the time. It is thus no accident that both Morgenthau and Mannheim played with the psychological underpinnings of social behaviour and normative structures – as, indeed, did Hans Kelsen and many others. In Chapters 2 and 3, I elaborated on how these ideas were successively introduced into some of Morgenthau's earlier writings, before also finding their way into his standard textbook. 'It is the very nature of politics to compel the actor on the political scene to use ideologies in order to disguise the immediate goal of his action', Morgenthau wrote in *Politics Among Nations*. And that goal was political power. At stake here were 'psychological forces' which 'engender the ideologies of international policies and make them weapons in the struggle for power on the international scene'.[30]

Mannheim's development of utopia is much more problematic, an issue that Mannheim was very much aware of. Indeed, right from the start of Chapter 4 of *Ideology and Utopia*, entitled 'The Utopian Mentality', Mannheim is at pains to spell out how the term utopia was in any way different to that of ideology. 'A state of mind is utopian when it is incongruous with the state of reality within which it occurs', Mannheim begins,[31] but he was very aware of the limitations of this definition, the logical conclusion of which was that the

28 See also W. Hofman, *Karl Mannheim zur Einführung* (Hamburg: Junius, 1996), pp. 91–3.
29 Morgenthau, *Politics Among Nations*, first edition, p. 61.
30 *Ibid.*, pp. 62–3.
31 Mannheim, *Ideology and Utopia*, p. 173.

ideological and utopian consciousness were structurally identical.[32] This is clear from the discussion that followed:

Ideologies are the situationally transcendent ideas which never succeed *de facto* in the realization of their projected contents. Though they often become the good-intentioned motives for the subjective conduct of the individual, when they are actually embodied in practice their meanings are most frequently distorted ... Utopias too transcend the social situation, for they too orient conduct towards elements which the situation, in so far as it is realized at the time, does not contain. But they are not ideologies, i.e. they are not ideologies in the measure and in so far as they succeed through counteractivity in transforming the existing historical reality into one more in accord with their own conceptions.[33]

Mannheim then literally gives up a few pages later: the only criterion on which to distinguish ideology from utopia was that of 'realization':

Ideas which later turned out to have been only distorted representations of a past or potential social order were ideological, while those which were adequately realized in the succeeding social order were relative utopias. The actualized realities of the past put an end to the conflict of mere opinions about what in earlier situationally transcendent ideas was relatively utopian bursting asunder the bonds of the existing order, and what was an ideology which merely served to conceal reality. The extent to which ideas are realized constitutes a *supplementary and retroactive standard* for making distinctions between facts which as long as they are contemporary are buried under the partisan conflict of opinion.[34]

In other words, ideas can have a utopian core and at the same time contain ideological elements: ideology and utopia can only be distinguished in terms of their effectiveness and moral quality on the level of intentions, but structurally and in the idea they are identical.[35] The important place that Mannheim continues to have in the literature on utopia is not because he proposed a novel way of distinguishing the two, but rather because he blended the two terms in a way that had not been done previously.[36]

---

32 See Hofman, *Karl Mannheim zur Einführung*, p. 108.
33 Mannheim, *Ideology and Utopia*, pp. 175–6.
34 *Ibid.*, p. 184; emphasis added.
35 Hofman, *Karl Mannheim zur Einführung*, p. 111.
36 See A. Neusüss, 'Schwierigkeiten einer Soziologie des utopischen Denkens', in Neusüss (ed.), *Utopie: Begriff und Phänomen des Utopischen* (Frankfurt a.M. and New York, NY: Campus, 1986), pp. 13–112, at 23.

I emphasize this point because it has an important bearing on the way we read *The Twenty Years' Crisis*, a book that Carr, under the obvious influence of Mannheim, had originally wanted to call 'Reality and Utopia'. Charles Jones, in his recent work on Carr, has thus also tried to juxtapose these two binary relations, arguing that when Carr 'adopted the main argument of *Ideology and Utopia*', he 'twisted its rhetorical structure almost out of recognition'.[37] Carr termed 'utopianism' what Mannheim had called 'ideology': namely, according to Jones, the 'rationalization, of those in power, of their privileged positions'. Realism, on the other hand, was not the 'diametrically opposed rationalization of political change' that Mannheim had called utopia, but rather incorporated Mannheim's 'technique of the sociology of knowledge':

In sliding from an account of the *Realpolitik* tradition to one of the sociology of knowledge, and bringing both under the term 'realism', Carr departs from the symmetry of Mannheim. He uses 'realism' to cover part of the conservative ideology that Mannheim labels 'ideology', but much more as a label for the sociology of knowledge, by which Mannheim had sought to transcend the sterile opposition of ideology and utopia. In short, the realism and utopianism of Part 2 of *The Twenty Years' Crisis* are not neatly counterposed rationalizations of conservatism and radical change in the rather simple way that a very different ideology and utopia had been for Mannheim.[38]

Referring back to the brief discussion of Mannheim's concepts above, it seems unclear whether Jones is accurate when he talks of 'symmetry' and 'opposition'. It is questionable if there ever was 'symmetry' in Mannheim between ideology and utopia, and certainly no 'sterile opposition' amounting to an 'antiphonal' distinction between conservatism and revisionism.[39] Be that as it may, however, important is Jones' valid claim that Carr's understanding of realism, influenced by Mannheim's approach, was not an advocacy of *Realpolitik*, but rather an application of Mannheim's sociology of knowledge. This is where the approaches of Morgenthau and Carr overlap significantly. Just like Morgenthau, Carr's realism is not so much based on Bismarckian conceptions of power politics as it is on a 'realistic'

---

37 Jones, 'Carr, Mannheim, and a Post-positivist Science of International Relations', p. 216.
38 *Ibid.*, p. 238.   39 *Ibid.*, p. 235.

assessment of the social forces at play in the establishment of norms, mores and morals, to use Morgenthau's vocabulary.

Yet such a realistic assessment of social forces was not possible, according to Morgenthau, without consciously making a moral decision about the nature of politics – and this, he charged, was precisely what the likes of Carr were not doing. Carr grouped everyone under the label 'utopian' who was, in his eyes, guilty of unjustified optimism, unqualified belief in obligatory arbitration, of playing down the failure of the League of Nations, and of advocating peaceful change through international legislation. Morgenthau's distinction between utopian and realist policies was on a different level of analysis: 'the utopian and realist positions in international affairs do not necessarily differ in the policies they advocate, but they part company over their general philosophies of politics and their way of thinking about matters political'.[40] Carr called utopian everything on the level of policy that he judged to be unrealistic; Morgenthau, much closer to Mannheim's conceptualization, labelled as utopian ideas that socially construct reality in such a way as to lead to an apolitical outlook on international relations that occludes the underlying power aspirations of states.

Unsurprisingly, Hersch Lauterpacht was one of Carr's main 'utopian' targets. According to Carr, the problems with the likes of Lauterpacht was that they asserted that all international disputes, irrespective of their nature, could be settled through the application of legal rules:

It is a pity that Professor Lauterpacht, having brilliantly conducted his analysis up to the point where the unwillingness of states is recognized as the limiting factor in the justiciability of international disputes, should have been content to leave it there, treating this 'unwillingness', in true utopian fashion, as perverse and undeserving of the attention of an international lawyer.[41]

Lauterpacht was well aware of Carr's jibing. The collected papers of Lauterpacht, edited by his son Sir Eli Lauterpacht,[42] contain both an

---

40 H. J. Morgenthau, 'Another "Great Debate": The National Interest of the United States', *American Political Science Review*, 46 (1952), pp. 961–88, at 978.
41 Carr, *The Twenty Years' Crisis*, p. 189; see also M. Koskenniemi, 'Hersch Lauterpacht (1897–1960)', in J. Beatson and R. Zimmermann (eds.), *Jurists Uprooted: German-Speaking Emigré Lawyers in Twentieth-century Britain* (Oxford University Press, 2004), pp. 601–61, at 630.
42 E. Lauterpacht (ed.), *International Law: Being the Collected Papers of Hersch Lauterpacht.* Four volumes (Cambridge University Press, 1975).

unpublished text, dated 1941, in which his father meticulously went through the way Carr had treated him in *The Twenty Years' Crisis*, as well as a lecture entitled 'Realism, Especially in International Relations', which Lauterpacht senior had held at a meeting of the Carlyle Club in 1953. The distinction between realism and idealism in the field of political action, Hersch Lauterpacht correctly pointed out, was not the same as the difference between realism and idealism in philosophy. Indeed, the realism/utopianism divide in International Relations was an odd one, in that nobody in their right mind would identify himself with the label utopian the way it was used there – indeed, he claimed, and not without reason, that what it effectively boils down to was: 'practically everyone who disagrees with Professor Carr is Utopian'.[43] Realism in the realm of politics, Lauterpacht argued, 'is nothing else than the method, or temper, or attitude most calculated to realize our desires. Who but a fool does not wish to be a realist in this sense?'[44] There was nothing in the writings of the so-called realists 'the opposite of which could not, with equal justice, be described as realism'.[45] Just as legal realism had been caricatured as being 'an essentially anti-democratic ideology to which no so-called realist would consciously have subscribed',[46] political realism was being boiled down to equally crude assertions.

Morgenthau would have undoubtedly agreed with Lauterpacht on this. Just as Lauterpacht felt misunderstood by Carr in Britain, so too did Morgenthau come to feel his ideas were abused by members of the political establishment in the United States – but, of course, in the opposite direction to Lauterpacht, as an ardent proponent of power politics. As Morgenthau himself admitted, *Politics Among Nations* was a polemical text.[47] Consciously written in the spirit of the times, it delivered frontal attacks against the 'idealists' believing in law and international institutions as the driving force in the attainment and maintenance of peace in international politics.

43 H. Lauterpacht, 'Professor Carr on International Morality' [1941], in E. Lauterpacht, *International Law, Being the Collected Papers of Hersch Lauterpacht. Volume 2: The Law of Peace, Part I: International Law in General*, pp. 67–92, at 69.

44 H. Lauterpacht, 'On Realism, Especially in International Relations' [1953], in E. Lauterpacht, *International Law, Volume 2*, pp. 52–66, at 54.

45 *Ibid.*, p. 57.

46 N. Duxbury, *Patterns of American Jurisprudence* (Oxford: Clarendon Press, 1995), p. 161.

47 H. J. Morgenthau, *Politics Among Nations: The Struggle for Power and Peace*. Second edition (New York, NY: Alfred A. Knopf, 1954), p. vii.

Yet Morgenthau never went as far as asserting that ethics and law had no place in the international realm, nor that international institutions were futile creations – what he did warn against, however, was what Oppenheim called the 'tyranny of phrases', which at times 'so turns the head that rules which absolutely never were rules of law are represented as such'.[48] Before Morgenthau knew it, however, his theory was boiled down to the formula 'might makes right', was branded immoral or amoral (many critics, it seems, did not know the difference), and taken to be an endorsement of Prussian-style *Realpolitik* by those he was criticizing. Yet such a vision of world politics was precisely what those in US foreign policy circles, grappling with the Korean War, the new superpower status of the United States, nuclear deterrence, and a lack of specialists to make sense of the regional and global dynamics of inter-state politics, were looking for to strengthen their cause. 'To Morgenthau's consternation', Lebow accurately writes, 'prominent representatives of that establishment came away with more or less the same understanding of *Politics Among Nations* as had idealists, only they endorsed its emphasis on power and alleged disparagement of ethics'.[49]

Indeed, a closer look at Morgenthau's writings reveals that his arguments were far more subtle (although arguably no less problematic) than has often been supposed. In large part due to his collaboration with Kennan's Policy Planning Department, the Morgenthau of 1950 onwards was an altogether different kettle of fish than the recent émigré who wrote *Scientific Man vs. Power Politics* and the first edition of *Politics Among Nations*. Now, Morgenthau fully identified with his new homeland and wrote in a passionate vein for the US public about 'our' country, 'our' foreign policy, 'our' national interest. What emerges is no longer the voice of the uprooted jurist, but rather the voice of an American public intellectual and policy pundit – an issue I will return to in the concluding chapter.

The aim of *In Defense of the National Interest* was to counter the generally held assumption, stemming from 'the specific experiences of

---

48 L. Oppenheim, *The Future of International Law* (Oxford: Clarendon Press, 1921), pp. 58–9; cited in H. J. Morgenthau, 'International Affairs', *The Review of Politics*, 10 (1948), pp. 493–7, at 493; see also Morgenthau, 'Positivism, Functionalism, and International Law', p. 266.

49 R. N. Lebow, *The Tragic Vision of Politics: Ethics, Interests and Orders* (Cambridge University Press, 2003), p. 39.

American history', that 'nations have a choice between power politics and another kind of foreign policy conforming to moral principles and not tainted by the desire for power'.[50] Such a view was, indeed, utopian. What was wrong with the 'internationalism' of the 1930s was that it triumphed 'in the moral terms of Wilsonianism',[51] ignorant of the political conditions under which it thrived. Maintaining that the national interest of the United States was 'identical with the interests of mankind itself', Wilsonianism effectively sought to neutralize and depoliticize, to use Carl Schmitt's vocabulary, all international relations. The result was a political naivety that inevitably ended in the disaster of the Second World War.

'There is a profound and neglected truth', the reader of *In Defense of the National Interest* is told, 'hidden in Hobbes's extreme dictum that the state creates morality as well as law and that there is neither morality nor law outside the state. Universal moral principles, such as justice or equality, are capable of guiding political action only to the extent that they have been given concrete content and have been related to political situations by society'.[52] This, Morgenthau pointed out in a subsequent article, was often interpreted as the assertion that there was no such thing as international law and morality. Yet his position, Morgenthau claimed, was 'the exact opposite': 'I have always maintained that the actions of states are subject to universal moral principles and I have been careful to differentiate my position in this respect from Hobbes.'[53] To declare that a political action could not have a moral purpose was positively absurd, Morgenthau charged; the choice was not one between moral principles and the national interest, but between 'one set of moral principles *divorced* from political reality, and another set of moral principles *derived* from political reality'.[54] Rather than restoring a new balance of power after the First World War, Woodrow Wilson had sought to put an end to the idea of a balance of power altogether, instead replacing it with an internationalist juridical positivism that was 'only too eager to remodel the word of the law after idealistic assumptions whose universal validity [was] taken for granted ... Grandiose legalistic schemes purporting to solve the ills of the world have replaced

50 Morgenthau, *In Defense of the National Interest*, pp. 12–13.
51 *Ibid.*, p. 30.   52 *Ibid.*, p. 34.
53 Morgenthau, 'Another "Great Debate"', p. 983.
54 Morgenthau, *In Defense of the National Interest*, p. 33; emphasis added.

the less spectacular, painstaking search for the actual laws and the facts underlying them'.[55] As Lassa Oppenheim had already pointed out, and Morgenthau frequently repeated, there is no international law where there is not also a community of interests or a balance of power.[56] But where such a balance is maintained, in pursuit of the national interests of the states involved, it is not utopian to focus on 'the actual laws and the facts underlying them', as Morgenthau expressed it. Contra Carr, the contest between utopianism and realism is one between two types of political morality, 'one taking as its standard universal moral principles abstractly formulated, the other weighing these principles against the moral requirements of concrete political action, their relative merits to be decided by a prudent evaluation of the political consequences to which they are likely to lead'.[57]

Virtue and leadership

Prudence was a term Morgenthau would often resort to in his later writings: 'There can be no political morality without prudence, that is, without consideration of the political consequences of seemingly moral action.'[58] Indeed, the 'art' of statecraft, rather than the 'scientism' of academic political theory, was what was most needed for the United States in the new era of bipolarity that was unfolding. Already in 1948, Morgenthau ended *Politics Among Nations* with two chapters on diplomacy, and *In Defense of the National Interest* and numerous journal articles and commentaries he then went on to assert that a negotiated settlement with the Soviet Union was the only way to avoid the nuclear fallout of a third world war. As William Scheuerman has nicely laid out, Morgenthau was genuinely concerned about the way the Truman administration had reacted

---

55 Morgenthau, 'Positivism, Functionalism, and International Law', p. 283. See also Morgenthau, *Scientific Man vs. Power Politics*, p. 40, where he writes: 'All the scheme and devices by which great humanitarians and shrewd politicians endeavoured to organize the relations between states on the basis of law, have failed to stand the trial of history. Instead of asking whether the devices were adequate to the problems which they were supposed to solve, the internationalists take the appropriateness of the devices for granted and blame the facts for the failure ... Not unlike the sorcerers of primitive ages, they attempt to exorcise social evils by the indefatigable repetition of magic formulas.'

56 *Ibid.*, p. 275; see also Chapter 2, pp. 68–73.

57 Morgenthau, 'Another "Great Debate"', p. 988.   58 *Ibid.*, p. 986.

to news of Soviet nuclear tests, charging that by embracing 'smug and increasingly reckless illusions about US military, as well as political and moral superiority',[59] the errors of the inter-war years were being repeated. Rather than face the reality of a negotiated settlement, President Truman was merely a 'typical representative of a deeply neurotic political culture'[60] that refused to reflect upon the Soviet threat in realistic, political terms, but only in the moralistic and ultimately sentimentalist terms of good versus evil, virtue against vice. Akin to the legalism of the League of Nations era, too much emphasis was again being placed on the pacifying potential of the United Nations.

The understanding of the functions which the United Nations can perform for the preservation of peace under present conditions is hampered by ... the tendency to look at the legal provisions of the Charter and the institutions derived from them as though they were self-sufficient entities which receive their political meaning and their ability to perform political functions from their own literal content without reference to the political environment within and with regard to which they are supposed to operate.[61]

Once again, the domestic analogy with municipal law was resulting in 'grandiose legalistic schemes purporting to solve the ills of the world' that were ultimately subverting 'the actual laws and the facts underlying them'.[62]

It was out of this call for prudent superpower negotiations that Morgenthau's focus on the 'primacy of the national interest' emerged. Nuclear war could only be prevented through 'realistic statecraft', and this entailed, for Morgenthau, the recognition that only a foreign policy upholding the 'moral dignity' of its own national interest would avoid the 'intellectual error' and 'perversion' of the moralizing approach.[63] Until the conditions for a world state had been attained, the only way forward was to learn the lessons of Chamberlain's disastrous policy of appeasement[64] and clearly

---

59 Scheuerman, *Hans Morgenthau*, p. 71.   60 *Ibid.*, p. 75.
61 H. J. Morgenthau, 'Political Limitations of the United Nations', in Morgenthau, *The Impasse of American Foreign Policy* (University of Chicago Press, 1962), pp. 112–18, at 112.
62 Morgenthau, 'Positivism, Functionalism, and International Law', p. 283.
63 Morgenthau, *In Defense of the National Interest*, pp. 33–4.
64 In *Scientific Man vs. Power Politics*, pp. 102–3, Morgenthau writes: 'Chamberlain's waving a piece of paper with Hitler's peace pledge as guarantee of "peace in our time"

distinguish between primary and secondary interests. A focus on the latter would not only buy time, but would also begin to pave the way for US–Russian collaboration on issues that could be cut loose from the ideological divide that had engulfed public discourse.[65]

Much of the recent 'texts as inspirations' literature on Morgenthau has consequently argued that what lies behind Morgenthau's call for realistic statecraft is Max Weber's ethic of responsibility.[66] In short, a state's legitimate pursuit of its national interest must entail a prudent foreign policy based on a consequentialist ethic that sets the limits on state action. The most sophisticated 'redescription' of Morgenthau's thought on this matter has recently been formulated by Michael C. Williams, who uses his own conceptualization of 'wilful' realism to examine the link between an ethic of responsibility and the national interest, and how such an understanding relates to recent neo-conservative strands in US foreign policy.[67] Yet as I seek to argue in this section, the flipside of this argument is Morgenthau's legalism critique, formulated, implicitly, as breeding *irresponsibility* – that is, providing the statesman with a fig leaf behind which to hide on crucial issues of foreign policy.

Morgenthau's reference to Machiavelli in his review of E. H. Carr can help us begin to elaborate this point. Standard renditions of 'Machiavellianism', in particular in International Relations, boil Machiavelli's thought down to the assertion that history is a sequence of cause and effect, and that morality is a product of power. This is indeed the way Carr, for one, described it in *The Twenty Years' Crisis*.[68] As with other canonical authors, we can again observe a situation in which the field of International Relations uses Machiavelli as a place marker for an extreme position, caricatured

is a tragic symbol of this period if intellectual history, which believed in the miraculous power of the legal formula through its inherent qualities to drive out the evil and improve the conditions of man.'

65 See Scheuerman, *Hans Morgenthau*, p. 79.

66 See M. Weber, 'Politics as a Vocation', in Weber, *The Vocation Lectures*. Edited and with an Introduction by D. Owen and T. B. Strong (Indianapolis, IN: Hackett, 2004), pp. 32–94, in particular pp. 83–4 and 91–2.

67 See M. C. Williams, *The Realist Tradition and the Limits of International Relations* (Cambridge University Press, 2005); M. C. Williams, 'What is the National Interest?: The Neoconservative Challenge in IR Theory', *European Journal of International Relations*, 11 (2005), pp. 307–37; B. Schmidt and M. C. Williams, 'The Bush Doctrine and the Iraq War: Neoconservatives vs. Realists', *Security Studies*, 17 (2008), pp. 1–30.

68 Carr, *The Twenty Years' Crisis*, pp. 62–3.

to the point of breaking all ties with its original author and showing little awareness of the complex secondary literature that may have been produced in a variety of disciplines.

Morgenthau, it seems, had a more sophisticated understanding of Machiavelli, as the last two sentences of his critique of Carr – 'It is a dangerous thing to be a Machiavelli. It is a disastrous thing to be a Machiavelli without *virtù*'[69] – undoubtedly attest to. What is more, Morgenthau also entitled a 1945 article 'The Machiavellian Utopia',[70] in which, while discussing Hans Kelsen's *Peace Through Law*,[71] he compares Machiavelli's 'utopian' belief that the unification of Italy could be achieved through 'any one of those small sovereigns' clever handling of the mechanics of political action' with proceedings at the 1944 Dumbarton Oaks Conference.[72] We also know that Morgenthau wanted to write a book on Machiavelli in 1927, until he came across Friedrich Meinecke's *Die Idee der Staatsräson*:[73] 'Have given up the plan for the Machiavelli, as Meinecke's book on the Raison d'Etat already contains much the same thing', he wrote in his diary in August 1929.[74] All this strengthens the assumption that Morgenthau's reference to Machiavelli's *virtù* in his review of Carr was not an act of cursory name-dropping.

Machiavelli's political theory revolved around the concepts of *necessità*, *fortuna* and *virtù*. *Necessità* captured the insight that historiography, no longer the representation of divine intervention in time, did not simply become the accumulation of singular events. Indeed, the focus of many interpretations emphasizing Machiavelli's understanding of history as being a sequence of cause and effect is based on the insight that one of the major achievements of Machiavelli is to move reflections in the philosophy of history away from *providentia Dei* towards a more deterministic conception formulated through the notion of *necessità*. But while *necessità* was a 'necessary' condition for the realization of one's aims in history, it was not a

---

69 Morgenthau, 'The Political Science of E. H. Carr', p. 134.
70 H. J. Morgenthau, 'The Machiavellian Utopia', *Ethics*, 55 (1945), pp. 145–7.
71 H. Kelsen, *Peace Through Law* (Chapel Hill, NC: University of North Carolina Press, 1944).
72 Morgenthau, 'The Machiavellian Utopia', p. 145.
73 F. Meinecke, *Die Idee der Staatsräson in der neueren Geschichte* [1924], *Werke*, Vol. 1 (Munich: R. Oldenbourg, 1957).
74 Cited in C. Frei, *Hans J. Morgenthau: An Intellectual Biography* (Baton Rouge, LA: Louisiana State University Press, 2001), p. 123.

sufficient condition.[75] Such success required the *virtù* of political action.

If *necessità* corresponded to everything that was political invariable, *fortuna* denoted exactly the opposite, namely an historical factor without measurable causality nor perceivable finality. By the time Machiavelli employed the term *fortuna*, it had already developed over the centuries until it was a long way off from the Greek τύχη, and from the connotation associated with the Roman goddess Fortuna. For the Italians of Machiavelli's time, the notion of *fortuna* was well expressed in the slogan '*Mutuant ad fortunas maris*' in the context of bottomry: *fortuna* was synonymous with a storm at sea, and thus paradigmatic for sudden and uncontrolled changes in human affairs.[76] And just as dams and aqueducts can be built to counter the storm and rising tides, so too can political wisdom, *virtù*, be used to constrain the forces of *fortuna* on the political scene. *Fortuna* rears its head where *virtù* is absent: *dove non è ordinate virtù a resisterle*. For Machiavelli *fortuna* is not a constant, but strengthens and weakens in proportion to the degree of ingenuity and know-how of the political actor.[77]

The very complex notion of *virtù* (which cannot simply be translated as 'virtue' in English) encapsulates the shift in Renaissance philosophy from the actions of God to those of the individual. For Machiavelli, *virtù* represented all that was required of an individual and a people in order to fulfil the goal of the self-preservation and stability of political community.[78] *Virtù* combines competence (the German *Tüchtigkeit* is useful here) with energy, a worldly dynamic that goes against the grain of medieval philosophy in that it puts into question the whole issue of fate, as well as the deontological ethic on which it was based. But contrary to many interpretations, this does not make *virtù* amoral or immoral. On the contrary: *virtù* is the opposite of corruptibility, *corruzione*.[79] The *uomo virtuoso*, far from being an amoral actor, works against the corruptibility of

---

75 H. Münkler, *Machiavelli: Die Begründung des politischen Denkens der Neuzeit aus der Krise der Republik Florenz* (Frankfurt a.M.: S. Fischer, 2004), p. 248.

76 *Ibid.*, p. 301.   77 *Ibid.*, pp. 302–4.

78 *Ibid.*, p. 313; also H.-J. Diesner, *Virtù, Fortuna und das Prinzip Hoffnung bei Machiavelli* (Nachrichten der Akademie der Wissenschaften in Göttingen; I. Philologisch-historische Klasse, Jahrgang 1993, Nr. 5) (Göttingen: Vandenhoeck & Ruprecht, 1993), p. 178.

79 Münkler, *Machiavelli*, p. 317.

man to consolidate political stability in the republic. Through law
and education, the *virtù* of a participatory citizenry (in contrast to
the Roman *virtus* of the feudal nobility) was to be strengthened in
order to restrain the natural tendency towards moral corruption and
decadence.

Necessità and *fortuna*, then, need to be balanced by the *virtù* of the
statesman. Morgenthau's charge, expressed in his critique of Carr,
was that power corrupts both the actor on the political scene as
well as the observer if they do not retain a certain 'transcendent
standard of ethics'. That is precisely the difference between what
Morgenthau called 'a Machiavelli' *tout court*, and 'a Machiavelli
without *virtù*'. Pointing to the aspirations of power did not mean,
as many of Morgenthau commentators often supposed, sliding into
an amoral struggle for power as the only form of political action.
Indeed, Morgenthau complained in the preface to both the second
and third editions of *Politics Among Nations* that it was 'not pleasant
for an author to be blamed for ideas he has not only never expressed,
but which he has explicitly and repeatedly refuted and which are
repugnant to him'.[80] Power, Morgenthau kept insisting, was not to
be equated with material strength. On the contrary, what he termed
power had much to do with particular ideologies (in Mannheim's
sense) and with the *virtù* of the individual involved – either in theory
or in practice – with political action.

Morgenthau's legalism critique is closely linked with this understanding of *virtù*, in relation to the idea of responsible statecraft. At
the heart of this critique lay the anxiety that the indeterminacy of
law can become an excuse for irresponsible action (or inaction). I
believe that Morgenthau's use of the term legalism entails a per-
formative aspect of law that he never properly articulated, but that
goes to the heart of his unease with the 'dominant doctrine' of legal
formalism. Thanks to some of the work of Jürgen Habermas, it is
perhaps possible to redescribe Morgenthau's legalism critique in
slightly more explicit terms today.

In his daunting monograph, *Faktizität und Geltung*, Habermas
seeks to unpack the intricate relationship(s) between the rule of
law and democracy, and thus also the fundamental links between

---

80 Morgenthau, *Politics Among Nations*, second edition, 'Foreword'; emphasis added.

law, politics and morality.[81] Norms of law and morality both have the function of regulating inter-personal conflicts in a way that secures the autonomy of those involved in an egalitarian manner. But whereas moral self-determination is a unitary concept, according to which each individual adheres to those norms that he or she deems, following his or her own impartial judgment, to be binding, the self-determination of the citizen is split into private and public autonomy. Subjective rights unlink legal persons from moral principles and give them a certain freedom of action, within specified limits: everything is permitted that is not forbidden. While there is a symmetry of rights and obligations in morality, legal obligations are only a consequence of the maintenance of conceptually prioritized entitlements.[82]

In other words, as Scott Veitch recently argued, 'the juridical form permeates, structures and organises the available range of normative understandings, expectations and responses' in society.[83] This means, according to Habermas, conceiving of law as a functional complement to morality: positive law '*relieves* the judging and acting person of the considerable cognitive, motivational and ... organizational demands of morality centred on the individual's conscience'.[84] And this is also why the mantle of positive law may well breed irresponsibility and lead to the type of legalism that Morgenthau was talking of. The dominant doctrine of formalism releases the statesman from making decisions according to the complex and possibly conflicting demands of moral and shared responsibility. It offers a framework according to which sensitive decisions 'in the national interest' can be qualified and legitimized in a way that occludes the claims to universality that Morgenthau – and Carl Schmitt – were so acutely aware of. Herein lies the corruption of the political actor, corrupted by the acquisition of power to believe that this power brings with it

---

81 J. Habermas, *Faktizität und Geltung. Beiträge zur Diskurstheorie des Rechts und des demokratischen Rechtsstaats* (Frankfurt a.M.: Suhrkamp, 1992). Published in English as *Between Facts and Norms: Contributions to a Discourse Theory of Law and Democracy* (Cambridge, MA: MIT Press, 1996).

82 Habermas, *Between Facts and Norms*, pp. 450–3; also 118–19.

83 S. Veitch, *Law and Irresponsibility: On the Legitimation of Human Suffering* (Abingdon: Routledge-Cavendish, 2007), p. 26.

84 Habermas, *Between Facts and Norms*, p. 452; emphasis in the original. Also Veitch, *Law and Irresponsibility*, p. 26.

superior morality as well. And this tendency, Morgenthau insisted, had to be resisted at every turn:

> For the light-hearted assumption that what one's own nation aims at and does is morally good and that those who oppose that nation's policies are evil is morally indefensible and intellectually untenable and leads in practice to that distortion of judgement, born of the blindness of crusading frenzy, which has been the curse of nations from the beginning of time.[85]

Romanticism

In his review of Carr, then, Morgenthau took his critique of the corruptibility of the political actor and transposed it onto the observer as well, whose perception of political actions also runs the risk, Morgenthau pointed out, of being corrupted by power without a transcending standard of ethics. He continues: 'Mr. Carr might have learned that lesson from the fate of the political romantics of whom the outstanding representatives are Adam Müller and Carl Schmitt.'[86]

I am inclined to assert that this is one of the most remarkable sentences to have come from Morgenthau's pen. If ever the likes of Michael Williams, Chris Brown or William Scheuerman are looking for an entry point into making the case that Morgenthau knew Schmitt's work inside out, this is it. The sentence undoubtedly makes reference to Schmitt's remarkable and provocative book of 1919, entitled *Politische Romantik*,[87] in which its author dealt extensively with the figure of Adam Müller (1779–1829), an otherwise unknown quantity outside of literary circles. Indeed, Schmitt acknowledges in the preface to the second edition of 1925 that much of the criticism he received for the book questioned why he made such a relatively unknown figure into the representative of nineteenth-century romanticism.[88] Whether writing a book about political romanticism makes Schmitt himself a romantic, as Morgenthau seems to suggest – or rather, whether elements of romanticism pervade the work of Schmitt – is certainly an interesting proposition. It will not be

---

85 Morgenthau, 'Another "Great Debate"', p. 984.
86 Morgenthau, 'The Political Science of E. H. Carr', p. 134.
87 C. Schmitt, *Politische Romantik* [1919] (Berlin: Duncker & Humblot, 1998); based on the second edition of 1925.
88 *Ibid.*, p. 21.

dealt with here, however, as such an endeavour will deter us from focusing on the subject at hand.[89]

The path from Morgenthau's sentence in 1945 and Schmitt's 1919 treatise once again passes via Karl Mannheim. In 1925, the young Mannheim handed in the thesis for his habilitation at the faculty of philosophy of the Ruprecht Karl University in Heidelberg. It ran under the title *Altkonservatismus: Ein Beitrag zur Soziologie des Wissens*, and dealt extensively with romanticism and a certain Adam Müller – clearly, as visible from the footnotes, under the influence of the book by Schmitt.[90] As I already mentioned, Morgenthau was in contact with Mannheim in Frankfurt and was undoubtedly aware of the latter's habilitation. Moreover, in 1927 Mannheim published a short version of his manuscript in the *Archiv für Sozialwissenschaft und Sozialpolitik*,[91] the same year Schmitt published the 'Concept of the Political' in precisely this journal (in the next issue, in fact). Morgenthau simply must have seen it. This is worth mentioning because Schmitt was, of course, by far the only scholar writing on the issue of romanticism. Not surprisingly, there is quite a healthy literature on romanticism in the fields of aesthetics, cultural history and literature dealing with the nineteenth-century phenomenon or movement of that name. Indeed, this is also how Karl Mannheim engaged with romanticism in his habilitation, identifying it as a particular moment within the history of conservatism.[92] But seen from

---

89 Suffice it to say that even in *Politische Romantik* itself, Schmitt does leave himself open to the criticism that he applies the same types of 'aesthetic' rhetorical and stylistic embellishments that he marks out as being representative of the work of Adam Müller – after all, romanticizing an issue is as much about language as it is about substance. But we are getting ahead of ourselves here. At this point, let it simply be said that it is at times difficult to pinpoint in the text where sneering elaborations of Adam Müller stop and Schmitt's own views takes over.

90 The manuscript was posthumously published as K. Mannheim, *Konservatismus: Ein Beitrag zur Soziologie des Wissens*. Edited by D. Kettler, V. Meja and N. Stehr (Frankfurt a.M.: Suhrkamp, 1984).

91 K. Mannheim, 'Das konservative Denken. Soziologische Beiträge zum Werden des politisch-historischen Denkens in Deutschland', *Archiv für Sozialwissenschaft und Sozialpolitik*, 57 (1927), pp. 68–142 and 470–95.

92 Mannheim talks of '*der romantisch-ständische Standort*', an expression that is hopelessly difficult to translate. *Standort* means location or position, while *Stand*, the way it is used here, has produced an entire literature in itself – also in English; see J. Böröcz, '*Stand* Reconstructed: Contingent Closure and Institutional Change', *Sociological Theory*, 15 (1997), pp. 215–48 – given that it is a key term in the German sociological literature. It is also of significance in the works of Max Weber, where it is often translated as 'status group'.

this angle, Schmitt's book is rather unique in trying to define romanticism outside of its nineteenth-century connotations, and from the perspective of law.

Romanticism, Schmitt pointed out, was one of those empty containers that are filled with various contents on a case-by-case basis.[93] The term has often been taken to be about the goodness in human nature, '*la bonté naturelle*', especially in the French literature. Other conceptual approximations relate romanticism to conservatism, mysticism, political restoration, or take it simply as the negative reaction to all forms of rationalism. While containing elements of the puzzle, such dogmatic-moralistic abstractions occluded, Schmitt and Mannheim both argued, the historical particularity of nineteenth-century romanticism – in other words, it is only via a socio-historical contextualization that it is possible to distil the defining characteristics of what romanticism is as such, and what the politicization of this cultural and societal vision engenders.

The historical analysis is too complex to be outlined here. Suffice it to say that for the aristocrats of the restoration, such as Prince von Metternich (1773–1859), 'romantic' was equated with liberalism and humanitarianism – human rights, tolerance, individual freedoms, all this meant revolution, Rousseauism, unbridled subjectivism and ultimately romanticism.[94] Conceptually, Schmitt thus conceived of the romantic position via the notion of *occasio*, the negation of any sort of *causa*. Romanticism is, according to Schmitt, 'subjectified occasionalism', i.e. the declaration of the individual as the highest instance, rather than the state, God or the people. The 'magic hand of chance' creates endless possibilities and thus always only 'occasional world', a world without substance or functional inter-linkage, without a last judgment, without being bound by a norm. Indeed, the notion of norms is 'unromantic tyranny', for the romantic is not able and willing to take a decision. Hence, the romantic position is inherently incompatible with any moral, legal or political standard.[95] The distinction between the real and the possible leaves the romantic in a state of utter despair, with numerous realities ironically playing around simultaneously within him. But

93 Schmitt, *Politische Romantik*, p. 35.
94 *Ibid.*, p. 27. The view was also shared by Karl Marx (1818–83).
95 *Ibid.*, p. 29.

his passivity also makes the romantic personify the state as a 'beauti-fied' individual – the romantic lacks any notion of limits, both of the individual and of the state. Adam Müller, the bourgeois aspiring to attain the ranks of the nobility, thus becomes the typical romantic, the apologist of the aristocracy and thus the Middle Ages, the all-endorsing pantheist – meaning, for the philosopher Karl Wilhelm Friedrich von Schlegel (1872–1929), a 'realist of the worst kind', 'ein schlimmer Realist'.[96]

For Morgenthau, Carr was one of these 'terrible realists' as well – Schlegel obviously uses the term in its philosophical version, but in the context of pantheism, it overlaps to an extent with the realism Carr was advocating and Morgenthau was criticizing. As Morgenthau points out in his review, the problem with Carr's argu-ment is that it is not founded on any sort of deontological prin-ciples, 'no transcendent point of view from which to survey the political scene and to appraise the phenomenon of power'.[97] This is the inherent apologist element of political romanticism: unable to decide, the 'political moralist transforms himself into a utopian of power'. Carr, lacking a 'transcendent standard of ethics', thus bases his argument in *The Twenty Years' Crisis* on 'a relativistic, instrumen-talist conception of morality'. In Machiavelli's political theory, at least, the forces of *necessità* and *fortuna* are balanced by the *virtù* of the statesman. Unable to offer more than the call for 'a compromi-se between morality and power', however, Carr makes himself into a crude apologist of the state as the holder of superior morality as well. This is exactly what Morgenthau was so worried about, and

96 *Ibid.*, p. 129. Again, this is not the place to go into an exploration of whether Schmitt was a romantic himself, as Morgenthau seems to suggest, but it is perhaps no coinci-dence that Schmitt should spend so much energy on Adam Müller. After all, Schmitt's biography shows very similar tendencies: of upon his own admission 'modest descent' (his family were Catholic migrants from the Lorraine who came down the Mosel to settle in the dominantly Protestant town of Plettenberg in Westphalia), Schmitt, somewhat of a child prodigy, managed to break out of his social surroundings and head to the Friedrich Wilhelm University in Berlin. Conditions were so overwhelming and becoming socially accepted was so difficult, however, that after two semesters he withdrew to Munich and then even to Strasbourg to complete his studies. By the time he wrote *Politische Romantik* in 1919, he had even entered into ill-fated wedlock with a lady who claimed to be Serbian nobility – he even adopted her name: the author of the first edition of the book was a certain Carl Schmitt-Dorotić; see G. Balakrishnan, *The Enemy: An Intellectual Portrait of Carl Schmitt* (London: Verso, 2000), pp. 11–27.
97 Morgenthau, 'The Political Science of E. H. Carr', p. 134.

what lies at the heart of what he called legalism and moralism. As he makes clear in the fifth principle in *Politics Among Nations*, the task of political realism is precisely to expose all efforts that try to equate the moral aspirations of a particular state with 'the moral laws that govern the universe'. For if this is not done, Morgenthau argued, one would end up with as many standards of ethics as there are national interests: 'Instead of the universality of an ethics to which all nations adhere, we have in the end the particularity of national ethics which claim the right to, and aspire toward, universal recognition. There are then as many ethical codes claiming universality as there are politically active nations.'[98]

Nonetheless, Morgenthau was himself facing the critique of being a romantic, but from a rather different angle: the pen of Karl Popper (1902–94). In the second edition of *The Open Society and Its Enemies*, Karl Popper added a lengthy footnote discussing Morgenthau's argument in *Scientific Man vs. Power Politics* that the usage of rational methods for the establishment of international peace was a 'Utopian dream'.[99] Morgenthau's position, Popper claimed, 'can be summed up as that of a disappointed historicist': Morgenthau was correct in believing that historical prediction was impossible, but wrong in the assumption that predictability was the only field to which the scientific method, or 'reason', could be applied. He was mistaken in caricaturing the sciences, be they natural or social, as being engaged in the prediction of trends. Neither branches had ever had such aims, and 'the realization that these aims are not realizable will disappoint only the historicist'. Morgenthau's error, according to Popper, was to assume that historical prophesy was the basis of rational politics. Of course, many political scientists were deluding themselves into thinking that they could predict social events with a high degree of certainty, but the consequence of this observation was not the rejection of the scientific method:

Morgenthau ridicules all attempts to bring power under the control of reason, and to suppress war, as springing from a rationalism and scientism which is inapplicable to society by its very essence. But clearly, he proves too much. Civil peace has been established in many societies, in spite of that

---

98 H. J. Morgenthau, 'The Twilight of International Morality', *Ethics*, 58 (1948), pp. 79–99, at 96.
99 Karl Popper, *The Open Society and its Enemies*. Second edition [1952], published in one volume (London and New York, NY: Routledge, 2002), p. 661.

essential lust for power which according to Morgenthau's theory, should prevent it. He admits the fact, of course, but does not see that it destroys the theoretical basis of his romantic contentions.[100]

Popper's portrayal of Morgenthau as a disappointed historicist is rather pertinent, in particular with regard to the rather confused *Scientific Man vs. Power Politics*, discussed in Chapter 4.[101] There, Morgenthau lumps all scientific approaches to the study of politics under the heading of 'rationalism', and claims that the resulting 'scientism' was misplaced because it focused solely on historical prediction. But according to the way Carl Schmitt conceptualized political romanticism, however, Morgenthau was not a romantic. Yes, he was a conservative, even though, as Lebow correctly argues, he did become more 'optimistic' about political change with age.[102] And yes, if one defines romanticism simply as the denial of all forms of rationalism, as does Karl Popper, then Morgenthau may have been entertaining romantic contentions. But as Schmitt told his readers, the interesting and defining feature of the political romantic is indecision. The romantic can be a conservative one minute and call for revolution the next. Morgenthau's biography does not follow that pattern, regardless of what inconsistencies one might inevitably find in his work. Carr, on the other hand, is a perfect fit, and Charles Jones is spot on in his brilliant characterization of him in the last pages of his book, *E. H. Carr and International Relations: A Duty to Lie*:

Admiring the Soviet ally and favouring social revolution at home, he [Carr] pursued an essentially conservative purpose: the preservation of British power and the extension of British political culture through meritocratic forms of government. He supped with a very long spoon, commending far-reaching changes in the lives of others while leaving his own daily round and that of the mandarin class to which he belonged quite undisturbed. His vision was therefore romantic in the double sense of being built from the tension of irreconcilable desires and constituted by a subjective aestheticisation of everyday events.[103]

100 *Ibid.*, p. 662.
101 Popper had already characterized Morgenthau a 'disappointed historicist' in an address delivered to the Plenary Session of the Tenth International Congress of Philosophy in Amsterdam in 1948; see K. Popper, *Conjectures and Refutations: The Growth of Scientific Knowledge* [1963] (London and New York, NY: Routledge, 2002), pp. 452–466, at 458.
102 Lebow, *The Tragic Vision of Politics*, p. 254.
103 Jones, *E. H. Carr*, p. 161.

Morgenthau was of an altogether different demeanour. Laborious and ponderous, he meticulously structured his arguments and delivered them with good German rigour (and a heavy German accent). There were no sudden flourishes, no rush of blood to the head in moments of intellectual or political enthusiasm. His Jewish heritage, which he cultivated rather than played down, only added to his focus on principles. The notion of 'speaking truth to power' captures this well. 'While military strength and political power are the preconditions for lasting national greatness', Morgenthau wrote late in his career, 'the substance of that greatness springs from the hidden sources of intellect and morale, from ideas and values'.[104] What he loosely termed a 'transcendent standard of ethics' was at the core of Morgenthau's thought. In Lebow's formulation, it was derived from the recognition 'that great powers are often their own worst enemies because success and the hubris it engenders encourage actors to see themselves outside of and above their community, and thus in turn blinds them to the need for self-restraint'.[105] 'The history of political thought', Morgenthau wrote, 'is the history of the moral evaluation of political power'.[106]

Conclusion

Ever since his 1929 dissertation on the justiciability of disputes, Morgenthau was arguing for a more realistic appraisal of the relationship between law and politics in international relations. It was futile to discuss dispute settlement mechanisms without acknowledging the underlying tensions that were a result of asymmetries in the distribution of power. It made no sense to speak of the validity of norms without taking into account the empirical reality of their enforcement. And it was pernicious to uphold a formalist legal doctrine that was only instrumentalized to suit the requirements of one or more superpowers seeking to depoliticize their underlying claims to ideational supremacy. Seen from this angle, the common thread running through Morgenthau's writings is the worry about legal

104 H. J. Morgenthau, *A New Foreign Policy for the United States* (New York, NY: Praeger, 1969), p. 221.
105 Lebow, *The Tragic Vision of Politics*, p. 258.
106 H. J. Morgenthau, 'The Evil of Politics and the Ethics of Evil', *Ethics*, 56 (1945), pp. 1 18, at 1.

formalism, a worry that is a defining feature of twentieth-century legal theoretical discourse. As Duncan Kennedy writes:

Formal law is part of the drama of governance, the trivial or murderous drama of breaking eggs to make omelettes. The critical use of the term formalism, against the abuse of deduction and the fantasy of gaplessness in legal discourse, is part of the twentieth-century battle between those who have wanted to depoliticize the drama as much as possible, through reason, and those who have seen it as inevitably a dangerous improvisation.[107]

Morgenthau's 'traditionalism'[108] falls squarely into the latter group. For all that has been written on Morgenthau's advocacy of a Weberian consequentialist ethic of responsibility to formulate a foreign policy 'in defence of the national interest', key to Morgenthau's thought is nonetheless the belief that states 'are subject to the moral law'.[109] It shines through in his belief, taken from Hans Kelsen, in a hierarchy of norms culminating in an a-legal basic norm – a norm that, by definition, cannot be conceived of consequentially. It is evident in the way he faults Carr for not having a transcendent standard of ethics from which to analyse politics, and in the way he employs the terminology of moralism and legalism to warn against the corruptibility of political actors who are prone towards hiding their interests behind an ideological discourse that takes on utopian characteristics if coupled with the (socially constructed) conviction that this discourse can lay claim to universality. The fact that Morgenthau's thought varyingly incorporates a seemingly irreconcilable array of theoretical positions – Kelsen's theory of norms, (deontological) natural law premises, legal realism – is precisely the result of his effort to grapple with law's indeterminacy from the perspective of his Weimar heritage of legal formalism.

107 D. Kennedy, 'Legal Formalism', in N. J. Smelser and P. B. Baltes (eds.), *Encyclopedia of the Social & Behavioral Sciences* (Amsterdam: Elsevier, 2001), pp. 8634–8, at 8637.
108 M. Koskenniemi, *The Gentle Civilizer of Nations: The Rise and Fall of International Law 1870–1960* (Cambridge University Press, 2002), p. 499.
109 Morgenthau, 'Another "Great Debate"', p. 984.

6   The legacy of legal formalism

The purpose of this book was not to present a comprehensive rede-scription of Morgenthau's thought, nor to assess the influence of his writings on academic and policy discourse in the United States. Rather, it attempted to emphasize the under-studied juridical dimension of Morgenthau's ideas, thereby highlighting the way many of their origins were occluded by standard renditions of Morgenthau that continue to apply him as an un-scientific precursor to more sophisticated theories of political realism subsequently generated. From a contemporary Political Science perspective, Morgenthau's approach was certainly 'un-scientific', to say the least, and the teacher of introductory courses to International Relations theory has every right to use Morgenthau as exemplary of a 'classical' version of 'human nature realism' based on the six principles added to the second edition of *Politics Among Nations*. Were it not for those six principles of realism and the success of that textbook, it is doubtful whether we would still be talking of Morgenthau today, and even more doubtful that he would be considered a 'canonical' thinker in International Relations. Grumble as he might about being misunderstood, even Morgenthau would have to accept that fact.

But casting Morgenthau aside as an easy-to-place anachronism does not help contemporary ambitions to offer a more critical approach to the way the field of International Relations has been writing its own 'disciplinary history' and has appropriated certain 'classical' thinkers for that purpose. The current 'cottage industry' rehabilitating Morgenthau, which I discussed in Chapter 1, is thus a welcome development. Yet the endeavour to generate a more sophisticated, contextualized understanding of Morgenthau nonetheless seems to turn in a circle: most attempts to 'situate' the early Morgenthau continue to be based on the assertions Morgenthau expressed in his autobiographical fragment and the interview with Bernhard Johnson,[1] which seem to contain all the material required to comfortably place Morgenthau in the familiar territory of anglophone International Relations. As Ulrik Enemark Peterson wrote in 1999, traditional interpretations of Morgenthau 'fail to grasp the proper meaning of and relation between his core concepts because their hermeneutic horizon remains defined by what has famously been described as "the rich tradition of political realism" and the widespread assumption that Morgenthau was primarily "an American thinker"'.[2] Most contemporary (re)interpretations, I would charge, do not fare much better. While there is growing enthusiasm about pointing to Morgenthau's European roots, no one seems eager to step out of the comfort zone and into the realm of public law debates, a task that inevitably entails trying to decipher writings in foreign languages on obscure legal issues. Out of this frustration with the contemporary 'cottage industry' on Morgenthau emerged the present book.

Chapter 2 explored how the distinction between 'disputes' and 'tensions', the basis for Morgenthau's reflections on the balance of power, stemmed from his doctorate on the limits to the justiciability of disputes in international law. Like Lassa Oppenheim before him, Morgenthau argued that a stable distribution of power was a prerequisite for international law to function in cases where vital interests were at stake. Of course, international law worked for most cases most of the time. But it was the exceptional, 'political' cases that deserved extra attention, those of such an 'intensity' that states were unwilling to resort to third-party settlement. As his reviewers were eager to point out, however, his work was far from being stunningly original. It was solid, rigorous stuff, but that was it. His subsequent focus on the concept of power, and the threefold distinction between policies that seek to maintain, increase or demonstrate power, were the result of his efforts to reply to the criticisms he received, in particular from Hersch Lauterpacht. These three

---

1 H. J. Morgenthau, 'Fragment of an Intellectual Autobiography: 1904–1932' and 'Interview with Bernhard Johnson', in K. W. Thompson and R. J. Meyers (eds.), *Truth and Tragedy. A Tribute to Hans J. Morgenthau*. Second edition with new Postscript (New Brunswick, NJ: Transaction Books), pp. 1–17 and 333–86.
2 U. E. Peterson, 'Breathing Nietzsche's Air: New Reflections on Morgenthau's Concepts of Power and Human Nature', *Alternatives*, 24 (1999), pp. 83–119, at 85.

different manifestations of power would then respectively correspond to policies of the status quo, of imperialism and of prestige in
Politics Among Nations. From the point of view of international legal
scholarship, his reaction constituted a '*salto mortale*' that forsook
international law for a non-legal focus on 'power aspirations' and
'social forces'. This move, Morgenthau later recalled, earned him
the charge of being a cynic:

> I was called a cynic for the first time in 1929, after the signature of the
> Kellogg–Briand Pact in which all the nations of the world pledged them-
> selves to forego war as an instrument of international policy. War was
> outlawed, and hence war had become impossible. Such was at least the
> consensus of the authorities. Those who then pointed to the impotence of a
> legal formula in the face of the formidable social forces which make for war
> were declared to be 'lacking in imagination' or to be outright cynics.[3]

With hindsight, however, forsaking the disciplinary framework of
(formalist) legal scholarship was precisely what differentiated him
from many of his peers, and what would form the basis for his subsequent career in the United States.

Chapter 3 shifted the focus to Morgenthau's *Habilitationsschrift*,
the published version of which, *La réalité des normes*, was the attempt
to refine and elaborate a particular element of Hans Kelsen's theory
of norms, namely what Morgenthau called the 'reality of norms',
or the '*Da-Sein*' of the '*Sollen*', a cue he had taken from his mentor Arthur Baumgarten. Again, Morgenthau's attempt to differentiate his own work from that of Kelsen lacked originality, though,
and contrary to his own account of his institutional struggle with
the University of Geneva, Paul Guggenheim was arguably right in
being disappointed with the manuscript Morgenthau submitted. It
was indeed not very original, obscure in very Baumgartenian fashion, and terribly written. Essentially, the reality of a norm was its
empirical manifestation through the presence of an enforceable
sanction. Morgenthau adopted Kelsen's monistic notion of an hierarchical system of norms culminating in an a-legal basic norm,
and argued that international law was thus a 'primitive' type of law
because it was decentralized: the holders of validity and the subjects

---

3 H. J. Morgenthau, 'About Cynicism, Perfectionism, and Realism in International
Affairs', in Morgenthau, *The Decline of Democratic Politics* (University of Chicago Press,
1962), pp. 127–30, at 127.

of international law were one and the same. Morgenthau repeated this assertion in *Politics Among Nations*, and also adapted the differentiation between morals, mores and legal norms to denote international morality, world public opinion and international law on the level of relations among states. His musings about the desirability of aspiring to a world state also stem from Kelsen's conceptualization of international law. And crucially, it was the formalist, Kelsenian understanding of law that would have a lasting impact on Morgenthau, leading to his anxiety over the 'dominant doctrine' as being a legalistic device that occluded the social forces that generate both order and law.[4]

Chapter 4 then reflected on the potential points of convergence between Morgenthau's call for a 'radical legal realism' and the legal realist agenda that represented the early twentieth-century culmination of progressivist US legal thought. During the mid-1930s, however, circumstances in the United States had changed considerably, with the advent of totalitarianism in Europe and an overall 'crisis of democratic theory' putting a damper on public portrayals of the virtues of legal realism. By the time Morgenthau arrived on the scene, legal realism was of ill repute, and he unsuccessfully tried to repackage his research agenda under the guise of 'functionalism'. At the University of Chicago, Morgenthau found himself completely at odds with the behaviouralist movement of the Merriam faction. What is more, Lasswell, perhaps Merriam's most gifted disciple, was, together with the international lawyer Myers McDougal at Yale, implementing the functionalist approach Morgenthau himself had called for, but using a notion of 'empiricism' that was alien to him. Outraged at the barbarity of the 'scientism' he was witnessing around him, Morgenthau, the 'disappointed historicist', resorted to looking down with disdain on the riff-raff attempting to tinker with techniques of 'social engineering' – although it is uncertain from his writings whether he knew what exactly his peers meant by this term, nor that he had any precise idea of what the 'scientism' he was looking down upon actually entailed. At the University of Chicago, Morgenthau was an anachronism: he was unable to wear his new hat of Professor of Political Science competently, yet in the presence

4 H. J. Morgenthau, *Scientific Man vs. Power Politics* (University of Chicago Press, 1946), pp. 103–4.

of someone of the calibre of Leo Strauss, he was not able to fall
back upon the role of political theorist either. Political action, he
grumbled, was about the 'art' of responsible statecraft. Morgenthau
would never engage in legal scholarship again.

Chapter 5 then tackled Morgenthau's notion of 'legalism', a
term he would employ repeatedly in most of his publications in
the 1940s and early 1950s. His critique of E. H. Carr was taken
as a useful thread to flesh out Morgenthau's own understanding
of realism in international relations – an understanding, based on
the concept of the 'national interest', that was, when all is said and
done, quite similar to the one espoused by Hersch Lauterpacht.
By focusing on some of the central themes in the work of
Machiavelli, Mannheim and Schmitt, the chapter showed that
what Morgenthau termed 'legalism' and 'moralism' was not synonymous with the claims that international law was irrelevant and
that political action boiled down to amoral power politics. On the
contrary, Morgenthau's 'realistic' view of international relations
was founded on a 'transcendent standard of ethics' that warned
against the 'depoliticizing' and 'neutralizing' tendencies of a hegemonic superpower attempting to universalize its own ideational
supremacy. Ultimately, Morgenthau's legalism critique entailed
the anxiety that the 'dominant doctrine' of legal formalism promotes irresponsible action by releasing the statesman from making decisions that correspond to the demands of morality. As the
fifth principle of a realist theory of international politics asserts in
Politics Among Nations, the task of political realism is to expose all
attempts to equate the 'moral aspirations of a particular state' with
the 'moral laws that govern the universe'.

Changes of emphasis

Contrary to mainstream conceptions, *Politics Among Nations* was
not a book on what today would be called International Relations
theory, constituted in the vein of Political Science. It was a book
on the practical limitations to the use of law in the international
realm, written at a time when peaceful change seemed an increasingly futile endeavour and the bipolar stalemate that was to become
the Cold War an ominous reality. Students of international law had
to be aware of this reality, and textbooks were drawn up attempting

to describe the contemporary international scene. One thinks of Wolfgang G. Friedmann's *Introduction to World Politics*, Georg Schwarzenberger's *Power Politics* or Gerhart Niemeyer's *Law Without Force*.[5] These are works written by international lawyers, not political scientists, and were never intended to be anything other than a commentary on – and not a theory of – international politics. In this regard, it is useful to cite Morgenthau's review of the first edition of Schwarzenberger's *Power Politics*, in, tellingly, the *American Journal of International Law*:

> Whoever published a volume ten years ago on the general problems of international affairs, the forces determining them, and their possible solutions, could not fail to indicate in the title the importance of international law or the League of Nations for his subject matter. Dr. Schwarzenberger himself, together with Professor Keeton, dealt with this subject as late as 1939 under the title *Making International Law Work*. His more recent 'Introduction to the Study of International Relations and Post-War Planning,' however, he simply calls *Power Politics*. Yet the new title indicates a change of emphasis rather than a new approach.[6]

'A change of emphasis rather than a new approach': neither Schwarzenberger nor Morgenthau intended to frame a *theory* of political power the way Charles Merriam and his students, for instance, had envisioned. Let the added first chapter of the second edition of *Politics Among Nations* on a realist theory of international politics, and especially Morgenthau's use of the word 'theory', not deceive us: the book is not akin to the work of Harold Lasswell or Karl Deutsch – Chapter 4 should have insisted on that point sufficiently. *Politics Among Nations* served a polemical purpose, Morgenthau himself noted, and the print run of the book – compared to Schwarzenberger's *Power Politics*, for instance – pays tribute to what extent he managed to captivate his audience. *Politics Among Nations* was not so much more successful because Morgenthau had developed a 'proper theory' of international relations in it, as Stephanie

---

5 W. Friedmann, *An Introduction to World Politics* (London: Macmillan, 1951); G. Schwarzenberger, *Power Politics: An Introduction to the Study of International Relations and Post-War Planning* (London: Jonathan Cape, 1941); G. Niemeyer, *Law Without Force: The Function of Politics in International Law* (Princeton University Press, 1941); see also Morgenthau's useful review of Niemeyer's book in the *Iowa Law Review*, 27 (1942), pp. 350–5.

6 H. J. Morgenthau, 'Review of G. Schwarzenberger, *Power Politics*', *American Journal of International Law*, 36 (1942), pp. 351–52, at 351.

Steinle has argued,[7] but because it got into the hands of a US political establishment looking for ways to legitimize the new role of the
United States in the post-war international system. That establishment found what they were looking for in *Politics Among Nations*.

It is highly informative to accumulate the various editions of
Politics Among Nations and study its life cycle. Apart from the numerous changes effected in the later editions by Kenneth W. Thompson,
Morgenthau's long-term colleague, friend and editor, the most
prominent modification is of course the addition, in the second
edition, of the introductory chapter entitled 'A Realist Theory of
International Politics'. In consultation with his editors at Alfred A.
Knopf, Morgenthau added the 'Six Principles of Political Realism'
that would become the staple diet of International Relations under-
graduates for decades, and that are still taken to be the culmination
of Morgenthau's achievement – and even there, the focus of attention has in general been the first and second principles, namely that
politics is governed by objective laws having their roots in human
nature and that realism's key concept is that of interest defined
in terms of power. Readers, it seems, did not really know what to
make of the statement that realism is aware of the moral significance of political action (the fourth principle), or that it represents
'a distinctive intellectual and moral attitude to matters political'
(the sixth).

In any event, the first edition of *Politics Among Nations* had an
altogether different complexion to it. In an opening section entitled
'International Politics: A Dual Approach', Morgenthau started off
by telling his readers that the purpose of the book was twofold: 'The
first is to detect and understand the forces which determine political relations among nations, and to comprehend the ways in which
those forces act upon each other and upon international political
relations and institutions.'[8] Yet because of the predominance of
the United States in the post-Second World War scene, reflecting
on international politics in the United States equated to studying
US foreign policy: 'Since in this world situation the United States
holds a position of predominant power and, hence, of foremost

---

7 S. Steinle, '"Plus ça change, plus c'est la même chose": Georg Schwarzenberger's *Power
   Politics*', *Journal of the History of International Law*, 5 (2003), pp. 387–402, at 399.
8 H. J. Morgenthau, *Politics Among Nations: The Struggle for Power and Peace*. First edition
   (New York, NY: Alfred A. Knopf, 1948), p. 7.

responsibility, the understanding of the forces which mould inter-national politics and of the factors which determine its course has become for the United States more than an interesting intellec-tual occupation. It has become a vital necessity.'[9] For this reason, Morgenthau proposed to structure the book around two central concepts, power and peace:

> In a world whose moving force is the aspiration for power of sovereign nations, peace can only be maintained by two devices: One is the self-regulatory mechanism of the social forces which manifests itself in the struggle for power on the international scene, that is, the balance of power. The other consists of normative limitations upon that struggle in the form of international law, international morality, and world public opinion.[10]

For those of us who have now studied Morgenthau's earlier works, it all sounds terribly familiar. But is this the 'classic' Morgenthau of the introductory International Relations course? Surely not. Indeed, Morgenthau was soon bitterly aggrieved at the extent to which he was quoted out of context and misinterpreted as endorsing a theory that made all political action into a struggle for power on the basis of material capabilities. Yet Morgenthau was also a survivor and an opportunist, for his frustrations did not prevent him from reinfor-cing the misinterpretations with talk of a 'realist theory of inter-national politics' in the second edition. He continued to 'find solace in Montesquieu's similar experience' of it being the fate of authors 'to be criticized for ideas one has never held',[11] but when the options were academic obscurity or considerable public prominence – in particular given the hard time he was receiving from his 'scientistic' colleagues at Chicago – the choice for Morgenthau was nonetheless an easy one. If the book sells better by reiterating and emphasizing what your readers declare you to have said, then so be it.

Americanization

I have focused so much on *Politics Among Nations* not because it is the only notable work Morgenthau published, but because it is the pri-mary vehicle with which the émigré scholar performed his cultural

---

9 *Ibid.*, p. 8.   10 *Ibid.*, p. 9.

11 H. J. Morgenthau, *Politics Among Nations: The Struggle for Power and Peace*. Third edi-tion (New York, NY: Alfred A. Knopf, 1960), Preface.

assimilation. Because of the fact that it was a textbook, and that it had to deliver a comprehensive-as-possible overview of international politics for the undergraduate student, it was the publication for which Morgenthau drew most extensively from his earlier writings. His other books of the period, *Scientific Man vs. Power Politics* and *In Defense of the National Interest*, were much shorter texts that were written with a different purpose in mind, and where the 'process of Americanization' was easier to implement. This process, as Robbie Shilliam points out, entailed Morgenthau anglicizing the sources of his argument, 'thus making German philosophy speak predominantly through the mouths of British and American historical personalities'.[12] Even Max Weber, the omnipresent ghost haunting the writings of all the émigrés with a background in history, law or sociology, is not mentioned at all in the first edition of *Politics Among Nations*, nor in *Scientific Man vs. Power Politics*. Only once Weber had been sufficiently introduced to a US audience – by Talcott Parsons (1902–1979) at Harvard and by a number of Morgenthau's émigré colleagues at Chicago, notably Max Rheinstein and Edward Shils (1910–1995) – did Morgenthau deem it acceptable to add a citation from Weber to subsequent editions of *Politics Among Nations*.[13]

As Herbert A. Strauss has pointed out, emigration is, in the final analysis, a very individual occurrence, and it is pernicious to think about collective exile or emigration as if all the German-Jewish academics moving to the United States or Britain had a common experience of one sort or another.[14] For a start, one is faced with a significant sample bias because of the fact that one only has the success stories to analyse, those scholars who managed to find a new academic position and were able to continue their research and

---

12 R. Shilliam, *German Thought and International Relations: The Rise and Fall of a Liberal Project* (Basingstoke: Palgrave Macmillan, 2009), p. 194.
13 Under the third principle of realism one now reads the following Weber citation: 'Interests (material and ideal), not ideas, dominate directly the actions of men. Yet the "images of the world" created by these ideas have very often served as switches determining the tracks on which the dynamism of interests kept actions moving'; Morgenthau, *Politics Among Nations*, third edition, p. 9. For a discussion see S. P. Turner, 'Hans J. Morgenthau and the Legacy of Max Weber', in D. Bell (ed.), *Political Thought and International Relations: Variations on a Realist Theme* (Oxford University Press, 2009), pp. 63–82.
14 H. A. Strauss, 'Wissenschaftsemigration als Forschungsproblem', in H. A. Strauss, K. Fischer, C. Hoffmann and A. Söllner (eds.), *Die Emigration der Wissenschaften nach 1933: Disziplingeschichtliche Studien* (Munich, etc.: K. G. Saur, 1991), pp. 7–23, at 15.

teaching in one form or another. All the others who fell through the cracks – and there were plenty of them – have also slipped off the radar screen of those studying this issue. But perhaps more important still is the way each scholar tried to tackle the daunting task of making his or her thoughts compatible with the new institutional and cultural setting. As Stephen Turner highlights, '[c]ommunicating with an American audience required appealing to a new set of philosophical, literary, and historical sources, as well as historical experiences'.[15] For Morgenthau and his fellow jurist émigrés, this task was particularly demanding because the field of Political Science, in which many of them found themselves, did not exist in the Germany they had left behind.[16] The result is a trial-and-error approach in which Morgenthau 'tested' a variety of arguments and viewpoints on his new audience until he had identified a tenable position. Petersen seems to be on the mark when he writes:

Assuming that someone arrives as a virtually clean slate in a foreign culture and then quite simply adopts the fundamental assumptions of that culture wholesale when he is in his mid- to late thirties seems to me pretty heroic. This, of course, is not to say that he [Morgenthau] did not change or modify elements of his thought in the light of this new experience, but I find it unlikely in the extreme that anybody would be able to, or want to, completely reinvent themselves at such an age, at least not without sacrificing their moral and intellectual integrity. The assumption I make is to my mind the more reasonable one that Morgenthau probably did change elements of his thought but that the basic assumptions and overall problematic remained basically the same.[17]

Indeed, when gearing up to write *Politics Among Nations*, Morgenthau was still worrying about the inadequacy of legal formalism, and about its inherent weakness of not being able to specify the factors that determine whether law is valid or not. Morgenthau's legal heritage is the idea that international law is synonymous with formal dispute settlement mechanisms. The logic in *Politics Among Nations* is hence still that you need a balance of power (and not a bipolar stalemate) in order for international disputes to be justiciable. Since that structure is hopelessly undermined in the face of one

15 S. Turner, 'Hans J. Morgenthau and the Legacy of Max Weber', p. 63.
16 See G. Stourzh, 'Die deutschsprachige Emigration in den Vereinigten Staaten', *Jahrbuch für Amerikastudien*, 10 (1965), pp. 59–77, at 69–70.
17 Peterson, 'Breathing Nietzsche's Air', p. 112.

or more superpowers transforming their 'national interest' into at
least regional hegemonic aspirations, international law came to be
seen as largely irrelevant to the study of international relations. As
Koskenniemi has consequently argued, it is precisely the absence
of an image of law as being inherently valid that is 'a product of the
Weimar heritage in American international relations theory'.[18]

The disastrous consequences of the legalist internationalism of
the inter-war period had resulted in a veritable aversion to international law – in both academic and policy circles. As Chimni writes,
'the phenomenon of overestimating international law called forth
and legitimised the opposite – the complete underestimate of law
and legal institutions'.[19] Morgenthau's writings, with their emphasis
on power and their critique of the 'noble experiment of Geneva'[20]
played no insignificant part in that trend. The dominant doctrine of
formalism had led to a legalism 'to which the history of the world
appeared as a succession of legal cases handled most unintelligently
by an unenlightened humanity'.[21] Morgenthau's solution was to
separate law from politics by positing that politics was an autonomous sphere ruled by the lust for power having its roots in human
nature. As Stanley Hoffmann explained:

Eager to educate the heathen, not merely to joust with fellow literati,
Morgenthau quite deliberately couched his work in the terms of general
propositions and grounded them in history ... He wanted to be normative,
but to root his norms in the realities of politics, not in the aspirations of
politicians or in the constructs of lawyers.[22]

The success of Morgenthau's endeavour to decouple legal formalism from an understanding of the realities of politics is reflected
in the fact that much of international legal scholarship has been
sidelined in International Relations ever since. As Judith N. Shklar
argues, thanks to the likes of Morgenthau the formalism of juristic thought took root among its professed opponents: the same

18 M. Koskenniemi, *The Gentle Civilizer of Nations: The Rise and Fall of International Law 1870–1960* (Cambridge University Press, 2002), p. 495.
19 B. S. Chimni, *International Law and World Order: A Critique of Contemporary Approaches* (New Delhi: Sage Publications, 1993), p. 24.
20 Morgenthau, 'About Cynicism, Perfectionism, and Realism in International Affairs', p. 128.
21 *Ibid.*
22 S. Hoffmann, 'An American Social Science: International Relations', *Daedalus*, 106 (1977), pp. 41–60, at 44.

arguments that legal theoreticians used to separate law from morality were then used by political realists to preserve politics from both law and morality. 'The realistic picture of politics is, in fact, that of legalism gone sour'.[23]

Morgenthau's legalism critique is significant because it points to the ways in which formal law brings the spectre of universalization onto itself by dint of its own argumentative structure – and therefore also goes some way towards explaining Koskenniemi's 'culture of dynamism' that is engrossed in the language and methods of Political Science. In that sense, the 'political ideology of Geneva' in the 1920s was not all that different from the 'political ideology of Washington' in the immediate post-war period. For in both cases, the United States took a lead in establishing international law and institutions, although not always signing the ensuing treaty. It promoted but did not join the League of Nations, and similarly did not ratify the 1951 Convention Relating to the Status of Refugees or the Convention on the Rights of the Child.[24] The United States declares itself the promoter of a certain set of 'universal' values, but its status as hegemon prevents it from accepting to be bound by specific obligations these values may result in. As Morgenthau expressed it so well, 'American globalism assumes the existence of one valid legal order whose content is defined by the United States and which reflects the contents of American foreign policy'.[25] International law is at once both relevant and irrelevant because it is conveniently conceived of as formal law one day and as an informal regime of like-minded states the next.

As I highlighted in Chapter 5, an important change of language occurred in his writings once Morgenthau became a consultant to George Kennan's Policy Planning Staff. From *In Defense of the National Interest* onwards, the émigré legal scholar was gradually turning himself into a proponent of the US cause. At times, he may have been somewhat of a lonely voice – as, indeed, was the case when

---

23 J. N. Shklar, *Legalism: Law, Morals, and Political Trials* (Cambridge, MA: Harvard University Press, 1986), p. 126.

24 See S. V. Scott, 'Is There Room for International Law in *Realpolitik?*: Accounting for the US "Attitude" Towards International Law', *Review of International Studies*, 30 (2004), pp. 71–88.

25 H. J. Morgenthau, 'Emergent Problems of United States Foreign Policy', in K. Deutsch and S. Hoffman (eds.), *The Relevance of International Law* (Garden City, NY: Anchor Books, 1971), pp. 67–79, at 71.

he advocated vigorously for a negotiated settlement with the Soviet Union at the beginning of the 1950s – but the *Denkstil* of the jurist was all the while being adapted to the new circumstances. Once we reach *The Purpose of American Politics* in 1960,[26] Morgenthau's 'Americanization' seems complete. From a glance at the index, one would never guess that the book's author was a German-Jewish émigré steeped in *Staatsrechtslehre* and *Völkerrecht*. Neither the names of those cited nor the subjects discussed give any indication of Morgenthau's heritage. That this heritage is nonetheless still there is beyond doubt, and Shilliam is probably right when he argues that Morgenthau 'began to re-interpret the founding myths that constituted the American psyche – American exceptionalism, the American dream, and the American frontier – as part of the grand-narrative of the tragedy of liberal individualism that he had formulated out of his Weimar experience'.[27] But the late Morgenthau of the 1960s and 1970s is not the Morgenthau that is remembered as the classical realist in International Relations theory. In academic terms, Morgenthau had made his mark a decade earlier.

'When I address a group of lawyers I am always a little ill at ease. I do not feel exactly like a fugitive from justice, but like a fugitive from the law, because this is where I started, and from this I got away and went into other fields of enterprise.'[28] With these words, Morgenthau began a lecture to the Commercial Law League of America in 1965. Indeed, he had come a long way since emigrating in 1937. Though not being able to make the intellectual shift to Political Science at the University of Chicago, *Politics Among Nations* had gone on to become the most successful textbook in its field. And instead of engaging in academic debates – be they in International Law or Political Science – Morgenthau used the success of his textbook to further his role as a distinguished commentator on international affairs.

In the late 1960s, a survey of US State Department personnel dealing with the role of law in its administration of foreign policy included an 'academic familiarity' question.[29] The idea was to see

---

26 H. J. Morgenthau, *The Purpose of American Politics* (New York: Vintage Books, 1960).
27 Shilliam, *German Thought and International Relations*, p. 194.
28 H. J. Morgenthau, 'Law, Politics and the United Nations', *Commercial Law Journal*, 70 (1965), pp. 121–4 and 135.
29 J.W. Outland, 'The Decision-Maker and the Scholar: Who Reads Whom', *International Lawyer*, 4 (1970), pp. 859–70.

'who reads whom' among members of the Legal Adviser's Office, Foreign Service officers with a legal training, and those without. Morgenthau came out on top, not only on the list of International Relations scholars (as opposed to those identified with International Law), but on the overall ranking as well. Quincy Wright came a distant second. In the fall of 1968, another survey, this time on the issue of 'disciplinary culture' within the field of International Relations, questioned 500 political scientists specializing in the field.[30] Topping the list of scholarly works mentioned by respondents is *Politics Among Nations*, which was mentioned by one-third of all respondents and mentioned by more than twice as many as the second-ranked work, Morton A. Kaplan's *Systems and Process in International Politics*.[31] In the list of scholars mentioned, Morgenthau dominates the list once again, being mentioned by 47 per cent of all respondents, as opposed to Karl Deutsch, who comes second at 25 per cent.

Morgenthau's popularity was not based on scholarly innovation, cutting-edge research or astute theory-building, but on his skills as public intellectual. What made Morgenthau's emigration a success story was not his assimilation into the academic *Denkkollektiv* of his new field of Political Science, but his sensibilities for what was required to be heard by an audience of policy practitioners and commentators. He was 'both adviser and nettle' to the Pentagon and US State Department,[32] and for many the 'leading academic opponent of Johnson's policy towards Vietnam'.[33] Indeed, it was in particular Morgenthau's opposition to the war that also sparked a prolonged debate amongst the US public over the role of the intellectual, or scholar, in decision-making.[34] When asked about the function of the intellectual in society, Morgenthau replied: 'The intellectual's function is threefold, that is, there are three types. First, the expert who does not question the goals, only seeks the improvement of the means. Second, the ideologist who invests policy with the appeal of

30 R. B. Finnegan, 'The Field of International Relations: A View From Within', *Towson State Journal of International Affairs*, 7 (1972), pp. 1–24.
31 M. A. Kaplan, *Systems and Process in International Politics* (New York, NY: John Wiley & Sons, 1957).
32 H. Winsor, 'Why Aid to the Third World Failed', *The Globe and Mail* (25 July 1969), p. 7.
33 Neue Zürcher Zeitung, 'Washingtons Chinapolitik: Abschluß der Hearings im Senat', 31 March 1966, p. 1.
34 See, for instance, R. Kirk, 'The Scholar Is Not a Lion or a Fox', *The New York Times Magazine*, 1 May 1966, pp. 28–9 and 111–12.

virtue and wisdom. Third, the prophet who must serve outside the policy-making body as critic and seer.'[35] Morgenthau had, over the years, taken on all three functions himself.

Redescription

'Much of the appeal of functional jurisprudence', Martti Koskenniemi writes, 'has emerged from a disappointment with formalism's failure to fulfill the expectation that rules and processes would contain readymade solutions to social conflict, and the apparent arrogance of a profession that refused to acknowledge this failure'.[36] Morgenthau's rule-scepticism and his emphasis on social forces and the power aspirations of states, I have argued, is also a result of this disappointment, coupled with institutional and methodological barriers that deterred him from pursuing the functionalist agenda that he, too, was advocating.

It is perhaps a similar arrogance to the one Koskenniemi was referring to in the legal profession that has prevented the field of International Relations to look beyond the confines of their *stahlhartes Gehäuse* and recognize Morgenthau for what he is. In a way, this is not surprising, for current generations of International Relations scholars, taught in the vein of Political Science and absorbed in its technical language of compliance, regimes and good governance, generally stay well away from any direct engagement with 'formal' international public law. This has meant that the renewed interest in Morgenthau has been a rather one-sided affair. Those in International Relations are much more comfortable talking about Carl von Clausewitz or Max Weber, than they are dealing with Hans Kelsen or James Brierly. The closest one comes to engaging with a jurist is by reading Carl Schmitt, and then he is only interesting because you can supposedly understand him without being a jurist. Talk about 'friend and foe', 'the political', or 'the exception' is still deemed compatible with contemporary debates about securitization and communitarian violence, while notions of justiciability or legal indeterminacy are much less so.

---

35 H. R. Rolph, 'Hans Morgenthau: Intellectual – Expert, Ideologist, Prophet', *The Stanford Daily* (24 May 1967).
36 Koskenniemi, *The Gentle Civilizer of Nations*, p. 496.

The 'redescription' undertaken in the above pages has tried to address this issue. I deliberately confined myself to making this one point, rather than trying to provide a more comprehensive picture of Morgenthau's thought that may have proved distracting. Morgenthau's voluminous work will continue to provide plenty of opportunities to grapple in novel ways with aspects of 'classical realism', or to serve Lebow's 'texts as inspirations' purpose and offer springboards for a variety of original arguments. A recent instance of both is Vibeke Schou Tjalve's fascinating new book I mentioned in Chapter 1. Tjalve argues that Morgenthau and Niebuhr were reacting to Dewey's pragmatism, which had 'turned out to be a vehicle for an empiricist reductionism and for a hollowing out of more humanist, septic, and fallibilist elements in the American mind'.[37] If such new rereadings and applications of Morgenthau's thought were to now remember his legal heritage – and in this case acknowledge the way Morgenthau grappled with the US pragmatist tradition through his engagement with the legal realist focus on law as an indeterminate form of social control – the task of my redescription will have been a success.

Of course, critics might argue that the criteria established in Chapter 1 about how such a 'redescription' differs from other interpretative approaches have not been adhered to. They might argue that what Chapters 2 to 5 have done is also an attempt to show 'the truth' behind Morgenthau, to highlight the 'real' interpretation of Morgenthau's writings, and that this exercise necessarily implies that the existing secondary literature is perceived as being 'wrong'. But let us not forget what the aim of the redescription was, namely to read texts as communicative actions, formulated in a particular period, that reacted with its descriptions to the society of that period. Redescriptions continuously transform necessity into contingency. Just as Morgenthau's writings were a product of and a reaction to the circumstances of a certain time and place, so the redescription offered in these pages is the product of a particular set of surrounding conditions. These conditions hinge on a vocabulary of compliance, soft law and governance that transforms the normative ambiguity of

---

37 V. S. Tjalve, *Realist Strategies of Republican Peace: Niebuhr, Morgenthau, and the Politics of Patriotic Dissent* (New York, NY and Basingstoke: Palgrave Macmillan, 2008), p. 42.

formalism into a 'culture of dynamism', thereby replacing normative disagreement with technical management and locating knowledge of the latter in the International Relations academy, steeped in
the methods of Political Science.[38]

The production of any work of this nature necessarily entails a
critical, differentiating engagement with texts already produced –
both primary and secondary sources – that are deemed relevant to
the study. It is not contrary to my aim of redescription to agree with
the literature that Max Weber certainly did influence Morgenthau's
thought, and that there are indeed obvious parallels to be drawn
with some of Morgenthau's ideas and the work of Carl Schmitt.
Yet it is equally informative to highlight the differences in their positions as it is to focus on the influence of one on the other,[39] and it is
even more enlightening to focus on sources of influences that have
arguably been occluded. The main characters of the play offered
in these pages are household names in legal scholarship, but generally non-entities in the International Relations literature – the
likes of Baumgarten, Guggenheim, Kelsen, Lauterpacht, Llewellyn,
McDougal, Nippold, Oppenheim, and Wehberg. Though receiving scarce mention in Morgenthau's US writings, these scholars
induced Morgenthau to produce the 'descriptions', in Luhmann's
sense, that he did.

38 See Koskenniemi, *The Gentle Civilizer of Nations*, in particular pp. 496–7.
39 For a commendable attempt to distil some of the shortcomings of Morgenthau's
   reading of Weber, and thus of the reception of Weber in International Relations,
   see T. Barkawi, 'Strategy as a Vocation: Weber, Morgenthau and Modern Strategic
   Studies', *Review of International Studies*, 24 (1998), pp. 159–84.

Name index

Subject index

Alabama arbitration, 46
apologism, 34–35, 40, 42, 47, 59, 74, 116, 144, 151, 170

behaviouralist social science, 28, 33, 106, 112, 115, 131, 135, 178
and traditionalists, 7, 142
Morgenthau's critique of, 138–42

Cases
Lochner v. *New York* (US Supreme Court), 109–11
Muller v. *Oregon* (US Supreme Court), 111
Nicaragua v. *United States of America* (I.C.J.), 47
classical legal thought, 106, 112
classical texts (appropriation and function of), 4, 5, 8, 13–18, 175–76
Cold War, 19, 101, 179
common law, 106–8
common sense, 135, 142–43
concreteness (scope) of international law, 34–36, 59, 136
crisis of democratic theory (US), 119, 132, 178

Darwinism, 108, 109
disputes (justiciability of), 34–35, 45–74, 95, 144, 156, 173, 176, 184
Dumbarton Oaks Conference, 163

émigré scholars, 4, 9, 13, 21, 22, 28, 119, 123–25
empiricism, 3, 12, 33, 86, 119, 133, 178, 190
ethics, 1, 17–18, 72, 126–27, 130, 150, 151, 158, 164–65, 167, 170–71, 173, 179
ethic of responsibility, 3, 162, 174
ethical relativism, 122

in foreign policy, 1–3

First World War, 21, 35, 42, 76, 112, 126, 159
foreign policy, 17, 136
and ethics, 2, 158–62, 174
decision-making, 4, 74
liberal foreign policy, 58
of the United States, 1, 3, 68, 135, 158, 162, 181, 186–87
policies of the status quo, imperialism, and prestige, 63, 69
formalism (legal), 40, 42, 53, 77, 86, 98, 103–4, 108, 115, 125, 144, 148, 165–66, 173–74, 177–78, 179, 184–86, 189, 191
functionalism, 125–30, 135–38, 145, 178, 189

Great Depression, 112, 123, 133–34

Hague Peace Conferences, 46

idealism, 5–8, 26, 29, 36, 39, 56, 61, 157, 159
ideology, 85, 151–55, 157
'political ideology of Geneva', 126, 146, 186
indeterminacy of law, 47, 114, 115, 136, 165, 174, 189, 190
interests (of political actors), 3, 5, 34, 42, 44, 47, 60, 95, 120, 127, 149, 174
community of interests, 72, 130, 160
conflict of interests, 46, 54, 59
harmony of interests, 96
interest defined in terms of power, 4, 11, 12, 181
national interest, 3, 11, 12, 14, 29, 34, 147, 158–62, 166, 171, 174, 179, 184
vital interests, 45, 46, 52, 54, 176

196

9 781107 407688